Appel

Appel

A Canadian in the
French Foreign Legion

Joel Adam Struthers

WILFRID LAURIER
UNIVERSITY PRESS

Inspiring Lives.

Wilfrid Laurier University Press acknowledges the support of the Canada Council for the Arts for our publishing program. We acknowledge the financial support of the Government of Canada through the Canada Book Fund for our publishing activities. This work was supported by the Research Support Fund.

Library and Archives Canada Cataloguing in Publication

Struthers, Joel Adam, 1971–, author
    Appel : a Canadian in the French Foreign Legion / Joel Adam Struthers.

Includes bibliographical references and index.
Issued in print and electronic formats.
ISBN 978-1-77112-105-7 (softcover).—ISBN 978-1-77112-106-4 (EPUB).—
ISBN 978-1-77112-390-7 (PDF)

1. Struthers, Joel Adam, 1971–. 2. France. Armée. Légion étrangère—Biography
3. France. Armée. Légion étrangère—Military life. 4. Soldiers—France—Biography
5. Soldiers—Canada—Biography. 6. Autobiographies. I. Title.

UA703.L5 S77 2019   355.3′59092   C2018-902778-9
                                                 C2018-902779-7

Front-cover photo: G9 Ralentisseur-Stabilisateur-Extracteur (RSE) certification, ÉTAP, near Pau, France. Image courtesy of the author. Cover design by Blakeley Words+Pictures. Interior design by James Leahy.

This book is printed on FSC®-certified paper. It contains recycled materials, and other controlled sources, is processed chlorine free, and is manufactured using biogas energy.

Printed in Canada

Contents

Foreword

In 1978, Simon Murray, former *caporal* of the 2e Régiment étranger de parachutistes, published his famous book *Legionnaire* telling of his five years of service in the regiment through the end of the Algerian war and the transition to peace after nearly forty years of constant operations. Since then, nothing of its kind has been written.

Forty years later, former Caporal Joel Struthers decided to follow his example and depict his time in the Corps. I would like to congratulate him for this decision and for having so honestly and openly unveiled this part of his life, including some private and unknown aspects of it.

His main merit lies in going beyond the action he valiantly saw in the Central African Republic, in Chad, and in the Congo to present us, without boasting, some rather unknown aspects of a *légionnaire*'s life. Indeed, Joel takes the reader through his daily life as a légionnaire, from the very first day at the recruitment post to the last nights in Aubagne, before going back to a past he had put aside for six years. Travelling through these pages, you will discover how a restless young Canadian turned himself into a professional soldier, and then a pathfinder immersed in a system that, even if could always be improved, remains a reference in terms of soldiering. You will appreciate the quasi-monastic life—made of satisfaction, celebration, hard training, operational commitments, but also of routine and service—of these soldiers who decided to leave everything they had to come and serve in the Legion. And finally you will discover from the inside this esprit de corps that empowers the Corps and helps these *hommes sans noms* to cope with the tensions of their new lives.

Joel left the service in September 2000. Since then, the Legion has been confronted by a long series of new commitments, challenges, and technological evolutions. The Legion has evolved, as it has always done, be it in Indochina or in Algeria. After Afghanistan, Iraq, Mali, and the Central African Republic (on numerous occasions), the appearance of the current Legion is different—more sophisticated and experienced than ever. But the heart of the organization has remained the same. The légionnaires still are unknown and, as always, remarkable young men seeking new lives and new challenges, popping in at a recruitment post, staying for a few years, and then leaving for something else. Joel is a good example of what a légionnaire is and will always be.

May his book help the reader to travel through this unknown world and to discover who these men really are.

—Colonel Benoît Desmeulles, commanding officer
 2ᵉ Régiment étranger de parachutistes (2012–14)
 Paris, October 30, 2017

Preface

Only a few stories exist about what it is like to join and serve with la Légion étrangère (French Foreign Legion), and most are written by questionable characters, deserters, or liars—sometimes a mix of all three. It's true that a mystique exists with the Legion, as do misconceptions and pure fiction. The French Foreign Legion is a professional fighting force, a part of the French military, and governed under the republic's military law. I served in the Legion's ranks, and this is a légionnaire's story. And it's dedicated to légionnaires who served or continue to serve honourably.

Acronyms and Abbreviations

1st Cie — 1st Company: Urban Combat
2nd Cie — 2nd Company: Mountain Warfare
3rd Cie — 3rd Company: Amphibious Warfare
4th Cie — 4th Company: Sniper and Explosives
5th Cie — 5th Company: Service Support Company
1er BEP — 1er Bataillon étranger de parachutistes
2e BEP — 2e Bataillon étranger de parachutistes
1er RCP — 1er Régiment de chasseurs parachutistes
1er RE — 1er Régiment étranger
1er REC — 1er Régiment étranger cavalarie
4e RE — 4e Régiment étranger
2e REI — 2e Régiment étranger d'infanterie
1er REP — 1er Régiment étranger de parachutistes
2e REP — 2e Régiment étranger de parachutistes
1er RHP — 1er Régiment de hussards parachutistes
1er RPIMa — 1er Régiment de parachutistes d'infanterie de marine
1er RTP — 1er Régiment du train parachutiste
8e RPIMa — 8e Régiment de parachutistes d'infanterie de marine
2iC — second-in-command
11e CCTP — 11e Compagnie de commandement et de transmissions parachutiste
13e RDP — 13e Régiment de dragons parachutistes
17e RGP — 17e Régiment du génie parachutiste
35e RAP — 35e Régiment d'artillerie parachutistes
159e RIA-CNAM — Régiment d'infanterie alpine—Centre national aguerrissement combat montagne

AD — Accidental discharge
BSM — Brevet skieur militaire
B2 — Deuxième bureau
CASOGHE — Certificat d'aptitude au saut opérationnel à grande hauteur en équipe
CASOGHI — Certificat d'aptitude au saut opérationnel à grande hauteur en individuel
CCS — Compagnie de commandement et des services
CEA — Compagnie d'éclairage et d'appui; its sections are Section Milan; Section autonome de défense anti-aérienne (SADAA); Section de mortier lourd (SML); Section escadron de reconnaissance (SER); and Groupe des commandos parachutistes (GCP)
CEITO — Centre d'entraînement de l'infanterie au tir opérationnel
CME — Certificats militaires élémentaires
CNAM — Centre national aguerissement combat montagne
CNEC — Centre nationale d'entraînement commando
CO — Commanding officer
COS — Commandement des opérations spéciales (Special Operations Command)
CTE — Certificat technique élémentaire
DGSE — Direction générale de la sécurité extérieur
DZ — Drop zone
EPMS — Aide moniteur éducation physique militaire et sportive
ÉTAP — École des troupes aéroportées
FAMAS — 5.56mm assault rifle
FAR — Force d'action rapide
FIBUA — Fighting in built-up areas
FLNC — Front de libération nationale corse
GCP — Groupe des commandos parachutistes
GIGN — Groupe d'intervention de la gendarmerie nationale
GQ — James Gregory and Raymond Quilter—GQ Parachute Company Ltd.

KIA — Killed in action
MP — Military Police
NCO — Non-commissioned officers
NVG — Night-vision goggles
OP — Observation post
PC — Parcours du combattant
P4 — Soft-skinned Peugeot four-wheel-drive
PFP — Partnership for Peace Programme
PLD — Permission longue durée
PPCLI — Princess Patricia's Canadian Light Infantry
PRLE — Poste de recrutement de la Légion étrangère
RSE — Ralentisseur-Stabilisateur-Extracteur
RPIMa — Regiment de parachutistes d'infanterie de marine
SAMU — Service d'aide médicale urgente
SEPP — Section d'entretien et de pliage des parachutes
SNCM — Société nationale maritime corse méditerranée
SOGH — Saut opérationnel à grande hauteur
SPIE — Special patrol insertion/extraction
TAP — Test troupes aéroportées
TRM — Transport Renault militaire
USDIFRA — Union syndicale de défense des intérêts des français retiés d'Algérie
VAB — Véhicule de l'avant blindé
VIH — Vancouver Island Helicopters
VLRA — Véhicules de liaison, de reconnaissance et d'appui (reconnaissance, escort, and support variant)
VOX — Voice-activated radio

Prologue

Open ground covered in tall elephant grass swaying in the wind, a makeshift barricade of burned-out cars, and a single-track dirt road are all that lie between us and the rebel checkpoint and stronghold 500 metres ahead of us.

I am one of a dozen men here who form the Groupe des commandos parachutistes (GCP) of the 2e Régiment étranger de parachutistes (2e REP), and we are gathered in an abandoned bullet-riddled building in Bangui, capital of the Central African Republic (CAR). The derelict structure, located in the heart of the Bea-Rex-Kptene 92 Housing Zone, serves as our observation post (OP), allowing our section to keep our eyes and weapons trained on the rebels.

Their position consists of the single-lane Pont Jackson (Jackson Bridge)—a narrow crossing over a dried-up riverbed—plus a bunker complex concealed among the trees to the left of the bridge and two adjacent buildings they use as barracks and a command post. The city's main artery, Avenue Point Kilometre Zero (PK Zero), serves as the boundary between the rebel lines and those of the government forces and their French allies. It also roughly divides Bangui into two zones. The narrow dirt avenue leads into a housing complex. Here, the bunker gives the rebels a defensive position with a full view of the bridge as well as the buildings they occupy. Tonight, that rebel position is our target.

In the sweaty and poorly lit confines of our OP, the twelve of us crowd around a series of aerial reconnaissance photos taken earlier that day by a French Air Force Jaguar. The images provide a vivid and detailed view of the ground we have to cover and the objectives we are to take. At times gesturing to specific points on the photos,

Capitaine Raoul issues orders: at 0200 hours a Super Puma helicopter of the Commandement des opérations spéciales (COS), armed with a 20mm cannon, would engage a rebel position at the city's main power station. This was the key objective of the operation, and it would be our cue to assault Pont Jackson.

The section's véhicule de l'avant blindé (VAB), a 14-ton armoured personnel carrier, would lead the assault, punching through the barricade and flushing out the rebels from the bunker complex and nearby buildings. Then it would advance up the main avenue of the housing complex into rebel-controlled territory. The VAB would provide covering fire from its turret with the 50-calibre machine gun, while the rest of the section follows in two soft-skinned Peugeot four-wheel-drives (P4s).

Once Capitaine Raoul is sure we clearly understand our positions and responsibilities, he tells us to get the vehicles and equipment prepared and positioned. The P4s are open-top convertibles armed with rear-mounted 7.62mm machine guns. Individually, and depending on each team member's specialty, we are armed with an assortment of weapons, including FAMAS 5.56mm assault rifles, FN Minimi 5.56mm support weapons, 9mm Beretta 92 pistols, and grenades. I take up position behind the wheel of the first P4 following the VAB. Our vehicles are concealed inside the OP's fenced courtyard, and from there we are to drive directly onto PK Zero.

Bangui, usually a city buzzing with activity even at night, is deathly quiet. Many residents have fled or are hiding indoors, fearful of being caught by the rebels. Only the odd crack of gunfire and crump of mortar explosions in the distance cut through the stillness. Ready, we sit in silence, each man wrapped in his own thoughts. The only display of tension is the repeated glancing at watches as the minutes tick by, closing in on 0200 hours.

My own responsibility is to follow the VAB as closely as possible to ensure maximum cover. The P4 has no armour, and when the VAB breaks off to the right and takes up a covering-fire position, I am to break left and assault one of the rebel-held buildings. That is the theory, at least.

The Central African night is hot and humid. The sky is clear and starlit. I am sweating under the weight of my body armour and the personal webbing that holds eight full magazines, four fragmentation grenades, two additional AC 58 grenades, and water bottles. With less than a year in the regiment, and only two years in the Legion, I suddenly find myself shouldering a massive responsibility. The onus is on me not to screw up or let my teammates down. They are all more experienced than I am, with several years in the unit and many operations behind them. Adrenaline flooding my veins, I am acutely aware of my immediate environment. And I'm certain that before any of the others, I hear the thump of the Puma's rotor blades in the distance.

This is it.

CHAPTER ONE

The Road to France

"If your son is going to draw that symbol, perhaps he should do it properly," said the waiter in a condescending tone. It was 1977, and I was a six-year-old sitting with my parents in a restaurant located on the Franco-German border. I'd drawn the bad guys' Nazi swastika backwards.

My parents met as students at Canadian Forces Base (CFB) Petawawa in Ontario, Canada, and started dating in Grade 11. As the son of a fighter pilot in the Canadian Air Force, I lived an itinerant lifestyle, moving from one CFB to another. In 1989, when my father retired as the commanding officer of 441 Tactical Fighter Squadron, CFB Cold Lake, Alberta, we settled down in British Columbia, Canada.

Ours is a military family, with a lineage that dates back to the 1800s. On my mother's side, my great-great-great uncle George Albert Ravenhill served with the Royal Scots Fusiliers during the Boer War in South Africa.[1] He was awarded the Victoria Cross after saving a gun crew at the Battle of Colenso in 1899, and later served in France during the First World War. Sadly, he fell on hard times after enduring the effects of shell shock. As a result, he had to make the difficult decision to send three of his children to Canada to be fostered.

Another distant family member, Will Walks, enlisted in the Canadian Expeditionary Force after finishing his veterinary schooling and cared for war horses in France during the First World War. Eventually, he married his French mademoiselle and brought her back to Ontario. But she soon persuaded him to return to France, where he continued taking care of farm animals in Noyon, north of Paris. When the Second World War came around, he assisted in the French "maquis rescue" of no fewer than thirty downed Allied airmen who had parachuted into farmers' fields. After receiving phone calls from excited farmers, Walks transported the airmen on the back of his motorbike after dark, hiding them in his home until they could be passed on to the next underground contact for their trip across the English Channel.

My maternal grandfather, Major-General A. James Tedlie,[2] was awarded the Distinguished Service Order for his actions with the British Columbia Regiment in the tank battle for Todtenhügal, Germany, during the closing phases of the Second World War. In the field, the ribbon to the Order was pinned on his uniform by Field Marshal Viscount Montgomery. Later, my grandfather received his medal from King George VI at Buckingham Palace.

On my father's side of the family, my great-grandfather served in the First World War as a medical doctor,[3] overseeing Chinese labourers who were shipped to France via Canada to dig the trenches along the front. And my paternal grandfather, Colonel David Struthers, was a D-Day veteran of the Bernières-sur-Mer landings, Juno Beach, the invasion of Holland, and Korea. He later served as military attaché to the Canadian Embassy in Beijing, China, during China's Cultural Revolution, eventually retiring from the Royal Canadian Artillery. He was the one who let me take my Christmas gift to church during our visit to Belgium, where he was serving the North Atlantic Treaty Organization (NATO) as the Canadian attaché for Emergency Canada. Sitting there, as an eight-year-old with a plastic handgun hidden under my jacket, was, well, awesome. Our visit to the site of the Battle of Waterloo was less of a thrill, but it was my introduction to a different history, and one that I knew nothing about.

From my earliest days, I remember being interested in everything military. At school, I spent most of my time in class drawing castles, tanks, and airplanes. I visited countless museums and castles, and played in old trenches and bunkers all over Europe. Once, I found a key in a tower of the walled city of Rothenburg ob der Tauber, in Bavaria. I was certain it would open a dungeon. My fascination with the military deepened with age. So did my interest in sports.

My mother was very athletic, and she enrolled me, from an early age, in soccer, baseball, judo, swimming, and hockey. She was also an avid animal lover, and I became one too. Aside from my mother, my role models were predominantly fighter pilots and soldiers— my dad and his friends, as well as my friends' dads, and my grandfathers. Even my hockey coaches were soldiers. The military was in my blood.

As a teenager, a slight chip on my shoulder started to develop while my family was living in Alberta. I was the top scorer in the Alberta Midget AAA Hockey League. I could hit too, and I wasn't afraid to stick up for my myself or my teammates. But unlike the typical jock, I was more reserved and introverted. At six feet, I was big, but I hadn't filled out yet.

After my first season playing AAA hockey, I was invited to the Western Hockey League's Regina Pats tryout camp, but my parents didn't let me attend because my school marks were too low. The fact that I had been expelled from high school for a week for fighting hadn't helped my cause. The following season, I made the Lloydminster Blazers in the Alberta Junior Hockey League, but that achievement was short-lived. My game had changed: I was trying to be the enforcer, and no one told me I didn't have the size or the chin to be that guy.

I was often ejected for fighting and watched the remaining minutes from the stands with my new girlfriend. Jamie and I had met at the high school in Lloyd, where I was attending class—well, supposed to be attending. I enjoyed her company. I had girlfriends prior, but we didn't really hang out the same way. I recall one evening while speaking on the phone late into the night I asked if she could hold. I ran the five or six blocks from my billets to her house as fast as I could. When she opened the door, I had a handful of leaves for her, with an explanation that I hadn't seen any flowers in the neighbour's lawns on my way over. She accepted the leaves with a smile.

Eventually, I was released from the Blazers, and the trouble started when I was fresh out of Langley Secondary School without hockey, experiencing a loss of direction. A mix of immaturity, trying to impress friends and girls, and reacting to other idiots all took their toll. I was hanging out with the wrong crowd and these so-called friends were leading me nowhere. The final twist in my downward spiral came when I was confronted by an RCMP special investigations officer, revolver drawn.

I was lucky I didn't end up in prison. My parents were at odds with what to do and I could see that my behaviour was hurting them. They had brought me up to respect others and to be account-able for my actions. I realized that I needed to change—and fast—so I contacted the Canadian Armed Forces recruitment centre in Vancouver.

Unfortunately, the Canadian Armed Forces was no longer accept-ing applicants for regular force infantry positions. My only option was to join a Canadian reserve unit and hope to be at the front of the recruitment line when the regular forces started to expand. I signed up with the Royal Westminster Regiment (Westies) based in New Westminster, British Columbia. The Westies were assigned to support the Canadian Airborne Regiment, setting me on the path to become a paratrooper, something I was interested in.

By this time, I was already twenty-one. Reservists do most of their training in the summer, and I reported to CFB Wainwright near Edmonton, Alberta, home to Princess Patricia's Canadian Light Infantry (PPCLI). It was May 1993, and along with a group of other militiamen, I was going to attend Battle School, which would be my first real taste of an infantry soldier's life. I was impressed by some of the course's non-commissioned officers (NCOs) and their demeanour, and I liked the military way of doing things. Every-thing was organized: we paraded, marched, shot, endured frequent inspections, and engaged in battle drills and exercises. The course itself wasn't too physically challenging, but during those mentally tough moments out on the dry and dusty prairies, I would just put my head down and soldier on. The experience confirmed in my mind that this was my vocation. I felt at home.

After completing Battle School, I waited for the parachute jump course at CFB Edmonton. But the Canadian Airborne Regiment was in jeopardy, its future cast under the dark cloud of controversy and politics following the Somalia Affair, which eventually led to the disbanding of the Airborne Regiment. During the public inquiry into the Somalia Affair, word was that the Westies were going to lose its airborne tasking and instead retrain for an anti-tank role, which didn't exactly inspire me. Enthusiasm within our unit was low at that point.

By now, my family knew that the lack of positive direction in my life was getting to me. I had called a US Army recruiter about joining, but the recruitment process would take a long time. Working at the Vancouver International Airport loading luggage and parading at the Westies twice a week wasn't cutting it. I needed more, and the sooner the better.

During my time at PPCLI Battle School, one of our NCOs mentioned that a colleague of his had recently returned from France after serving in the French Foreign Legion's parachute regiment. I was intrigued. True, I had heard of the Legion before, but never really thought more of it or took it seriously, to be honest. But more recently, the idea of being able to join an airborne regiment in a foreign country piqued my sense of adventure, something that was seriously lacking in my life.

I eventually wrote to the French Foreign Legion's headquarters in France, expressing my interest in joining.[4] This brought a quick reply from the Legion, outlining its organizational structure, enlistment requirements, pay scales, and the addresses of its various recruiting depots—all located in France.

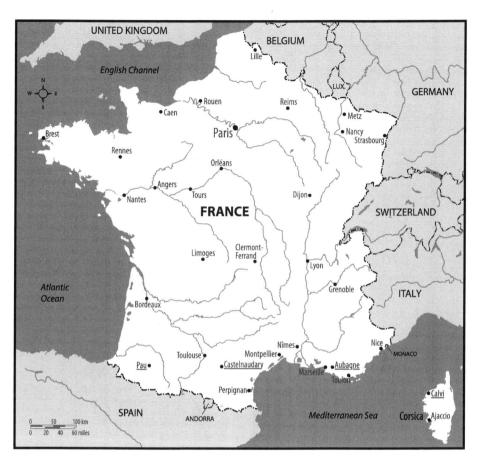

Map of France. (*Credit:* Mike Bechthold)

CHAPTER TWO

Strasbourg

La Légion étrangère is known the world over, and fixed in the popular mind are images of 1930s-era légionnaires wearing the characteristic white kepi caps, trudging across African deserts under a merciless sun to defend an outpost. These men were petty thieves and criminals with dark pasts, as well as deserters from foreign armies who had found a new home and a life in the ranks of the Legion. Some would call these men mercenaries. What caught my attention, though, were history books filled with black-and-white photos of the Legion's 1er Bataillon étranger de parachutistes (1er BEP) and 2e Bataillon étranger de parachutistes (2e BEP) jumping in French Indochina.[5]

The Legion I was interested in joining had evolved into a modern, elite fighting force. But when I looked for books on the Legion, I found few relevant to modern day. There was a scarcity of quality and depth to many of the accounts, and since some were written by deserters, their perspectives were questionable. I read and really enjoyed *Légionnaire*, written by Simon Murray, and a reference on the Legion, albeit covering its activities during the 1960s in Algeria, North Africa.

My maternal grandfather questioned my idea of joining the Legion, but he empathized with my frustration. He said, "If you are going to do this, Joel, represent your country well." Janel, my girlfriend, wasn't convinced either. We had been together for some time, and she didn't understand my motivations or abrupt decision to leave. But I was restless and not willing to settle for an average life. My mind was made up: I was going to France to join the Legion.

My father, retired from the Canadian Air Force, was now flying for a commercial airline. In September 1994, I flew with him to Düsseldorf, Germany, in the cockpit jump seat of a Boeing 757. On a clear and cold morning at the Düsseldorf airport, Dad looked at me sternly and shook my hand. He wished me luck, saying, "Call us when you get the chance."

I made my way to the train station to continue my journey to Strasbourg, France. Second thoughts, anxiety, and excitement were fighting in my mind, but there was no way I was turning back. Riding the train and watching the German countryside speed by brought back memories of my childhood spent on Canadian Forces bases in Baden-Baden and Lahr. My father had flown the CF-104 Starfighter, nicknamed the "widow-maker." I remember hearing sirens signalling training alerts in the middle of the night, the constant sonic booms, and a classmate being ushered out of school after her father was killed in a crash.

I had made German friends and spoke German fluently at a young age. I learned French in the Canadian military school system, played hockey, and skied in the Alps. These were my formative years. Good years.

Outside the Strasbourg train station, I waved down a taxi, and in rusty French explained my destination to the driver: the Legion's recruitment depot. Looking surprised, he turned to me and asked, "Are you certain? La Légion is a tough life." When I said yes, he replied, "You crazy?" Then he turned back around, put the car in gear, and accelerated into Strasbourg's evening traffic.

The Strasbourg Legion recruitment depot was a First World War–era whitewashed three-storey building facing a large parade ground. A partially abandoned barracks, it's now used as a Poste de recrutement de la Légion étrangère (PRLE). With the Cold War over, there was no longer a need for large military units and therefore sprawling military barracks.

The entrance to the PRLE was a metal door set into a 3-metre-high wall topped with razor wire. A solitary light glared down from above. Inscribed on the door were three words: Legio Patria Nostra. The Legion Is Our Fatherland.

My hand hovered over the well-worn push-button doorbell. No turning back now, I thought. Still, I hesitated. Despite having come all this way, joining the French Foreign Legion wasn't the kind of choice you make every day. Retreating across the street, I sat down on the cold stone steps of a church, eyeing the Legion door. The old street lights illuminated my view. An hour passed. There was no movement from anywhere, just my restless feet and the trees rustling in the evening's cold wind. The PRLE seemed just as abandoned as the rest of the barracks.

Finally, I stood up. Enough stalling, I told myself. I crossed the street, walked to the door, and rang the doorbell. It didn't make any noise. After what seemed like minutes, a large man, taller than me—and a lot more imposing, dressed in a khaki-green army combat uniform—finally opened the door. He asked to see my passport. I handed it to him.

"You join Legion?" he asked, in broken English.

"Oui," I replied.

He glanced at my passport again. "Canadian?"

"Oui."

He motioned me inside, closed the door behind me, and then he led me to what appeared to be a waiting room cluttered with old chairs and a battered wooden table. The smell of cigarettes lingered in the air, and the dim lighting reminded me of wartime offices in all the old movies I had watched since I was a kid. The walls were covered with Legion posters, old and new portraits of légionnaires, and photos of the men on deployment throughout the world. It was a lot to take in. I felt uncertainty about what lay ahead and nervous excitement in the adventure of it all.

The *caporal-chef* selected a videocassette, in English, from a box on the table, put it into an antiquated VCR, and turned on the television in a corner of the room. He told me to sit down and watch the video, then call him once it had ended. The video started off with a group of légionnaires, white kepis on their heads, singing as they slowly marched down a road. A brief outline of the Legion's history and significant battles followed.

King Louis-Philippe founded the Legion on March 10, 1831,[6] to advance France's colonial efforts. In the twentieth century, scenes of légionnaires on exercise and engaged in operations in the former Yugoslavia, Africa, and the jungles of South America promised adventure. I found the footage fascinating and encouraging, notably the shots of the Legion's parachute regiment jumping, the 2e Régiment étranger de parachutistes (2e REP). It painted a picture of a modern, professional fighting force, a far cry from old fortresses in the desert. It was also a relief. I had no fallback: it was all or nothing. When the tape ended, I called for the caporal-chef.

He directed me to another room. Sitting behind a battered desk that looked like it had seen its fair share of action, an NCO, a sergent, tapped away at a beat-up antique typewriter. He was smaller in stature than the caporal-chef and older, probably in his early forties. He gestured for me to sit down. In broken English, he asked me my age, nationality, parents' names, and my reason for leaving Canada. Was I wanted in connection with any criminal offences? Did I have any prior military experience?

All of this was worked through methodically. The sergent smoked as he typed, hunting and pecking at the keys with a single finger while sternly looking me in the eyes with every question, like some human lie detector. My initial impressions were that the Legion was an austere and no-nonsense environment, if the buildings and légionnaires I had just met were anything to go by.

As we painstakingly went through the paperwork, I looked around the room. While it was functional, it was old and worn. In Canada, the military recruitment facilities were more modern, yet this place seemed like a time warp. But I was in Europe, and these solid buildings had served the military for the past one hundred years. They were probably good for a few hundred more. With the basics out of the way, the sergent moved on to the big question:

"Why do you want to join the Legion?" he asked.

"I want to soldier," I replied.

No one can do a poker face like a Foreign Legion recruitment NCO. Without speaking, he placed a document in front of me that stated my acceptance into the pre-volunteer phase of the Legion's initial five-year contract. He motioned for me to sign it, marking my first major step into the ranks of the Legion. I was aware of the initial five-year commitment; the letter I received from the Legion prior to flying to France clearly outlined what was expected. Without hesitation, I leaned forward and signed the document. It was September 8, 1994.

The caporal-chef then led me upstairs to a third-floor living area. It was a large, open space with a long dining table in the middle that could seat a dozen people. Two guys in civilian clothes were sitting on a couch, smoking cigarettes, and watching TV. I assumed they were new recruits like me. They didn't stand out in any way. Both were of average stature, and neither looked overly athletic or tough. Sizing them up in my brief look, I thought, if that's my competition, I'm good.

Adjacent to the dining and living space was the sleeping area, which consisted of three six-man bedrooms. The single beds were old-fashioned metal-framed affairs. On each, sheets were rolled into two long sleeves placed in an X formation on top of a green wool blanket. The mattress lay upright on its side, resting on top of the bedsprings. This, caporal-chef said, was *lit en batterie*, battery style. As he showed me around the quarters, he told me how certain areas were to be maintained, including my bed, which was to be prepared in this manner. I was the third recruit who started that day, and I was told to introduce myself to the other two men sitting on the couch. One guy was Romanian; the other, French.

In broken English, Stefan (the Romanian) said that a group of new volunteers had just left that morning. We would do the same in a week's time. The Frenchman seemed like he had an attitude, as if he was at home and we were the imposters. Perhaps it was the language barrier and because he spoke the Legion's language. I just ignored him.

I didn't sleep much that night. Partly because of jet lag, and also because the day's events were a little surreal and somewhat depressing. Before flying to France, I had spent a lot of time thinking about life in the French Foreign Legion, but not about its recruitment phase. This was something I didn't know much about. My unease wasn't about being a foreigner. That was a familiar experience from the get-go. My first year of school was at a German kindergarten. I had also spent a year of grade school in Bracknell, in West London, England, when my father was attending the Royal Airforce Command, and Advanced Staff Course during the Falklands War in 1982. What could be worse? Joining the French Foreign Legion, or going to public school in a jacket and tie in a country where no one plays hockey?

During my childhood, I also spent the winters skiing in the French Alps with French military ski instructors and French Air Force pilots who were learning to ski. I was the only child in my classes, but I was fluent enough in French at the time to talk to my instructors and course-mates.

A loud whistle woke me that first morning in the PRLE, with someone from down the hall yelling, "Reveille! Wake up!" After a shower and a simple breakfast of strong black coffee and baguettes cut into pieces, with butter, strawberry jam, and orange marmalade, the caporal-chef pointed out the cleaning supplies and mops in a corner of the common room. We were to start our day by scrubbing the building, floor by floor. This was the drill for the entire week—cleaning, followed by more cleaning. In the morning, we turned out in the courtyard to stand at attention for the raising of the French flag, the *tricolore*, and then again in the evening for its lowering.

Each day, several newcomers were led upstairs for introductions, and they later joined us in the routine of eating, cleaning, and watching music videos on TV. *A Girl Like You*, by Edwyn Collins, was one video that was on quite often, and seemed to stick in my memory.

Soon we numbered a dozen, all still wearing civilian clothes. Toward the end of the week, we bundled into a white minibus and set off to a nearby French military barracks for our first medical examination. A doctor closely measured and examined us from head to toe: our body weight, soundness of knees and ankles, arms and elbows, and heart rate. Even our teeth. As each man's examination was completed, he was ordered back aboard the minibus until all of us had been through the process.

Back at the recruitment depot, several men were ordered to pack up their belongings and leave. It seemed that poor teeth or previously broken limbs ensured dismissal. The rest of us were taken to an adjacent building that served as a storage area. Here, we turned in our civilian property and were issued second-hand green polyester tracksuits that looked like they were designed in the seventies. We were allowed to keep only our shoes and personal toiletries.

Each day, three of us were selected to help prepare our meals in the kitchen. While adequate, the food was certainly not representative of French cuisine, and most of it came out of tin cans. Despite this, mealtime was an opportunity to socialize. We were a pretty diverse group: French, Belgian, Croatian, Russian, Romanian, and Slovenian. And me, the only Canadian and true English-speaker. Those who shared a common language sometimes broke off into small groups, but at the table most of the conversation was in broken English, of which everybody seemed to have at least a basic understanding. Unsurprisingly, the topic of most conversations was the Legion and the various urban myths and legends surrounding it. Nothing more than fanciful bullshit, but it kept us busy.

I talked mostly with Stefan, and he confided that before joining the Legion he and several others had tried to stow away in a container from France to Belgium, bound for a freighter to Canada. He was intercepted in Belgium and sent back to France. Stefan couldn't understand why a Canadian would want to leave what he viewed as a land of plenty to join the Legion. For the first time, I realized that we weren't all there for the same reasons. I was looking for a military adventure. He, like many others, was looking for a way out.

Seven days passed, and after much cleaning we were reissued our civilian clothes for the evening's lowering of the *tricolore*. Afterwards, we got on a minibus that took us to the Strasbourg train station, where we boarded a train for the Foreign Legion's headquarters, the 1er Régiment étranger (1er RE), in Aubagne on France's Mediterranean coast. Created in 1841, the 1er RE is the Legion's oldest and most senior regiment. It's referred to as Maison Mère, Mother House of the Legion. The expression was inherited from the Legion's time based in Sidi Bel Abbès, Algeria.

Our group sat together in a railcar, feeling a little out of place amid the other passengers despite wearing our civilian clothes. As the hours passed and the train headed southward, the conversation among everyone increasingly led to what would happen to us when we arrived in Aubagne. I kept my thoughts to myself and watched the gradual change in light as morning arrived. My surroundings were very different, but at the same time, I was excited about the unknown to follow.

CHAPTER THREE

Aubagne

It was dawn when the train pulled into the station at Aubagne, and we were immediately marshalled together onto a Transport Renault militaire, military transport trucks known as TRMs. The feel of the TRMs' cold, hard steel benches in the open back was something I would become intimately familiar with in the years ahead.

During the short drive to our destination, everyone was deathly silent. Pulling off the main road, we passed through the front gates of the 1er RE. Two guards in immaculate uniforms, wearing white kepis and carrying assault rifles slung across their chests, snapped to attention at an order barked by an equally well-dressed sergent wearing a black kepi.

Inside the gates, we drove up a steep hill into a small fenced area adjacent to a parade square. This was the volunteer compound. As the trucks rolled to a stop, a caporal-chef shouted at us to dismount with our bags. We joined groups of volunteers from other recruitment centres, numbering well over one hundred, and lined up in single file on the parade square opposite the basement entrance of a single-storey building.

In an organized fashion, we entered what turned out to be the supply room and stood in line. Here, a caporal-chef ordered us to strip down to our underwear and put on green seventies-style tracksuits identical to those issued to us in Strasbourg. Our wallets, money, and watches were taken away and sealed inside individually labelled manila envelopes. Clothes and shoes were also taken from us and stored either in military duffel bags or, if they were deemed adequate, our civilian bags. We were then issued personal toiletries, T-shirts, a pair of white sports shorts, socks, underwear, a single towel, and a small padlock for our personal locker in the barrack rooms. Those without proper running shoes were handed hard-soled Adidas runners.

We were then directed back outside to the parade square. By now, the sun was rising and the small compound was crowded with a couple hundred volunteers dressed either in green tracksuits or green combat fatigues. A caporal-chef was standing on the stairs leading to the building's main entrance. Hispanic and short in stature, he wore a large pair of mirrored aviator sunglasses that dominated his face and gave him the look of a South American dictator. The caporal-chef barked out orders in a Spanish-tinged accent as we clumsily organized ourselves into several rows on the parade square, following the guys who already knew the drill.

Around us, men were speaking in a variety of languages unfamiliar to me. All orders and other information were given in French and quickly translated to the others by those who understood. A short time after forming up, we were allowed to take a break. I heard guys speaking English and walked over to them and introduced myself. Most of them had already spent three to four weeks in the compound. At any time, they warned, the Legion could kick you out with no reason given.

"What will we do here for three or four weeks?" I asked.

"Not much," one replied. "It's shite, mate."

The routine for the first week quickly became apparent: up at 0630 hours for roll call, or *appel* as it's called in French, followed by a collective march in loose formation to the kitchen hall for our typical breakfast of baguettes and coffee. An NCO, usually a sergent, was placed in charge of us for mealtimes. Only when he had seen that the last volunteer had received his allotted portion of food would he take his. Once he finished gulping it down, usually in record time, groups of fifty men were marched back to the compound, whether we had finished eating or not.

Back in barracks, we immediately set to making our beds in the required battery style, cleaning out our lockers and closing them. Then we cleaned the communal washrooms and hallways and emptied all the garbage containers. By 0730 hours, we once again formed up in ranks on the parade ground. Reading from clipboards, the NCO yelled out last names. As men were called forward, they formed up in ranks before the NCO who requested their presence. Those who didn't understand the commands were referred to as a "melon," or "simpleton."

Each of the half-dozen groups that resulted were marched off to be subjected to the many screening tests and medical reviews required. Not everyone was called forward. Those who weren't were split into manual-labour groups. Some were sent to one of the regiment's three mess halls to work in the kitchens, where they moved food stores and cleaned up after meals had been served. Others were put to work sweeping the roads and parade squares, or raking leaves and pruning the regiment's many trees and bushes.

The threat of being rejected hung over everyone, adding to the overall feeling of unease. Every afternoon, an NCO read out a list of names. You didn't want to hear your name. No matter how far you had advanced through the selection process, if your name was called out, it meant you didn't meet the Legion's criteria. No explanations were ever given. The men would gather their gear, be escorted to the regiment's front gates, and issued a train ticket back to the town where they had enlisted.

The series of medical examinations was similar to what I had experienced in Strasbourg, but more meticulous and invasive. Exams were done at the regiment's infirmary: our teeth, joints, and backs were scrutinized. My years spent playing hockey had left me with a collection of scars, including a prominent one on my forehead, which I was asked to account for. During the psychological examinations, we were ordered to stand to attention before several medical officers, who asked questions in either French or English. I was asked about my childhood and life up to joining the Legion. A translator was available for those who spoke neither language. Although my French was improving, most of the officers preferred to speak to me in passable English.

Once these tests were completed, we were taken in trucks to the Laveran military hospital in Marseille for further examinations and a range of blood tests. During the recruitment phase, some people were diagnosed with life-threatening illnesses or serious conditions that would have otherwise gone unnoticed. A Serbian recruit was rejected after they discovered he had a bullet wound.

Each of us was also subjected to an IQ evaluation. The results were critical in determining what courses or even career options we would be best suited for, and this information would follow us through our time in the Legion.

The final phase of the evaluation, referred to as "the Gestapo," was the most discussed among the potential recruits. The officer and NCOs conducting this phase were from the Legion's Deuxième bureau (B2), or internal security. This immediately dispelled one of the Legion's greatest myths: no questions asked. In fact, the Gestapo asked plenty of questions and dug deep, clearing our names through Interpol.

Then came the interviews. Twenty of us were lined up along a second-floor hallway. We stood silently, waiting until one by one our names were called out and we were told to enter the office for questioning. From day one rumours circulated, fuelling our paranoia. "Don't lie to the Gestapo; they know all!" It wasn't always the obvious things that suddenly snuffed out any prospects of a career in the Legion.

Sitting at the desk during my interview was an imposing NCO. He had a massive head and hands that dwarfed his typewriter. He spoke in clear English and instructed me to stand at ease. It was a Western military drill term. The NCO started with the basic questions I had been asked frequently during these past weeks: my name, country of origin, and the like. This repeated questioning was key to ensuring you were telling the truth.

Earlier, while waiting my turn outside, I overheard a recruit tell the NCO he had already answered the question, at which point the NCO shouted at him, "Just answer the fucking question!" In my case, he asked a lot of questions about the Canadian military reserves. Some of his questions were quite direct, asking for specifics and revealing a depth of knowledge that surprised me. At the end of my questioning, another NCO entered the room, and the two men exchanged words in a language I didn't recognize.

The next day, twenty of us were taken to Aubagne's athletics stadium for a physical fitness evaluation known as the Cooper test. It involved running as many laps of the stadium as you could in twelve minutes. Although the test wasn't difficult, several men failed. We weren't aware of the level we needed to pass; we were just told to run as fast for as long as we could until the whistle blew. It was the only physical fitness test of note we had during this recruitment phase, and it easily weeded out the unfit.

In our spare time, we tended to break out into our respective national or linguistic groups. I was the only Canadian recruit, but there were two English, two Irish, one Scottish, and an Australian. One of the English recruits stood out. He was easily six foot five. Apparently, his marital breakup had contributed to his decision to join the Legion, and he dropped occasional hints that he had served as a signaller in the British Special Air Services' reserve unit.

I hit it off with a Scottish recruit, Benny McDonald. Jock, as he was known, had served several years in a Scottish regiment of the British Army, and his arms and hands were covered with tattoos marking his time in the service.

Jock reminded me of a former classmate in England whom I'd had my first real fist fight with. On a school field trip to the Isle of Man, this large kid, referred to by others as a skinhead, apparently didn't like Canadians. Or maybe he just didn't like me. I had a crush on his girlfriend, and it was somewhat reciprocated. One evening in our hostel room, with his hand around my throat, he pushed me up against a wooden locker. I squeezed my eyes shut and threw a Hail Mary left that connected with his eye and sent him reeling. It was a eureka moment for me. Even our teacher didn't reprimand me.

The lack of physical exercise was getting on all our nerves, so we decided that each evening before dinner we would go for a run around the yard and mix in some push-ups and sit-ups. The yard had a set of pull-up bars and a rope tied to a tree. Both were there to relieve our boredom and help us prepare for the basic training phase, assuming we made it that far. Jock had been a sports monitor in the British Army, so he put us through some decent training circuits.

Each language group seemed to find its own place within the compound. The seven of us anglophones hung out near the main building. Although the Swedes and Norwegians all spoke excellent

English, we didn't mix with them much. The biggest groups hailed from the former Eastern-bloc countries: Russia, Poland, Ukraine, Romania, Hungary, Slovakia, and the Czech Republic. We commonly referred to them as *les communistes*, the communists. There were also several Serbians and a smaller number of Croatians from the ongoing Bosnian War. It wasn't uncommon for fights to break out between the Serbs and Croats. If a fight didn't end quickly, an NCO would break it up. Invariably, this was a ticket home for those involved.

Every second Friday of the month, a group of twenty-five to fifty volunteers were selected for basic training and shipped to Castelnaudary, home to the 4ᵉ Régiment étranger (4ᵉ RE). Three weeks in, it was with great relief that I was called out of the ranks with several others and issued second-hand combat pants, jacket, a belt, and boots. Our heads were shaved and we were moved to a cramped, smelly building in the volunteer compound, which we spent our time trying to clean. It was hard to imagine we were any closer to basic training except for the fact that we had been given a uniform and a new haircut.

A few days later, several of us from the group were issued a red plastic epaulette. We were now *rouge*, signifying that we had passed the Legion recruitment process and were bound for basic training. Known now as *les rouges*, we passed individually before a *colonel* in the regiment's HQ to sign our initial five-year contract with the Legion. We also received our Legion service numbers. Mine was *Matricule* 185-689.

What we didn't realize, though, was that an invisible vetting process continued behind closed doors. Every week, the recruitment cadre would assemble and assess the latest batch of candidates. Even those who passed all the tests still had to satisfy the cadre. Each man was discussed, not just his individual strengths and weaknesses, but also the cadre's overall impressions of him. This practice added an additional, more humane layer to the recruiting process rather than just set criteria.

At this point, a Legion myth was dispelled. For a short administrative period of time we were *hommes sans nom* (men without names), and those who needed an alias would be provided with one. This was dependent on each person's reason for joining the Legion, and what the Legion knew about us. The former Soviet-bloc recruits had no choice but to assume a *nom de guerre*, since serving in a foreign military was illegal in their countries and punishable by jail time. No Canadian laws forbade my choice to join the Legion, so I kept my name.

CHAPTER FOUR

Rouge

We were each assigned to a single barracks room for the final week prior to our departure to Castelnaudary, and issued two full sets of uniforms, new combats, boots, underwear, T-shirts, a backpack, canteens, new sportswear, runners, and toiletries.

Every morning, we gathered for parade to the right of the other volunteers who were still going through the recruitment process. Our group was then marched to the mess hall before the others. We spent most of our days finalizing all the administrative requirements and gathering the required kit. In the evenings, we were tasked with guarding the volunteer compound. Teamed up in threes, we took turns standing a two-hour watch. Simply armed with a flashlight and wooden baton, our duty was to ensure that no one left the compound. The remit was to stop deserters, although if caught, they would be kicked out anyway, so it seemed like a pointless exercise.

I was relieved to be through this first part. The thought of having to explain to others back home in Canada that I had failed to be accepted had gnawed at me.

One morning we were packed onto trucks and taken to Puyloubier, a village at the foot of Montagne Sainte-Victoire, northeast of Aubagne. An old château surrounded by vineyards, it houses Legion veterans. These were légionnaires who didn't have family or homes to return to in the civilian world. Most of these men had been injured in battle and were no longer fit for military duty or civilian life. Everyone at Puyloubier had an assigned duty, notably the production of award-winning wine, but some légionnaires made items such as small statuettes and paintings that were sold to support the home.

We were met with indifference by some of the veterans and greeted warmly by others. These old légionnaires were as curious about us as we were about them. On one occasion, while they were picking grapes, a veteran asked a recruit, "What did you do before you came here?" The recruit answered, "I was training to be a football coach." The veteran replied, "Ah, I knew a footballer. He got his legs blown off in Algeria."

Other veterans were suffering from post-traumatic stress disorder, and from time to time this manifested in violent outbursts. A friend told me how he had been chased around the kitchens by a knife-wielding veteran who, by all accounts, hadn't lost his killer instinct. Anecdotes aside, it was a one-of-a-kind place that did so much for those who had given their all.

For me, however, things soon took a turn for the worse. I came down with a fever the following day back in Aubagne. Although I tried to tough it out, I soon felt so ill that I reported to the NCO duty office. I was told, "Go back to your room and don't miss parade in the morning."

My condition worsened. I was diagnosed with chicken pox and segregated in a room at the regiment's infirmary for a week. Food was brought to me, and as each day dragged along, I spent my time trying not to scratch myself and worrying that this setback could result in my being rejected. But the medical officer assured me that once I recovered, I could join the next departing group. All I could think about was that the sooner I was out of the infirmary, the better.

While sitting in my room covered in red Betadine ointment to reduce the unrelenting itchiness, I was surprised to see Keith, a former member of the Royal Westminster Regiment, cleaning the infirmary hallway just outside my door. Although we were just brief acquaintances during my time with the Westies, it was more than strange to run into one another this way.

After a week in segregation, I was finally released and introduced to the latest group of rouges. The timing worked out well, since most of the English speakers I had befriended were rouge too. Jock, the two Irishmen—Fred O'Connor and Zafer Masalas, an Irish Cypriot—and the tall Brit, Alister, were all in my group. O'Connor was Mr. Average, but he was pale as the Irish can be, and he talked a lot. Masalas was practically the opposite. He was smaller, had a darker complexion, and was quiet. He mostly kept to himself, but he was a nice guy. Alister had a good sense of humour, but I sensed that he was a little flighty. Nothing going on seemed to sit well with him. The five of us went through the final week's program together, awaiting the arrival of our future training NCO and two caporals from the 4ᵉ Régiment étranger (4ᵉ RE).

When the NCO, Sergent Smit, and two French caporals finally arrived, they greeted us with looks that bordered on contempt. We stood to attention outside the main building on the parade square in our newly issued sportswear and were formally introduced to our training cadre.

Smit was a tall German. He was a big man, balding, and looked a little out of shape. That was surprising to me, but you never can tell. He was neither stocky nor built like a runner, but his facial expressions said a lot. He didn't seem like one to be messed with. Over the next few months, I'd confirm this first impression. We never learned the sergent's first name. It was "Sergent Smit, or get hit." The caporals were of average stature, and both were in good shape. They offered no smiles and were all business.

That morning, we ran outside the regiment through residential areas and along country roads. All seemed to be going well. Then I started hearing noises coming from the guys at the back. Those lagging behind were being kicked and tripped up by the caporals, who were also showering them with verbal abuse. The run wasn't difficult, but some of the men suffered. I kept up with the pack and was left alone. Masalas was a good runner, and he held his own at the front.

We spent the rest of the day finalizing the acquisition of our kit and fitting our uniforms and green berets, as well as the famous *kepi blanc*, a légionnaire's hallmark. The kepi's origins date back to 1914 or earlier. During the North African campaigns of the 1930s,[7] the original beige kepi cover would be bleached white by the African sun. And like many things in the military, this soon became symbolic. Tradition then followed that a légionnaire's kepi was white. An NCO wears a black kepi, as do the officers, although theirs differ slightly in appearance, defined by a series of silver or gold braid around the trim.

The next day, we were told we were going to Malmousque, and we boarded a truck for the leave centre for légionnaires on time off or on a medical rehabilitation program. The centre is within walking distance of Marseille's old port area and its buzzing nightlife. We certainly weren't there to rest, and we were tasked with the inevitable cleaning and other duties. The highlight of the day was our truck drive through the busy city streets, getting a glimpse of the outside world again. Although I hadn't spent much time in garrison, it already seemed like an eternity. It was alarming how quickly I had become detached from my previous life and tethered to a new one that was still being shaped.

While cleaning the centre, two guys in our group were caught speaking Polish to each other. Although talking in any language besides French had been accepted over the past few weeks, we soon learned that it was no longer tolerated. To demonstrate his displeasure, a caporal kneed one of the Poles in his midsection, and then ordered him to do push-ups. While he was doing push-ups, the caporal kicked him in his ribs, demanding that he pick up the pace. This was our first taste of the Legion's discipline—and a revelation.

CHAPTER FIVE

Castel

After breakfast, and as much of it as I could cram down my throat, twenty-five of us raw recruits left the 1er RE gates. It was October 21, 1994, and close to six weeks since I had arrived in Strasbourg. We bundled into a large white Legion bus headed to Marseille's train station to travel to Castel, home of the 4^e RE. As we drove toward the Mediterranean coast, we caught views of the distant brilliant blue sea in the early-morning sun. The space and scenery were jarring in contrast to the claustrophobia and depressing atmosphere of the Aubagne recruitment centre. At the station, a swarm of morning commuters rushed to catch their trains. We followed Smit to ours, clad in our new uniforms and green berets, each sporting a newly issued 4^e RE cap badge.

After being directed to our compartments, we split up into our respective language-based groups, or "mafias" as they were commonly referred, to hang out with the guys who had become the closest thing we had to friends. Smit had made it clear that he would not tolerate anyone speaking anything other than French unless he asked a direct question in another language. Silence was preferable, we were told; however, we were prohibited from sleeping during the five-hour train ride.

As the train clanked out of the busy station, I watched the city sights go by. The last month's recruitment phase had been stressful and at times boring. Finally heading to basic training seemed like a step in the right direction.

Smit began moving from one compartment to the next, and he eventually entered ours, greeting the English mafia. In clear English, he asked if we had any questions, and Jock asked what we could expect over the next four months. Smit dispelled the bullshit rumours we had heard back at the recruit compound. He said we would be assigned to the 3rd Company (3 Cie) for our basic training. To start, that would take place over four weeks at the 3rd Company's training facility, known as La Ferme, The Farm. We would be isolated at The Farm for the duration of this phase to ensure we were fully immersed in the lifestyle and discipline fundamental to the Legion.

That evening, the train pulled into Castelnaudary, a small town in southwestern France on the famous Canal du Midi, where two TRMs were waiting for us. We climbed into the back of the military trucks, which wound noisily through the narrow, tree-lined streets and gazed silently at the sidewalk cafés, shops, and homes all locked up for the night. We knew this would be our last look at civilization for a while.

Quartier du Capitaine Danjou, home to the 4ᵉ RE, stands on the outskirts of Castelnaudary close to the canal. Its name honours the memory of Capitaine Jean Danjou, who was killed during the Battle of Camarón (Camerone) in Mexico.[8] As we would soon learn, the Battle of Camerone symbolizes the Legion.

On April 30, 1863, Capitaine Jean Danjou's reconnaissance team of sixty-two légionnaires and three officers were attacked by two thousand Mexican infantry and cavalry. Capitaine Danjou, in a tactic typical of the time, formed his men into a defensive square. The Mexican cavalry charged the square and at one hundred yards had their charge shattered in the first volley of Legion musket fire. The Mexicans quickly withdrew.

Capitaine Danjou ordered a retreat to a nearby farmhouse from where the légionnaires fought off repeated attacks by the Mexicans, who had called reinforcements. From the outset, the situation was hopeless. The farmhouse was surrounded. Now, numbering several thousand men, the Mexicans called for the légionnaires to surrender. They refused. At this point, Capitaine Danjou is said to have made each man swear to fight to the death, a concept that's rather obscure nowadays. Capitaine Danjou, who had lost a hand in another campaign (he wore a prosthetic one made of wood), was struck by a musket ball and killed. His second-in-command,

Lieutenant Maudet, took over and continued fighting. As the day wore on, the légionnaires became low on ammunition. Most were dead or wounded. Only a handful of légionnaires remained.

At this point, and depending on whose account you believe, the Mexicans either overran the position or the légionnaires fixed bayonets and charged. A fast-thinking Mexican officer asked the three remaining légionnaires to surrender. They agreed. But only if the Mexicans promised to provide immediate care for their wounded. When the three survivors were brought before the Mexican colonel in command, he is reported to have said, "These are not men. They are demons."

The Battle of Camerone came to symbolize the ultimate example of the Legion's battle ethic, sense of duty, loyalty, and determination to fulfil a mission. Capitaine Danjou's wooden hand was recovered from the battle, and it's now on display in the 1er RE museum. The phrase *"Faire Camerone,"* or to do Camerone, is often used by légionnaires as an analogy for any situation where the odds are against them.

Unlike Aubagne or the garrison where I had enlisted, the Quartier du Capitaine Danjou (or Castel, as it is referred to) was built in the late 1980s, replacing an older *casern* in the town's centre. The new garrison is composed of four company buildings situated around a parade square, an indoor shooting range, athletics track, gym, various training buildings, and a château. The regiment's headquarters is set directly across from the main gate, overlooking the centre of the parade square.

When the TRMs stopped, the two caporals immediately jumped out of the cabs and began yelling at us to disembark. We all scrambled down, throwing our backpacks and kit bags to the ground, and formed up in three rows. Another caporal, who had been waiting for us to arrive, quickly made it understood that we had better be on the third-floor hallway of the barracks with our kit before he reached it.

Backpacks on and kit bags in hand, we rushed in a mob up the company building's cramped stairwell. Another caporal met us there, yelling for everyone to immediately assume the push-up position. We dropped to the floor and did push-ups until we collapsed. Both caporals then started kicking us in our sides and screaming at us to get to our feet and stand to attention. We lined up in the hallway, rigidly at attention, and they counted us. Then they sent us back downstairs with our full kit, only to order us to turn around and run back up to the third floor. That was the routine for a good part of the evening, running up and down those damn stairs with our kit.

Finally, once we were all thoroughly familiar with the stairwell, we were divided into groups of six and assigned to a room where there was a single bed and a locker for each man. In a washroom attached to each room were three sinks and three showers. A small balcony off each room overlooked the large parade square. An orders board in the hallway displayed a diagram of how our kit was to be laid out and how our lockers were to be kept. The caporal advised us that there would be an inspection in one hour.

Our first lesson in how life would be as a recruit in Castel came via a ritual known as *appel*. All twenty-five of us lined up in the hallway along the wall, shoulders touching. We then counted off in French, each yelling the next number in succession, to ensure all section members were present and accounted for.

The caporal prowled up and down the ranks, inflicting immediate punishment in the form of a slap to the face or a knee to the stomach if there was a miscount. At one point, Alister, after receiving a verbal lashing and hard, open-handed slap across the face for getting his number wrong, said to the caporal, "But I don't speak French, Caporal." I couldn't help but laugh just a little. It's the French Foreign Legion, after all. I was damn lucky to have basic French knowledge on my side.

Appel would become a routine in our lives. Its intent was to quickly identify anyone who might have decided to desert. It was also a fast and effective way to gather a section together to issue orders. Our first morning appel, Alister and a Norwegian were missing—deserted. Apparently they had jumped the regiment wall just hours prior. This seemed strange to me. Like, what had they been expecting with basic training? They hadn't even lasted twenty-four hours in Castel.

Morning, noon, and night, our section, now twenty-three men, would form up and march from the company barracks to the mess hall. A caporal would set the pace, calling out the slow Legion pace at eighty-eight steps per minute. During the first few days, our attempts to maintain the timing, as well as the proper intervals between our rows, were ragged. In hindsight, it was comical. The other caporals, positioned at our sides, attempted to instill order by yelling at us and hitting anyone who fell out of step. Whether being struck and shouted at helped anyone improve was debatable. The pressure made some even more jumpy. Their marching only worsened and had a domino effect on those positioned behind. Some would go into meltdown and start swinging their arms in rhythm with their legs.

Our cue to assemble for the mealtime marches was when the duty-training caporal yelled "Rassemblement dehors!" or "Assemble outside!" We immediately lined up at attention, awaiting the arrival of our caporals, who then put us through a short regimen of push-ups, intended to warm up our arms and encourage our appetites, before marching us to the mess hall.

The first visit to the mess hall provided a chance to size up légionnaires, most of whom were somewhere in their second to fourth month of basic training. Castel is also where légionnaires from the operational regiments are sent for their caporal, or sergent's course, and specialized training in everything from communications, IT to mechanics and medical training.

In the mess hall, a number of légionnaires were wearing the 2e Régiment étranger de parachutistes (2e REP referred to as "Le REP") cap badge depicting a winged hand holding a sword. I immediately noticed they were in excellent physical condition and carried themselves in a manner that stood out from the rest of us. They had an air of proven confidence. I wanted that cap badge too.

We lined up for food, and armed with our stainless-steel trays, were ordered to take a table as a section. As in Aubagne, our caporal received his food tray after the rest of us, and he would eat with the other caporals while keeping an eagle eye on us. That first day, none of us had finished our meals before he walked up and ordered us to follow him outside. We quickly learned to eat very fast or risk starving.

Some of the guys tried smuggling food back to their rooms, but the caporals were well versed in this tactic and made us turn out our

pockets. The usual contraband was dessert, and the penalty was pre-
dictable: a hard slap to the side of the head. Then the entire section
was made to do push-ups right outside the mess hall until we collapsed. When it wasn't possible for us to do a single more push-up,
we were made to assume stress positions in push-up stance, knees
off the ground, with our asses in the air. Anyone who faltered and
dropped was kicked until he managed to regain his stance. After a
few incidents, nobody tried smuggling food out of the mess hall,
and the caporal stopped inspecting our pockets.

Our evenings were usually spent taking basic French lessons in
the company's classroom, followed by washing and ironing our
combats and polishing our boots. At 2100 hours, the caporals would
inspect our rooms, along with the section hallway, stairs, and washrooms. We were then to form up in the hallway and the duty caporal
would announce whether we were to wear our combats or tracksuits for the evening appel at 2200 hours.

At 2200 hours sharp, after a whistle from the *bureau de semaine*
with an added shout of "appel" down the hallways, the arrival
of the company duty sergent was preceded by the shouted order,
"Garde-à-vous!" or "Attention!" from our caporal. We immediately snapped to attention, each slapping our legs with our hand
in one collective crack. The caporal then presented the section for
review, announcing that the 3rd Company, 3rd Section was present
for inspection. Next, he announced his rank, name, time of service,
and current function. In response, the duty sergent saluted and then
strolled down the line, counting us off one by one and giving each
of us a short punch to the solar plexus. The trick was to not flinch or
he would stop and do it again.

When all were accounted for, he inspected the quarters with
emphasis on the floor in hopes of finding black polish that had
scuffed off our boots. If all was acceptable, the sergent released the
section back to the caporal. Once appel was complete, anyone who
had made mistakes during the day could expect punishment detail
and, invariably, the entire section would be disciplined too.

The punishments varied and largely came down to the caporal's
imagination. *Revue Caméléon* involved everyone changing into a
given uniform, and back in the hallway for appel as fast as possible.

The first to arrive in the hallway had to do push-ups until the last guys arrived. Others were not quite as amusing, as anyone who has cleaned a toilet cubicle with a toothbrush can testify. If we were lucky enough to have avoided a punishable error, we were free to hit the showers and then go to bed. The punishments had their place. They helped build the collective spirit, fostering mutual support, which is key to any military unit.

At 0600 hours, the sound of a whistle announced the start of our day. The duty sergent and caporal dictated the rhythm of our days with regular whistle blasts—morning reveille, each appel, parade, meal, and the three daily building cleanings—followed by shouts along the hallways announcing the proper timings for specific activities. The moment the morning whistle sounded, we jumped out of our beds and rushed to the hallway to be counted. Once everyone was accounted for, we made our beds, changed into our uniforms, gathered downstairs, and the caporal marched us to the parade square for presentation to the duty sergent. Afterwards, he marched us in formation, by section or company, to the mess hall for breakfast.

After eating, we showered and shaved, ironed our clothes, and polished our boots until morning parade at 0730 hours. After presentation to the duty sergent, the caporal informed us of the day's activities. This usually consisted of physical exercise in the morning and classroom work during the afternoon, which concentrated on French lessons and Legion history. The main goal at this point was to ingrain in our minds the French military rank system. NCOs checked our abilities to remember the junior, NCO, and officer ranks, and properly pronounce them by having us stand and individually recite in their order: *engagé volontaire, légionnaire deuxième classe, légionnaire première classe, caporal, caporal-chef, sergent, sergent-chef, adjudant, adjudant-chef,* and *major.*

The officer rank structure started with *sous-lieutenant,* followed by *lieutenant, capitaine, commandant, lieutenant-colonel, colonel,* and *général.* Officers, who were graduates of the École spéciale militaire de Saint-Cyr, begin their careers as young sous-lieutenants and usually spend most of the careers in the Legion. The Legion is commanded by a brigadier general at the 1er RE. Each Legion regiment is commanded by either a lieutenant-colonel or colonel. Companies are commanded by capitaines, and company sections by lieutenants. They can also be commanded by a senior NCO, a sergent-chef, or adjudant, the latter of which was the case with our section.

While the Legion is part of the French military, it retains its own history, traditions, and discipline. Within the French military, it is understood that a légionnaire differs from a regular soldier in that the expectations and discipline are higher. When I joined, the French military still operated mandatory service, a throwback to the Cold War. The French military possessed a relatively small number of professional and deployable military units, of which the Legion was a part. Known as the Force d'action rapide (FAR), the rapid reaction force, it was the spearhead of the French army.

A légionnaire's initial contract is five years, with an opportunity to leave after completion of the four-month basic training phase if one felt the Legion wasn't for him. On completion of the five years with a good service record, a one- to three-year extension is offered. Fifteen years' service was required to qualify for a military pension.

A légionnaire's pay was fair, averaging 1000 euros per month. Overseas tours and postings resulted in substantial pay increases. When based in mainland France, légionnaires are subject to income tax deductions. The norm is for légionnaires to spend two years of the original five-year contract overseas.

On arrival in Castel, we were provided with a bank account and a personal debit card issued by La Poste, the French Post Office banking program. Our monthly wages were transferred directly into our accounts. This was a new form of payment for the Legion. Historically, pay was doled out at a monthly money parade where each légionnaire presented himself to the paymaster, holding out his kepi into which the appropriate number of French francs was dropped.

CHAPTER SIX

The Farm

Two weeks into our time in Castel, the second allotment of men arrived from Aubagne, bringing our section to full strength of fifty recruits. Our section leader, Sergent-Chef Sébastien, a Spaniard, had returned from leave to take command. A Turkish and a French sergent also joined the section.

Each training company in Castel has its own farm. We set off to ours: Raissac. Before boarding the trucks, we were told that those who finished their breakfast faster than the rest would have a chance to use the phones in the mess hall foyer. I made a dash, taking the opportunity to call home for the first time. Despite the time difference, I got through and told my parents that I was fine, I was in the Legion, and warned them that it was unlikely I'd be able to call them again any time soon. As I put the phone back on its hook, I suddenly felt a long way from home.

The next four weeks would be our first real challenge in basic training. Its purpose was to weed out anyone deemed unfit for the Legion. We would be presented with our white kepis only when we completed The Farm.

The drive through the countryside offered a welcome change of scenery, and after about two hours we arrived at Raissac, which stood alone in the middle of a large open field, flanked by several steep hills with a long tree-lined drive leading up to it. In normal circumstances, it would have been picturesque.

Although we had been told that our destination was The Farm, it had never occurred to me that this literally was the case. There was nothing military about the place at all. It looked precisely like any of the dozens of other farmhouses we had passed along the way.

Castelnaudary, southwestern France, 4ᵉ Régiment étranger, 3rd Company, Raissac Training Farm. (*Credit:* 4ᵉ Régiment étranger)

Mainly because it was, complete with cattle sheds, a waterhole, and other typically French farm buildings. Looking out to the nearby hills, I noticed they were marked by a series of well-worn paths I would become intimately acquainted with. As the trucks rumbled up the long driveway, I thought to myself, "OK, four weeks. One day at a time."

The farmhouse was a split-level building. The left-hand side provided accommodation for the training staff in the form of a traditional stone-built farmhouse, which again looked no different from a regular home. It included a separate dining area and living space that was well furnished with couches and chairs arranged around a TV and large fireplace. The centre to right-hand side of the building consisted of a large eating area, kitchen, a classroom, accommodations, washrooms, and showers for légionnaires in training.

Our sleeping area at the far end of the building consisted of two large, open rooms with double bunks and small metal lockers. Between our living area and the kitchen was our classroom with desks, stools, and a large blackboard. Our first night was spent cleaning the eating area, kitchen, classroom, sleeping area, and arranging our individual lockers and kit.

Two new training caporals joined us at The Farm. Both came from the 2ᵉ REP and had drawn this assignment as part of their preparation for their sergent's course. The smaller of the two caporals was French Portuguese. He had a rat face. He just seemed mean, and I immediately felt like I needed to avoid him. Caporal Accante, a Romanian, was built like a boxer, complete with broken nose. As ex-Romanian military, he came across as fair and capable.

Together, the men would implement the NCO's orders. Our responses to them were to be limited to "Oui, caporal" or "Non, caporal." They imposed a strict routine that involved being called outside for appel, or *rassemblement*, easily a dozen times an hour. With each bellowed call to form up, the entire section dropped whatever it was doing and raced to line up outside our living area, facing our accommodation block. Here, we assumed the push-up position while waiting for any stragglers to arrive.

There was always someone caught by the rassemblement, busy on the toilet, or well away from the farmhouse on some assigned task. When nobody could continue doing push-ups, we assumed stress positions, normally crouching with knees bent, back braced against the farm wall, arms held out straight before us until everyone was present. That one was hell on the thighs.

The next day's orders were tacked to a board mounted on the wall, and each evening the caporals would read them out to ensure we all understood exactly what they expected. Cleaning details were established. Each day, three légionnaires were selected for kitchen duty. Two would do food preparation while the third served the NCOs their meals. All the food was carefully measured, and stealing any was a serious offence. After our first meal a Russian working the kitchen was caught with a yogurt container he'd pilfered, and we were made to watch while he was forced to eat the entire carton of yogurt stored in the kitchen refrigerator without pause.

Any error, collective or individual, resulted in a shared punishment. We were only as good as our weakest member, so those who were stronger had best help the less capable. But those of us who were stronger and more capable soon lost patience with the guys making our days a lot harder. It wasn't long before a clear hierarchy of ability became evident within our group.

That first morning in the classroom, the section was broken into three smaller instructional groups, each with its own sergent. Our head NCO briefed us on what we would be required to do over the next four weeks, both as a section and as individuals.

Immersed in our routine, we rose at 0600 hours or earlier for the *appel* outside. Jumping out of our sleeping bags (which we slept in on our beds' mattresses) each morning without time to get dressed, we formed up outside in our underwear. November mornings were cold, and push-ups, while half-naked in subzero temperatures in the rain, waiting for the last man to appear, quickly wore our collective patience thin.

The tough routine brought the expected result. During our first week, another Brit, an Australian, and a New Zealander from the latest group to join us were missing at morning appel. Once again, the realization that they had deserted struck me as odd. The caporals' reactions were minimal. They passed the information on to the duty sergent, who in turn informed Sergent-Chef Sébastien, who we assumed then informed the company CO back in Castel. Other than that, the desertion was not discussed.

Ultimately, no one wants a deserter in the ranks. I often wondered where these guys went, with no money, transport, ID, or civilian clothes, wandering the French countryside in green seventies-era tracksuits. It seemed like it was always the anglophones doing the deserting. I wondered who would be next.

Dismissed from morning appel, we shaved, put on our sports attire, and formed up for the morning parade and presentation to the day's duty sergent. We were fed a minimal amount at breakfast, which was a quick affair. Day two we went for a long run, followed by push-ups and sit-ups, and finished off with a rope climb in the cattle sheds. We were then split into three groups, depending on our individual athletic abilities. After the morning's physical fitness, we were given time to shower and change into our combats for the day's training.

At 1000 hours, we ate *casse-croûte*, generally a baguette sandwich of some type. It didn't matter—anything was appreciated. For classroom work and training purposes, we were broken down into *binômes*, or groups of two. This is a tradition that dates back to the Roman Legions whereby two soldiers were designated to guard each other's backs in battle.

We spent hours learning French vocabulary, both in and out of the classroom. The rules were that those who spoke the language were to make sure that everyone else understood. My French was coming along well enough, so I had an easier time, and I did my best to help Jock, O'Connor, and Masalas. They were keen to learn as it became apparent that those who were falling behind were often assigned cleaning details or kitchen duty. A large part of our training was classroom-based, and we soon dreaded the long hours in class, as well as our nemesis, Smit, who was our least favourite teacher. He was less patient and quicker to dole out punishment, preferring an open-handed hard slap to the head or a hard knee to the gut.

Hunger was a constant companion. The combination of physical fitness, long hours in the classroom, and the seemingly endless push-ups took its toll on everyone. We gauged the passage of the day in relation to mealtimes, and it was the expectation of the next meal that gave us the strength or drive to keep going. Not only was the food appreciated, for some, mealtimes were the only break when they could relax. It was clear that the calories burned off far exceeded those consumed, placing extra strain on our already overburdened minds and bodies. For some, this would be a defining factor in success or failure.

Each meal was preceded by the *apéro*, French slang for an aperitif; however, this did not consist of an alcoholic beverage as the name suggests. Instead, it was a cocktail of chin-ups, push-ups, sit-ups, and a 20-foot rope climb using only our arms. It was all about technique and upper-body strength, and it wasn't long before some of us were suffering from tennis elbow. Complaining about the pain didn't help. The caporals who oversaw the apero couldn't have cared less.

Afterwards, we were marched to the kitchen for our meagre ration of food—edible, but insufficient. The caporals made it a habit to offer extra helpings to those whom they thought had earned it during the day's training. While this caused some animosity, even the most grudging had to acknowledge that it was generally those who were doing well in the physical fitness end of things who got the reward. It was incentive to try harder.

Finally, we were introduced to the FAMAS 5.56mm assault rifle. By studying overhead-projector diagrams, we learned the names of the weapon's components and the breakdown and reassembly procedures while simultaneously identifying each component out loud. At first, the FAMAS seemed peculiar to me. It was small and quite different from the Canadian C7, but I came to appreciate how sturdy and trustworthy the FAMAS was.

While weapons training was something I took to eagerly, there was another cornerstone of training that gave me nothing but frustration: the numerous Legion marching songs. With many just struggling with simple French, like the words for *knife* and *fork*, having to memorize an entire song by heart and then sing it correctly in tune as a group was one of the toughest assignments we faced.

Marching songs are an important Legion tradition, and throughout its history, regiments have marched into battle singing. Most songs tell the stories of former campaigns and battles. Although I respected the Legion's history, I disliked the singing as it was completely alien to my concept of what soldiering should be. My previous exposure to army life had been an entirely different experience.

Our company song was one of the first ones we had to learn. "Contre les Viets" commemorates the bitterly fought war in French Indochina, present-day Vietnam. As you'd expect, the lyrics are patriotic, but typical of their time.

Contre les Viets

Contre les Viets, contre l'ennemi / Against the Viets, against the enemy

Partout où le devoir fait signe / Wherever duty calls

Soldats de France, soldats du pays / Soldiers of France, soldiers of the country

Nous remonterons vers les lignes / We will march toward the front

Légionnaires, le combat qui commence / Légionnaires, the battle that begins

Met dans nos âmes, enthousiasme et vaillance / Places enthusiasm and courage into our souls

Peuvent pleuvoir grenades et gravats / It may rain grenades and gravel

Notre victoire en aura plus d'éclat / Our victory will be sweeter

Et si la mort nous frappe en chemin / But if death strikes us down

Si nos doigts sanglants se crispent au sol / If our bloody fingers stiffen on the ground

Un dernier raid, adieu et demain / One last raid, farewell and tomorrow

Nous souhaiterons faire école / We will wish to train

Malgré les balles, malgré les obus / Despite the bullets and the shells

Sous les rafales et sous les bombes / Under fire and bombs

Nous avançons vers le même but / We will advance toward the same goal

Dédaignant l'appel de la tombe / Ignoring the call of the grave

There was a songbook called *Carnet des Chants*, which contained all the Legion marching songs, and it seemed like we spent more time singing than soldiering. Each song is sung so that the tune matches the slow pace of the Legion's march. In some songs, secondary singers are assigned for a specific tenor chorus filling the background.

The long evening rehearsals were hard to take, especially when Smit was playing maestro. However, to our surprise, and to Smit's, the hours of practice paid off. We found ourselves able to sing while marking time in the classroom. With that accomplished, it was now time to combine the songs with marching outside.

We spent entire days marching up and down the tree-lined drive in song, the sergents calling out for us to sing whatever song took their fancy. If we made a mistake, we were stopped and corrected. If we continued to screw up, we were told "marche canard," or duck walk. This meant squatting, hands on our heads, and waddling along until our burning thighs couldn't take it anymore. Over time, we developed muscles that could sustain the marche canard in song at the proper cadence.

Eventually, after what felt like an era, we had mastered half a dozen songs. That seemed to meet some quota, since suddenly the sergents forgot about singing, and the training moved onto other things. In hindsight, I now appreciate that every military unit maintains tradition since it creates a sense of identity, and in the case of the Legion, recalls the operations and wars fought. Songs are a map book of military history, and with an institution as steeped in tradition as the Legion, singing is an essential part. But I still couldn't get into it.

The singing, the language, the fitness—at a certain point, I felt that things were finally coming together. My training section's sergent, Timurhan, was from the 2ᵉ REP and I guessed he was in his thirties. Sergent Timurhan was of average stature and size, but he was in good physical condition and ran us hard.

I think he appreciated my willingness to put in the effort. For instance, if we were sent up the hillside trails for failing to do something correctly, I ran at those hills like I wanted to be the first to the top. He generally treated us fairly, but liked to harass people and talk shit if they didn't make the effort or get the results he wanted. One of his favourite sayings was, "France pays me to train you; they are wasting their money."

Every morning, Sergent Timurhan led the stronger running group, for which I had narrowly qualified. But I had been improving steadily. Shedding my extra pounds and muscle mass had made me leaner and faster. Jock and Masalas were both in good shape, and they were also members of this group. Before finding my own pace, I concentrated on sticking close to their heels. But I enjoyed the running and fitness sessions. Both were a reprieve from the classroom and a good way to release frustration.

Most of the recruits agreed that Legion training was far from what we had expected. The emphasis on singing and the constant hunger that gnawed at our guts didn't help. We were blissfully ignorant of the fact that this was part of the training. Things improved somewhat when we started concentrating on elementary combat skills. Although some of us had previous military experience, the majority did not. For those of us who had been through some military training, we soon learned that the Legion way is significantly different.

At first, we dug small, one-man trenches, and worked on our individual firing positions, going from a basic standing position to kneeling or prone, and did so for long periods of time. We trained on the *parcours du combattant* (PC), or assault course, which involved clearing twenty different obstacles using a specific technique for each. Initially, we did this wearing only our combats, but once we had mastered the techniques, we completed it in full combat gear, including our webbing and backpacks. On days when the physical and mental game was taking its toll on me, I would look up at the sky and think of home.

We also started marching for several hours at night as a complete section with our FAMAS, webbing, and backpacks. With each passing march, the duration extended until we spent most of a night marching, passing through local villages, forests, and fields. I enjoyed the marches and didn't find them too difficult, but some of the guys developed large blisters from the friction of our stiff leather boots. Nobody showed them much sympathy. Suffer in silence. That was the attitude.

Cumulative fatigue meant we were usually in a state of semi-sleep, simply following the man immediately in front of us. If the NCO stopped abruptly to examine an obstacle or check his map, everybody collided. Sometimes a guy would stumble into a ditch and two or three others would land right on top of him. I was usually assigned as the last man in the line of march. It was a good spot to be with nobody stepping on my heels.

Often Jock would drop back and join me, where out of the NCO's earshot we could speak in English without fear of being caught. I respected Jock. He had served in the British military and done several tours in Northern Ireland. Not only was he physically fit, he didn't have an attitude and was willing to help out guys. Most importantly, having another like-minded person around with a sense of humour was appreciated. We were able to laugh at the day's challenges, or bullshit, and he shared many anecdotes from his time in Northern Ireland, which as a novice soldier, I listened to.

After each night march, we would hit the cold showers and then crawl into our sleeping bags with only three to four hours before wake up. However, this didn't guarantee a full night's sleep since each group was required to stand guard, which meant two men had to be on watch for an hour. This exercise was to ensure nobody left The Farm, but there was an informal understanding among us that if someone was spotted trying to desert, we would look the other way. Two more guys did—a Spaniard and a Finn—and we never saw them again.

It was a tiresome truth that whenever we met one expectation, the NCOs would declare that we were weak in another. One evening, Smit announced a room inspection, and we all stood to attention by our lockers. I could hear the open-handed slaps and knees to the body given to those whose lockers he considered unacceptable. A Russian standing rigidly to my front had fear written all over his face.

Smit arrived, eyeing my bed and locker, and then gazed at me. With a smirk, he demanded, "Why is your locker such a colossal mess, Struthers?" Without waiting for an answer, he brought his hand up in slow motion, and with a decent swing hit me with an open-handed slap to the face. He then moved on to the next locker. The worst punishments were handed out to those caught with unwashed socks, underwear, or—sin of sins—food. Smit emptied most of our lockers' contents out onto the floor and pushed over a few bunks for added effect. With the room in ruins, he announced that he would be back in an hour. The next inspection was declared an equal disaster, and the place was ransacked again. This game went on all night until we were presented to the duty NCO the next morning. Playing along, the NCO declared that since we all looked well rested after a good night's sleep, we could go for a long run.

The weeks passed, and our physical fitness levels were way up. Our French was improving, and we could march singing whatever song was requested without too many mistakes. And despite my dislike of singing, the fact that we could march as a section collectively in song made me proud.

Our time at The Farm was finished. The final three days would involve a forced march, meaning a march of longer duration than what we had been used to. It was called *la marche kepi* because it was after this that you earned the right to wear the coveted white kepi and be promoted to the rank of *légionnaire deuxième classe*, second-class *légionnaire*.

That evening, after loading the trucks with our kit and farm stores, including a lot of leftover food, we shouldered our backpacks and weapons and headed off on the trail, following newly promoted Adjudant Sébastien, NCOs, and caporals. We marched from dusk till dawn, and during the day we built two-man fighting trenches that we slept in for a few hours. The third and final day, we formed up at noon and marched through heavy rain, arriving at a privately owned château. We changed into our clean combats, polished our boots, and strapped our FAMAS across our chests. The box from Aubagne with our kepis was brought out, our names were individually called, and our pre-sized kepis were handed to us. We were then told to stand in the ranks with our kepis in our right hands.

We awaited the 4ᵉ RE commanding officer's arrival. When his staff car pulled up, the order "Garde-à-vous!" was given, and as a section we came to attention. The CO walked up to face Adjudant Sébastien, who presented the section. Jock was then ordered to step forward and recite the first line of the Légionnaire's Code of Honour.[9] The rest of the section then joined in and recited the code in unison:

- Légionnaire, tu es un volontaire, servant la France avec honneur et fidélité. / Légionnaire, you are a volunteer serving France with honour and loyalty.
- Chaque légionnaire est ton frère d'armes, quelle que soit sa nationalité, sa race, ou sa religion. Tu lui manifestes toujours la solidarité étroite qui doit unir les membres d'une même famille. / Every légionnaire is your brother in arms, irrespective of his nationality, race, or religion. You will show him the same solidarity as that which bonds a family.
- Respectueux des traditions, attaché à tes chefs, la discipline et la camaraderie sont ta force, le courage et la loyauté tes vertus. /

Respectful of traditions, loyal to your commanders, discipline and camaraderie are your force, courage and loyalty your virtues.

☐ Fier de ton état de légionnaire, tu le montres dans ta tenue toujours élégante, ton comportement toujours digne mais modeste, ton casernement toujours net. / Proud of your status as a légionnaire, you express this through your uniform, always smart, your behaviour dignified but modest, and your quarters always clean.

☐ Soldat d'élite, tu t'entraînes avec rigueur, tu entretiens ton arme comme ton bien le plus précieux, tu as le souci constant de ta forme physique. / As an elite soldier, you train rigorously, you maintain your weapon as your most precious possession and you're always mindful of your physical condition.

☐ La mission est sacrée, tu l'exécutes jusqu'au bout et si besoin, en opérations, au péril de ta vie. / The mission is sacred; you will execute to the end at all costs.

☐ Au combat, tu agis sans passion et sans haine, tu respectes les ennemis vaincus, tu n'abandonnes jamais ni tes morts, ni tes blessés, ni tes armes. / In combat, you act without emotion or hatred, you respect the defeated enemy and you never abandon your dead, your wounded, or your weapons.

After completing the code, we were ordered to place our kepis on our heads and the order was given to present arms to the commanding officer. We were now légionnaires. The CO congratulated us, but reminded us that this was the beginning of a long road. Once the ceremony was completed, we each placed our FAMAS at our feet on its bipod and broke rank. After the regiment CO, company capitaine, NCOs, and caporals had helped themselves to food and drinks set out in the château's reception area, we were free to join in. We all ate what we could and drank a beer or two as fast as possible, knowing this break wouldn't last long. After four weeks of water, milk, and coffee, the beer was a refreshing change.

Sure enough, soon the slow, deep introduction of a song by an NCO was our cue to join in. Smit listened and watched us with narrowed eyes, waiting for someone to falter and forget the words. This was one of his favourite pastimes, and even when you knew the words, his piercing gaze could cause a momentary memory lapse. He would then slowly and deliberately walk toward the offender and stand at his side while he sang. If the words were wrong, a crisp slap followed. On that evening, Smit confined himself to merely glaring at anyone he suspected of missing a line.

After we cleared the tables, we boarded a waiting bus for our ride back to Castel. The beer had gone right to everyone's heads, and the bus heater's warmth meant we were all asleep within minutes. The NCOs woke us just as the bus entered Castel's outer parking lot. We dismounted, and with our FAMASs strapped to our chests and kepis on, marched into the 4e RE singing the 3rd Company song, "Contre les Viets."

No longer lowly recruits, forty-three civilians from varying back-grounds and languages had been shaped into a cohesive group who could work together—and all within a month. We had attained a level of physical fitness and discipline that most would consider impossible within such a short time frame.

CHAPTER SEVEN

3rd Company, 3rd Section

Regimental life was a relief. We were tired and hungry. Fortunately, the mess hall was our first stop that evening, and we were given ample time to eat dinner. Of course, we all ate too much and suffered the consequences, throwing up in the barrack toilets soon after.

The entire regiment would parade on Mondays, followed by a run with the regiment's CO, company commanders, NCOs, caporals, and légionnaires following behind. We were dressed in our combats without belt or beret for this regiment run, and within our ranks, we noticed a caporal back from leave, one we hadn't seen much of. He was one of the two caporals who had originally escorted us from Aubagne to Castel. But unlike the other caporal, who wore his rank on the front of his uniform, this guy wore a caporal rank brassard on his arm. This, I came to learn, identified him as a training caporal, commonly referred to as a *fut-fut*, which is a derogatory Arabic term used for a turnkey in prisons, inherited from the Legion's time in North Africa.

Training caporals were not popular among légionnaires, and they were commonly viewed as upstarts who had not earned their rank through service. This fut-fut, a tall and lanky Lithuanian with less than a year's service, as we had witnessed in Aubagne, was quick to dish out punishment to légionnaires. Soon, O'Connor seemed to be one of his favourites, and the fut-fut kneed him in the stomach that morning because his boots weren't properly blackened.

Company life was busy. We worked to a metronome of varying duties, which included some form of physical activity—parcours du combattant, swimming, soccer, hand-to-hand combat lessons, shooting at the regiment's indoor range—or the ever-popular classroom with Smit. At mealtimes, the duty sergent would march us to the mess hall, singing the company song. If he wasn't satisfied with our singing, we would continue past the mess hall until he was. All companies marched in song, and if we passed another section or course singing, we would invariably become mixed up, with men falling out of step and out of tune. What immediately followed was the all too familiar command of "Halte au chant!" or "Stop singing!" In some cases, this led to involuntary solo performances.

Midway through basic training, we passed in front of our company commander to volunteer for our regiment of choice once we had successfully completed basic. The general rule was that légionnaires who finished well had the option to pick what they wanted. Those who didn't would be sent to the less popular regiments, like the cavalry and engineers, although this wasn't always the case. For this, we worked on our individual presentations with the section caporals, sergents, and our adjudant prior to entering the capitaine's office.

When the time came, we stood along the wall waiting for our turn to enter the capitaine's office on the main floor of the company building. Finally, I was up. I asked for permission to enter, which was granted, and I walked inside taking several steps, then came to attention, saluted, removed my kepi, and presented myself:

"Légionnaire Struthers, un mois de service, 4e Régiment étranger, 3e compagnie, 3e section, section de l'Adjudant Sébastien, à vos ordres, mon capitaine."

The capitaine told me to stand at ease and then asked what my intentions were. I told him I was a volunteer for the 2e Régiment étranger de parachutistes, to which he replied, "Tu peux disposer." Dismissed. I placed my kepi back on my head, saluted, did a 180-degree turn, and left the office. That was it. I had no idea whether I would get my chosen regiment or not, but it felt like I was getting closer.

Training continued, including firing the FAMAS in the regiment's indoor range, and shooting support weapons at the outdoor ranges located throughout the region. All efforts were now geared toward our final evaluations, which would involve shooting, weapons handling, and general FAMAS knowledge. The physical testing would include a 1500-metre sprint, quickly followed by an 8-kilometre run in full combat gear, timed PC, rope climb, push-ups, sit-ups, chin-ups, and a swimming test. A written exam would assess our general knowledge of the French language and the Legion's history and regiments. At the time, the Legion had six regiments based in France; three overseas in French Guiana, South America; one in the Mayotte Islands in the Indian Ocean; and one in Djibouti, East Africa.

What was being taught at the 4e RE was the standard for all the Legion's regiments, so a légionnaire arriving at his new regiment had been taught the basic skills to survive in a combat infantry company. Additional specialized training would continue at a regimental level, or in some cases soldiers would return to Castel, depending on the type of training they required.

Like all regiments, companies shared the regimental guard duties and support services. The least favourite of these was Garde Vingt-Quatre, or Guard 24. A section sergent, two caporals, and eight légionnaires would guard the regiment's main entrance and perimeter in parade uniform, working two-hour shifts. Two légionnaires were positioned at the main gate; others were at the side gates. The caporals would monitor all arrivals and departures from the main gate, and the sergent would man the guard office, signing in guests and dealing with all the required administrative duties. Every time an NCO or officer passed through the gate, the two légionnaires on duty were required to stand to attention and present arms.

At first, our parade uniform was difficult to master. We were required to iron a series of creases into parts of the shirt and pants, following specific measurements. The evening before guard duty, our caporals and sergent would inspect our uniforms with a ruler and check our boots and kepi, which of course had to be spotless. Easier said than done when you combine black boot polish with a white kepi. Rule number one: boots are done last.

The following day, during the morning of Guard 24, the guard was presented to the company's duty NCO, then marched to the main gate and presented to the regimental duty NCO, who in turn verified the légionnaires' uniforms before commencing service.

Later in the day, the Guard 24 is presented to the regiment's commanding officer, with each légionnaire presenting himself to the CO and answering questions regarding training. This allowed the CO to monitor a company's training standards and progression, notably in the French language.

By now, we all knew each other well within the section, and we had become closer as a unit. When we arrived in Aubagne, each group had retreated into its various languages, so communication was extremely difficult. Speaking French helped create a bond, regardless of nationality. I got along well with the Russians, and in time we could laugh and share in our similar sense of humour. I also liked the Russians' air of superiority. With four or five men to a room, privacy was non-existent. We were exposed 24/7 to life in the section. The endless cycle of training and duties left no time for self-reflection; it was all about surviving and pulling your weight so the section didn't suffer.

Our final evaluation fell during Christmastime, which was an important holiday for the Legion. The celebrations included a two-day regimental sports competition between companies, followed by a regimental dinner on Christmas Eve.

Jock and I challenged each another during the evaluations, and we both did well. Masalas was at the infirmary. A blister covering his entire heel had gotten infected, so he was relegated to the next course once he recovered. We ran the 1500-metre sprint, followed by the 8-kilometre run in combats, with a backpack, webbing, and FAMAS, keeping up with Adjudant Sébastien until Jock's bad knees slowed him down and he fell behind. We raced each other's times on the parcours du combattant. In the shooting evaluation, the indoor facility had targets that were electronically actuated and fell when hit. I missed my second-to-last shot at 300 metres, and as I cursed myself, the target fell. Impossible! I quickly looked over my shoulder. There was Smit in the last shooting lane with his FAMAS, sporting a wry grin.

My first Legion Christmas brought with it moments where I questioned my reasons for joining; it certainly wasn't a soldier's life yet. My thoughts inevitably led to my past, the mistakes I'd made, family, and Janel. The Legion's approach was to remind everyone that it was their new family, and one to be celebrated in full traditional manner. Personally, I just wanted to get on with the training and soldiering. I didn't care about Christmas, and this wasn't my family. Decorations had to be put up and company bars were opened. A Legion catalogue was handed out from which each légionnaire could choose a gift, usually a pen knife, a multi-tool, or something similar. The caporals were charged with the task of recording each légionnaire's request; however, the novelty soon wore off, usually after order number four, as one individual who hesitated over gifts for too long soon discovered. "Right, you're getting the Legion towel," announced the caporal. A valued gift for years to come.

Christmas and basic training had taken its toll on many. Although he had finished second overall, Jock decided he was going home. This came as a surprise to me. After having been through so much, it never occurred to me that someone would just quit. Throughout the training, Jock had kept me entertained with his stories and acute sense of humour. He also pushed me to excel physically. I'll admit, compared to the others, his leaving made me stop to wonder why. Was he disappointed with the Legion after his experiences in the British Army? Perhaps his bad knees were the issue. He didn't say. Nor did a dozen others from the section who chose to leave the Legion and return to the life they had left behind in the civilian world.

One cold January morning, we all packed our kit bags and were put on a train back to Aubagne. The following morning, I was the first to pass in front of the colonel, having finished first in the course ranking. He asked me if I was interested in returning to Castel as a training caporal for two basic training courses, followed by my caporal's course (CME F1). Many French nationals or French-speaking légionnaires were chosen for this role. I had no interest in being a fut-fut; their lack of experience and knowledge usually meant they were delegated to secondary roles as runners for the real training caporals. There were some exceptions, but most took to the promotion with zeal, like our course fut-fut, dealing out harsh disciplinary measures to new légionnaires who were none the wiser. Eventually, these fut-futs would be sent to a regiment elsewhere and their past would come back to haunt them. Then the boot would be on the other foot, literally. Our fut-fut hadn't tried anything on me personally, but if we did cross paths I wouldn't forget his face or his ways.

Adjudant Sébastien knew I was hellbent on going to the 2e REP. I believe that it was his input that led to a more suitable course-mate being chosen to fill the fut-fut role. But my relief didn't last long. The colonel told me I would return to Castel for my military driver's qualification, and the Aide moniteur éducation physique militaire et sportive (EPMS), the sports monitor course. On successful completion of that, I would go to the 2e Régiment étranger de parachutistes (2e REP). I saluted the colonel, did my about-turn, and left his office.

To say I was disappointed was an understatement. Sure, the EPMS was considered a privileged course based on physical ability, from what I was being told. But it didn't help that O'Connor and others were off to the 2^e REP. I was envious, but at least I had avoided the bullshit fut-fut role.

CHAPTER EIGHT

Pieds-Noirs

The idea of going back to Castel was demoralizing. During my return, I contemplated throwing myself from the fast-moving train, but that certainly would have messed up my precisely ironed uniform and white kepi.

It was already February 2, 1995, and the EPMS course would run for six weeks. Before that, I finished my military driving qualification, which lasted two weeks and involved learning the French driving code and an introduction to driving the French military's P4, an unarmoured off-road vehicle manufactured by Peugeot, and the troop-carrying TRM 2000 and larger TRM 4000. Once that was completed, I would join the EPMS course intake of fifteen légionnaires, including two caporal-chefs and a handful of caporals. Légionnaire première-class Sevigne (a French national) and Légionnaire deuxième-classe Schubert (a Polish national) were both in a similar scenario as mine — fresh out of basic training from the 4ᵉ RE's other training companies.

Schubert spoke English well, and he and Sevigne were both good guys, so the three of us stuck together. EPMS was led by the head NCO for Castel's sports bureau, an adjudant. The entry tests began in earnest. They were similar to the physical fitness tests I had recently completed during basic training, but the minimum scores required to qualify for the EPMS course were higher. We had to complete the 8-kilometre run, with a 10-kilogram backpack and a weapon, under the forty-minute mark, and the PC in less than three minutes. I can't recall the exact EPMS scoring criteria, but a portion of the course also involved attaining a lifeguard qualification (BNSSA). Everyone was tested on his level of skill in the pool. A Russian caporal had competed at the Olympic level; the guy was a damn fish.

Everyone qualified, and we were billeted in an annex building for regiment support staff. No bureau de semaine, no duty sergent, no whistles. We ate our meals before the training companies did, wearing our newer Legion-issued green tracksuits. After basic training, this new and informal type of set-up was paradise to me.

We spent our mornings in the town's indoor pool, which was a lot smaller and more dated than what I was used to in Canada. Even my military-issue Speedos took some serious getting used to. Being mixed in with the locals felt odd to me. The smell of chlorine, the humidity, and older women wearing ancient swimming attire doing their morning laps added to the strangeness.

The adjudant was a firm believer in the backstroke, which was by far my least favourite stroke. I was caught sneaking into the front crawl often enough, followed by the adjudant yelling at me from across the pool. In the afternoon, we dried out in the classroom, studying the human respiratory system and ways to maximize its efficiency with cardiovascular training. Naturally, the curriculum was taught in French, but spoken at a much faster pace than I was accustomed to. This took concentration. After finishing up in the classroom, we headed outside for *corps-à-corps* (hand-to-hand combat training based on the Israeli Krav Maga self-defence system), orienteering, or perfecting our techniques on the regiment's parcours du combattant course.

Our hand-to-hand combat instructor's demonstrations were full-on. Despite his name, Sergent-Chef LeGros ("the big") was a small, wiry Frenchman. He was aggressive. During his demonstrations, he kicked a caporal in the groin while we all watched in awe. The sergent-chef then asked for the next volunteer. All our hands shot up immediately. We knew full well that if we didn't volunteer, we'd be chosen. The next guy was thrown to the ground hard, or something just as fun to watch.

Overall, our group was good. We trained hard and relaxed afterwards — a luxury. Despite this, some of the caporals were less inclined to talk to Servigne, Schubert, or me. No doubt because they had waited for or applied for this course after several years of service, only to be training with upstarts who might have been sent to fulfill some quota. Fortunately, our individual results spoke for themselves.

We also took advantage of the liberties offered to us on the weekends, travelling by train to the nearby city of Toulouse. It was a world apart—freedom, the French food, French girls, the fashion, the music, and the lively European atmosphere surrounding it all. I knew I was out of place, but I was captivated by everything—the mix of ethnic groups, the city's history, architecture, and even its unfamiliar smells. But I found myself acclimatizing to the French way. I would order café au lait and croissants in the mornings, and I enjoyed European pizzas with their thin crusts, accompanied by a glass of red wine, maybe even three or four.

Walking around a city in uniform with people looking at me was something I also had to get used to. Just *being* in a uniform was new. Making sure I didn't stain it while eating or spill wine on it when enjoying the spoils of Toulouse took some effort. Even avoiding other people's errors—a waitress spilling coffee or wine on the table could mean disaster! Setting your white kepi down was something to always consider; the surface had to be spotless and dry, and monitored with your life. I also found that French girls were less approachable compared to what I was used to. Maybe it was the uniform, or because I was a légionnaire and that meant something to them. Who knows?

I was close to completing the course when a French caporal-chef and I were tasked with placing chalk directional markings along the route of the upcoming regimental run, which followed the Canal du Midi. Driving the P4, the caporal-chef accelerated from a stop along its dirt path, and was a bit too heavy on the pedal. He lost control of it, and like in slow motion, we careened forward and smashed into a large tree, coming to a dead stop. My head hit the passenger side's metal handrail, knocking me senseless. After slowly coming around, I staggered out of the vehicle, dazed. The caporal-chef was slouched over in the driver's seat. He wasn't moving.

It was then that I felt the warmth of blood running down my face. Instinctively looking in the P4's side mirror, I could see that the skin along my hairline was split open. Feeling ill, I immediately sat down on the ground with my back against the P4's front tire. It felt like minutes had passed when the regiment's commanding officer and a handful of subordinates who were out for their morning run ran past the P4. The chief medical officer and another officer stopped to help, but the rest continued on.

Fifteen stitches and a night in the regiment's infirmary later, I passed before the regiment CO and received a suspended sentence of seven days in jail for failing to wear my seat belt. After spending a week in the infirmary, the caporal-chef was sentenced to thirty days in jail for destroying a regiment vehicle.

Back on the course, the adjudant was sympathetic to my situation and exempted me from the swimming because of my stitches. Nothing more was said about the matter. A French caporal from the 2^e REP's 3rd Company and I battled for the fastest 8-kilometre run and PC time. He won the PC by a mere two seconds, and later went on to break the Legion record. After a series of final tests, we all passed the course. Except for the caporal-chef in jail.

Returning to Aubagne (1er RE), Schubert and I passed before a colonel one after the other and we were both given lifeguarding duties at the regiment's swimming pool. In short, it would be a summer of yelling at the officers' and senior NCOs' children to stop running poolside. We were told that if we completed this task, we would be going to 2e Régiment étranger de parachutistes. I wasn't sure what to make of this lifeguarding deal; it certainly wasn't why I had joined the Legion. Taking it one day at a time, I resigned myself to a summer in Speedos.

One weekend, I recognized a face at the pool. It was the NCO who had done my Gestapo (B2) questioning. During the week while off-duty, I introduced myself to Sergent-Chef Macdonald (Mac), a Hungarian Canadian. Mac invited me to his Legion-issued apartment for one of his wife's home-cooked meals. Mac had served previously with the 2^e REP, and was former Canadian Army, and I welcomed his experience, advice, and overall knowledge, especially regarding the recruitment process.

The Legion was dealing with a high number of Eastern European applicants, many of whom were interested only in getting French nationality after spending five years of service in the Legion.

1er Régiment étranger, Bureau de sport—Operation Lifeguard. (*Credit:* Joel Struthers)

Following Russia's collapse in the late 1980s, Eastern Europe was in economic turmoil, so who could blame them for wanting a different life? Traditionally, the Legion benefited from whatever the socio-economic flavour was at the time. However, key in this endeavour was the Legion's ability to weed out the undesirables and decide which individual could be transformed into a professional soldier. On average, only one out of every twelve applicants made the cut.

One Saturday, Mac invited me to join his family on a hike, and we drove in his little French car to the foothills close to the village of Cuges-les-Pins. From there, we set off on foot with our backpacks. Mac's little three-year-old son sat on my shoulders until I felt warm liquid running down my back. In all fairness, he did say "pee-pee," which I unfortunately ignored. We eventually arrived at Château des Julhans, an old château in the foothills, surrounded by towering stone pines with their broad canopies. It was slightly dilapidated, but still an impressive structure to me. You just don't see things like that in Canada.

While I stood there taking in the view of the day's final rays of light streaming through the pine trees and silhouetting the château, an older man and his family approached us from the side of the château. We introduced ourselves, and Mac explained to me that the man was what the French referred to as a *pied-noir*,[10] a French national born in Algeria, North Africa. This was history I knew little about, aside from reading *Légionnaire*, but it was important in understanding the Legion, and the 2e REP in particular. Mac asked if we could camp on the château's grounds that night, and the gentleman agreed.

That evening, we sat around a campfire with the gentleman and his family, drinking wine and listening to his stories, like one in which he vividly described a battle where his regiment was saved by the Legion, which had apparently marched into the battle singing. He was emotional in telling it. He had been a French officer in the Algerian War (1954–62).

What I didn't fully understand at the time was that in 1961, dissident French regiments, including the Legion's 1er Régiment étranger de parachutistes (1er REP), had aligned with anti-Gaullists and seized power in Algiers during a coup d'état. In part, the 1er REP's objective was to jump into and seize Paris to remove President Charles de Gaulle from power.

The putsch[11]—a German term for a coup d'état, but used by the Legion—failed before it began, and the 1er REP was later disbanded. French officers and NCOs were sent back to France to serve their sentences in a military prison. France's political decision to grant Algeria independence in 1962 caught many pieds-noirs in the middle. Times were complicated and violent. Many pieds-noirs were unable to remain safely in Algeria; they felt betrayed by President de Gaulle and unwelcome in their homeland of France. Some, like the fellow we were sharing wine with, were released from military prison with nowhere to go. The colonial Algerian administration owned numerous châteaux in France, and some pieds-noirs made these their homes. Of course it was illegal, but these displaced people, known as the Union syndicale de défense des intérêts des français retiés d'Algérie (USDIFRA), were making a point. France wasn't interested in the problem, and the Algerian government was incapable of evicting them.

Our host was a putschist, and he had chosen this château as his home after serving his time in prison.

I was aware that the 1er BEP and 2e BEP served in French Indochina, and were later decimated at the Battle of Diên Biên Phu in 1954,[12] a confrontation between the French Far East Expeditionary Corps and Viet Minh communist-nationalists. Ultimately, the battle led to a massive French defeat and France's withdrawal from Indochina. The 1er REP was created in 1955 from reserves and volunteers, and garrisoned in the French Department of Algeria until their disbandment. The 2^e BEP was also enlarged to regiment size the same year and designated the 2^e REP fighting alongside the 1st and 3rd REP in Algeria until the regiments move to Calvi, Corsica (1967), and the only remaining parachute regiment in the Legion.

I'm not sure if Mac had purposely planned this history lesson, but the evening made an indelible mark on me.

My summer passed quickly enough, and I was given three weeks' leave and told that on my return I would be departing for the parachute regiment. Finally! I was relieved. Now, what to do with my time off? I wanted to go home and visit my friends and family, and maybe even Janel. But légionnaires are not permitted to depart France unless a proper request for leave is made well in advance.

Another roadblock: the Legion had my passport. I spoke with the Canadian Embassy in Paris, which informed me that it couldn't issue me a new passport if the original was in the Legion's possession.

Looking back, I should have just reported mine stolen, and I would have had a new passport in my hands within twenty-four hours. Instead, I would have to try to get home without it. Post-9/11 this might seem quite ludicrous; however, at the time it wasn't impossible.

I took the TGV high-speed train to Paris's Charles de Gaulle Airport, and I was soon speaking to a Canada Customs representative. I didn't really have a plan on how to explain my situation, but I decided I would just tell the truth. I showed the Customs official my Canadian birth certificate and Canadian social insurance card, which Mac had given to me under the radar. Neither of these pieces of ID had my photo on them, but the Customs official said that if I could make it through French Customs, she had no problem letting me board my flight to Canada. My father had pre-arranged a two-way ticket with the airline he flew for, advising them of my unusual situation.

After some tense moments waiting in line, and the unnerving feeling of not being able to get home, something one takes for granted, the French border police asked for my passport. I explained, in purposely broken French, that I was in France on holiday, and that I had lost my Canadian passport and was unable to replace it fast enough to make my unchangeable flight to Canada.

I was duly transferred to a room with two French Customs officials. After briefly outlining the "false facts," and explaining that the Canadian Customs official had no issue with me boarding my flight, they asked, "So you are Canadian?" I replied, "Yes" and provided them with my Canadian ID. They looked at one another, shrugging, and said, "Well it's not our problem once he's on the plane." I was cleared to get on the flight. A huge feeling of relief came over me once the airplane door closed, and we started rolling. But something I didn't even consider was that a légionnaire caught leaving or returning to France without proper regimental authorization would be held by the border police and returned to the Legion's military police. This would result in an automatic thirty-day jail term, possible reduction in rank, or even expulsion from the Legion itself—after serving the jail time, of course.

Unfortunately, home wasn't quite what I had expected. Seeing family was obviously great. But ultimately, things change with time, and people move on. Janel had a new boyfriend, and my friends were either working or going to school, not a lot of common interests or experiences. Trying to explain how I had spent my past year was difficult, if not pointless really. People just didn't get it. My time at home only reinforced my original goal: to jump from a military airplane.

Preoccupied with not being late for my return to the 1er RE, I had spoken with the Canadian passport office in Surrey, British Columbia, the day I arrived home. After numerous phone calls back and forth, I was informed that I would be issued a temporary passport that was to be returned to the Canadian embassy in Paris after my arrival in France. And I was told not to ask for something like this again. My request wasn't just somewhat out of the ordinary; in fact, the passport official mentioned that my ordeal had led to some diplomatic tensions. That seemed a little over the top to me, but I was just relieved to have a passport for my return to France.

When I arrived in France, I returned my temporary passport to the Canadian embassy as requested, then boarded the TGV at the Gare de Lyon train station, Paris, bound for Aubagne. Within a few days of arriving, and with no one the wiser, I was promoted to légionnaire première classe and received my transfer orders. I was on my way to the 2e Régiment étranger de parachutistes—Le REP.

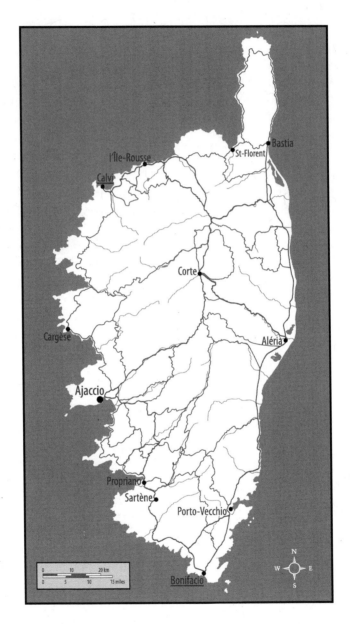

Map of Corsica, France. (*Credit:* Mike Bechthold)

CHAPTER NINE

Le REP

September 22, 1995, and just days after I returned from Canada, Schubert and I joined two rough-looking caporals returning from their posting in Djibouti, Africa, along with twenty légionnaires fresh out of basic, for the journey to Le REP (referred to as "the REP" by English speakers in the regiment). An NCO from the REP's 1st Company was there to accompany us, and he started barking orders from the get-go. Our transport bus left the 1er RE through its main gates, headed for the Port of Marseille. Here, we'd board an overnight ferry to Corsica, the birthplace of Napoléon Bonaparte,[13] before continuing to our destination, Calvi (Kalvi).

We were assigned to small two-person cabins, and I slept through the night to the soothing hum of the ship's engine, only to be woken by its horn early the next morning. Once I showered, shaved, and put on my uniform, I made my way up to the main deck to join the others. And what a view was waiting for me. As we approached the port city of Ajaccio (Aiacciu), the island's capital, I had my first look at Corsica. The French island suspended in the Mediterranean Sea was stunning. The city's simple buildings were surrounded by scrubby green hills and jagged mountain peaks that seemed to be just an arm's reach away.

My nose was filled with a hint of diesel and a new and intriguing smell. I had read in history books that when sailing to the island, Bonaparte knew when he was home because he could smell the aroma of maquis, an indigenous bush. Maquis is impregnable vegetation, and for this reason its name was adopted by the French Resistance during the Second World War.

Corsica also has a compelling political history, and its islanders have a fierce sense of identity, which manifested itself in the form of the Front de libération nationale corse (FLNC), and other armed splinter-separatist groups. Corsicans are extremely warm and hospitable people, but even now they undoubtedly have a very hard edge to them. Along the twisting road to Calvi, I could see FLNC graffiti on the walls of every town we drove through. It was hard to reconcile the views surrounding me—which varied from the angry-looking graffiti to the dramatic scenery of soaring mountain peaks, plunging cliffs, and white sandy beaches fringed with turquoise water—with my actual reason for being there, which was to join the toughest and most renowned regiment in the French Foreign Legion.

The regiment was a part of France's 11th parachute division rapid reaction force. It comprised fifteen hundred légionnaires, divided into six companies:

- □ 1st CIE—Urban Combat
- □ 2nd CIE—Mountain Warfare
- □ 3rd CIE—Amphibious Warfare
- □ 4th CIE—Sniper and Explosives
- □ CEA—Reconnaissance and Fire Support (Milan anti-tank, SADAA 20mm anti-aircraft, SML 81–120mm mortars, SER— Reconnaissance Platoon, G.C.P. SOGH Commando)
- □ CCS—Command and Service Company

Our bus finally arrived at Camp Raffalli in Calvi. Named for Colonel Barthélemy Raffalli, commanding officer of the 2e BEP[14] who was killed during the Indochina War, the regiment was set against the imposing backdrop of the Corsican mountains. The NCO ordered us to shut up and put on our kepis. As we drove through the gates, I could see armed légionnaires wearing khaki combats and flak jackets, unlike the dress uniform worn by guards in Aubagne or Castel.

A wave of both anxiousness and relief started to flood over me. It had been a year since I first arrived in Strasbourg.

We lined up outside the regiment duty NCO office with our kit bags at our sides. A caporal from the 1st Company was there to greet us. He introduced himself as Caporal Astudillo, speaking with a South American accent and rolling his *R*s to full effect. He wasn't particularly tall, built, or imposing. Astudillo then walked the ranks, carrying out a quick review. When he noticed my première-classe rank with EPMS badge, he stopped and asked if I was a fut-fut. I quickly answered, "Non, caporal." He replied, "Achtung." Careful. This was Legion-speak; it was short and to the point, in an almost undecipherable slang. To an outsider at least.

Dressed in our summer short-sleeved uniforms with dress shoes and kit bags, we toured the regiment at a slow run in formation. Astudillo stopped and pointed out each building of note—the infirmary, the mess hall, the combat company buildings—a mix of immaculately kept old and modern structures. Eventually, we arrived at a small single-storey barrack building that the caporal introduced to us as the Promo, short for Promotion Parachutiste. This was the REP's entry jump-course building. By now, we were also all feeling the effects of the run; uniform dress shoes were not designed for such a task.

Astudillo presented our group, Promo 706, to our awaiting jump monitor, a German NCO in charge of our promotion. Monitor Weiss was a large man, and he looked German too. My observation: he seemed impressed with his own rank. He informed, or more so, barked at us, that the 1st Company (1er CIE) was in Gabon, Africa, on tour. Our jump training would last four weeks, and once completed, we would join the 1st Company on its return. We were then issued our new cap badge of the winged hand grasping a sword—the French military paratrooper insignia—to put on our green berets.

Finally, we were returned to Astudillo's responsibility for the rest of the evening. From what I could tell, he was all business, and he led by example. Beds were quickly designated and kit bags squared away in our new barracks. Our first order of business was sewing attachments on our dress uniform shirts, which would accommodate our jump wings when the time came. The caporal demonstrated how this was to be done, and we all sat on our beds with needle and thread in hand while listening, strangely enough, to Sade's "Bullet Proof Soul" in the background. I wasn't expecting this type of music from a regiment caporal, but Sade's melodic voice did help one's focus.

Our next order of business was learning the regimental and company songs. The regiment's song "Le Diable marche avec nous," The Devil Marches with Us, as the name suggests, was the work of the devil to learn. It starts at an impossibly low, flat tone, which, if not executed properly, leads to everyone singing either too low or too high. This is where we witnessed Astudillo's patience falter for the first time, and experienced the many push-ups that followed.

The next morning, Monitor Weiss introduced us to Test troupes aéroportées (TAP), a physical fitness test involving push-ups, sit-ups, chin-ups, a 1500-metre sprint in full kit with backpack and FAMAS, followed by a similar 8-kilometre run (or twice around the regiment's drop zone), and to finish off, the timed PC. The standard was higher than basic training, but less than my EPMS. Légionnaires were given the Promo's four weeks to achieve the minimum requirements.

We were then introduced to the French parachute and *gaine*, a foldable bag that held our backpacks during the jump, along with a padded sleeve for our FAMAS. Both are attached to the parachute harness. The gaine is released during the ascent and it dangles beneath your harness on a 3-metre-long cord to avoid injuring a jumper when he impacts the ground, which can be violent. Using a slightly shortened, but to scale, model of a C-160 Transall aircraft (parts of which had been salvaged from one that had crashed in the mountains), we practised our jump drills over and over. Kitting up, boarding, sitting, standing, exiting, landing—there was a drill for each part.

My anticipation of the first jump increased as the course progressed. But our primary focus was our proficiency in taking off the parachute, removing the backpack and FAMAS from the gaine, quickly rolling up the purposely deployed parachute back into its harness, then running to a regrouping point with the parachute on our back, backpack resting on top of it, and FAMAS in hand, as fast as possible. The punishment for being slow to the regrouping point was push-ups. The emphasis was on being methodical. If you're rushed and the parachute is poorly packed, it will unfurl behind you as you run to the regrouping point. Well, you're fucked at that stage because you need to start over, and you've missed an acceptable time to make it to the regrouping point! An ex-paratrooper from the Belgium military, a thin Frenchman, and I were consistently the first three to arrive; however, I had my share of parachutes unravelling.

But the reward for our efforts—seven jumps and a successful TAP fitness test—is a numbered *brevet parachutiste* or paratrooper wings. Our training progressed in anticipation of a C-160 Transall, which was scheduled to arrive the next day. The final order of business before our first jump was painting an orange triangle on the back of our helmets, which we did outside the Promo barracks.

November 14, 1995: jump day had finally arrived. For instructional purposes, our gaines were each filled with a 11-kilogram box of sand and a wooden FAMAS. Trucks were loaded with our kit, but we first did a forty-five-minute run to the airport to rid us of any tension or pre-jump jitters. The fact of the matter is that jumping is simple. You step out the door of the plane, the parachute opens automatically, and you impact the ground. Mission accomplished. It was probably the fear of screwing up and losing face within the Promo that was foremost on people's minds. I know it affected my focus.

The regiment's loading area is situated next to Calvi International Airport. Here, we were issued parachutes in quick succession from the back of a Section d'entretien et de pliage des parachutes (SEPP) truck. Lining up in eight rows (two planeloads), we each placed our parachute and gaine with our helmet on the corrugated steel floor behind a white mark. Next, we left the line so that several légionnaires could ensure that the parachutes were all perfectly aligned, vertically and diagonally. A lot of effort and pride goes into this, but it's generally not completed before it's time to kit up.

As I stood to the side watching, I noticed the different colours of triangles painted on the backs of all the companies' helmets, with section numbers superimposed in white. Soon, the officer in charge of the day's jump gave the order "To your lines," followed by "Beginning with the helmet, kit up." We put on our helmets and parachutes, and our monitor checked our buckles and the tightness of the straps, giving us the OK one by one. Then he gave the group of us a step-by-step reminder of procedures to follow once we exited the aircraft.

Promo, loading C-160 Transall for our first jump, Calvi airport, Corsica. (*Credit*: Joel Struthers)

For our first jump, we wouldn't be using our gaines, and we were to deploy the reserve parachute once we stabilized under canopy. Suddenly, I heard the guy directly behind me utter "Curwa," which is "shit" in Polish. His reserve chute lay deployed at his feet. The poor fucker, I thought, and curwa, thankfully it wasn't mine. Monitor Weiss lost his mind, and after spewing some profanities, our course-mate ran off with the deployed reserve under his arm to the SEPP truck to be issued a replacement.

The noise of the C-160 increased as it approached the loading area, lowering its back ramp as it swung around. We boarded the plane in two columns. The jump monitors stood on the ramp, counting as we passed, and directing us to the front of the aircraft, either right or left. The cramped space, smell of aviation fuel, and turbine noise added to my anticipation and anxiety. I could feel the adrenaline pumping inside my veins, but we were also among the regiment's jumpers, so we acted accordingly; this wasn't a big deal. The ramp closed, the plane accelerated down the runway and took off, quickly climbing to 600 metres. The jump monitors opened the side doors, and the odour of aviation fuel filled the cabin once again.

The lead monitor stood halfway up the rear ramp, which gave him a view of the whole aircraft. On his signal, the two inside columns of men were ordered to stand, followed by hook-up. The monitors then checked each jumper, counting off every guy as they went down the line. The first jumper was then moved up to the door, and he assumed the position: one foot forward and both hands on either side of the door, waiting for the green light. In this position, you wouldn't see the light, but you heard the buzzer and felt a slap on your back, or even a push from the monitor, and his shout of "Go!" which rippled down the line.

Two columns of jumpers exited both of the rear side doors, and the monitors made sure everyone kept moving. They also collected the hooks and extractor straps at the door. When the last jumper had exited, the monitor poked his head out of the door to make sure that no one was hooked up on the aircraft's tail.

The C-160 did its circuit, and the next two rows of guys were out. Then it was the Promo's turn. Our exit was more staggered, with a one-second pause between jumpers. I was number three. I held my helmet and covered the red reserve chute handle attached to my front to prevent it from opening inadvertently as I exited the plane. Then I stepped into the void.

The wind roared in my ears, and then all went quiet as I silently counted, one … two … three. Then I felt a short, sharp pull on my harness as my main chute opened. I looked up to verify it had fully deployed. It was then crucial to deploy the reserve carefully, ensuring it didn't fall between your legs and open behind you, as this would result in a head-down position with your feet straight up in the air—not a good place to be on landing. Success! Then I looked down. A feeling of calm and quiet followed, with my course-mates floating to my sides.

With Calvi's citadel in the distance and the regiment below, my focus changed to the ground directly underneath me, which was fast approaching. Under canopy, our parachutes were semi-manoeuvrable, with two overhead toggles to counteract wind drift or help us avoid another jumper. However, our toggles were useless on this first jump with the reserve deployed as it didn't have any effect on the main chute. Two colliding parachutes can cause the higher chute to collapse, a dangerous predicament at most times, but especially when close to the ground. The biggest thing on my mind, though, was making it to that regrouping point first.

Although Astudillo would be the last out the door, he would also be quick. So would the Belgian—and they were. Those who arrived at the regrouping point after Astudillo were made to do push-ups with their parachutes on their backs. Once the Promo was accounted for with no broken bones, we climbed into the back of the waiting truck and returned to the Calvi airport for our second jump.

While waiting at the embarkation zone, I noticed a different-looking truck. It was a VLRA (*véhicule léger, de reconnaissance et d'appui*, or vehicle for reconnaissance, escort, and support variant), and légionnaires in khaki flight suits were disembarking. There were two officers and a mix of NCOs, caporal-chefs, and caporals. I asked Astudillo who they were. He explained that they were the Groupe des commandos parachutistes (GCP). The regiment's pathfinders, they were qualified in Saut opérationnel à grande hauteur (SOGH), which roughly translates to "operational jump from great height." Astudillo shared what he thought of them. "Show-offs," he said.

Within forty-eight hours, we finished our six jumps, including one at night, with our gaine and wooden FAMAS, to qualify for our jump wings. After making the quick transition from the red-lit interior of the C-160 to the dark, starry sky of Calvi with the regiment's lights below, my main chute deployed. Then I released my gaine and waited for the invisible ground to reach me. Thud! I heard the gaine hit the ground, and that meant to prepare for impact. Seconds later I hit the ground, too. Once I stood up (no broken bones!), I said to myself, "That hurts, but it's pretty fucking cool."

The following morning, Saturday, November 16, Monitor Weiss marched us onto the regiments parade square singing the regimental song. We were then presented to the commanding officer, Colonel Benoît Puga. He welcomed us to the REP and the para family. He also reminded us that the real work awaited us at our combat company. Several officers and senior NCOs then walked through the Promo and pinned the parachute wings to our chests. My brevet militaire de parachutistes numbered 588553. They also attached a red lanyard to our uniforms, which hangs off the left shoulder and under the armpit. It represents the Legion of Honour, which was awarded to the regiment for its actions in Indochina.

That evening, our Promo went into Calvi, a fortified medieval citadel surrounded by a more modern town, with shops, boutique hotels, and restaurants. Calvi is the birthplace of Christopher Columbus. It was also the first place since the start of the promo where we had a chance to blow off some steam. At a restaurant, our monitor Weiss briefed us on the rules and regulations we had to follow when visiting Calvi.

Part of this involved which restaurants and bars were approved for légionnaires. Some establishments were off limits because we weren't welcome. We also found out that the regiment's military police (MP) patrol Calvi by foot and vehicle, and we were required to salute them when they passed. Failure to do so would result in arrest. A légionnaire had to keep his uniform immaculate and wear his kepi at all times, except if seated at a restaurant or bar. The MPs would look for légionnaires who were drunk, not wearing their kepis, or having their uniform in disarray. Generally, all three. The MPs may also ask to see military identification and a légionnaire's *titre de permission*, or leave slip.

A titre de permission was a piece of paper that identified the légionnaire's name, rank, company, section, and date and time of leave. These were handwritten in the designated areas, using a ruler to ensure straight and legible writing. If you wanted to leave the regiment on an evening or weekend, you needed to submit a titre de permission to your duty caporal for review prior. If approved, these were signed and then submitted to your section lieutenant, and he approved and sent them to the company commanding officer for a final signature.

A légionnaire then presents to the company duty office at the appropriate timings prior to leaving the regiment in his dress uniform. The company duty sergent inspects the légionnaire's uniform, and if he approves, issues the leave slip. The final hurdle is at the regimental guardhouse, where the same uniform review happens and the regimental duty NCO checks your titre de permission.

Off-duty life was heavily regulated, and the MPs were quick to throw anyone in jail, which consisted of two cells behind the regiment's main gate guardhouse. If sentenced to actual jail time by your company captain or regiment CO for a variety of reasons, a légionnaire would have his head shaved and would be issued with an orange Hi-Viz vest to wear over his combats. Prisoners were taken on an 8-kilometre run each morning and then subjected to manual labour, keeping the regiment spic and span for the duration of the sentence, depending on the offence.

But tonight, all was good in Calvi. The beers were cold, and my uniform finally had a set of jump wings.

CHAPTER TEN

1st Company, 1st Section

On a Corsican mid-November morning in 1995, we packed our bags, cleaned the Promo barracks, put on our dress uniforms, and lined up outside the 1st Company CO's office to wait for our section assignments. The 1st Company, which specialized in urban warfare, was considered a no-bullshit company, or *gâteau*, which is Legion slang for having more muscle than brains. But I was just happy to be through the training and joining a Legion combat company.

When my turn came, Capitaine Gomart, former commanding officer of the regiment's GCP, informed me that I was joining the 1st Company's 1st Section, and I was dismissed. Next, I waited to see the 1st Section Lieutenant De Mesmay. Inside the small office he shared with the section NCOs, he told me to listen to the NCOs and caporals, work hard, not cause him any problems, and present myself to the section.

The company barracks were situated directly behind the company's main building. The first floor housed the company armoury and 3rd Section, and the second floor housed the 1st and 2nd sections. A tradition in the REP requires a new légionnaire to purchase two cases of beer prior to his joining a section. It would invariably be Kronenbourg, as the regimental foyer didn't sell anything else. (The Legion owned a majority stake in the beer company.) The légionnaire presents the cases of beer—cold—to his section office, first offering the officer and NCOs a beer, followed by his section caporals. This could vary from section to section, but the gist of it was to go buy beer. The légionnaires who chose not to buy beer paid a heavy price, which usually involved familiarization with a caporal's boot and the section's sanitation area. Then they were sent to buy beer.

I presented myself to the 1st Section duty NCO in the section hallway, and the duty caporal, Caporal Rake, who was formerly in the British parachute regiment. With beer case in hand, he provided me with some quick advice: "Toe the line, work hard." This simple insight into section life was pretty much the norm for all légionnaires. There was no room for discussion. But Rake, the section medic, seemed like a straight shooter and said that if I had any problems or questions, just ask.

My first responsibility was to replace my helmet's orange Promo triangle with a green one that had the number one superimposed in white, signifying 1st Company, 1st Section. The two other légionnaires joining the section had come straight from Castel, and they were sent to clean the section's toilets and hallways as their beers were passed around by the caporals and the duty NCO.

The 1st Section was predominately made up of Eastern blockers. After being shown to my room, where I bunked with five others, I began organizing my locker. A tall and somewhat awkward-looking New Zealander, Légionnaire Première-Classe Mars, introduced himself. Mars had been in the section for two years, and was the third and last member of the section's anglophone mafia. He told me that in the 1980s the company had been home to many former British soldiers who were disillusioned with their military after the Falklands War. They were a lively crowd, by all accounts. Some new and unpopular arrivals to the company were periodically thrown out the first-floor window — inside their lockers. This was referred to as their first company jump. That came to an end when a légionnaire was killed, apparently. Thankfully, times had changed.

Life in the company, however, didn't differ much from basic training. Appel was done at section and company levels on the company's parade squares and section hallways. In the mornings, the company would parade at 0720 hours. Section duty caporals would present to section duty sergeants, who would present to section head NCOs, who in turn would present to the section commanding officer, usually a lieutenant. Sections were then presented to the company head NCO, officer second-in-command (2iC), followed by the company capitaine at 0730 hours. It sounds long-winded, but it was actually a fast process. Unsurprisingly, a légionnaire's absenteeism from roll call or parade resulted in quick disciplinary action: seven days' jail for a single incident. In some cases it was longer, depending on the nature of the absence or repetitive behaviour.

On Monday mornings, the company would run up to the Chapelle Notre Dame de la Serra overlooking the Calvi Citadel, with an impressive view of the bay with its turquoise waters and white-sand beaches. Capitaine Gomart led our runs at a good pace to the very end, but generally, sections were released to their lieutenants.

Corsica had several jump zones, but the drop zone (DZ) directly behind the regiment was used most regularly. Our jumps focused on the operational aspects: a complete section, two columns exiting simultaneously through both doors. Once on the ground, we released our weapons and backpacks from the gaine, rolled up our parachutes, and made a dash to the regroup point.

On a typical jump day, it was possible to make two to three jumps, with an additional night jump. We could expect to jump, on average, every second week. Less thrilling, but a major facet of section life, were the regimental duties, which included Guard 24, kitchen, SEPP, or infirmary duties. Each company took its turn covering these basic but vital services for a week at a time to keep the regiment sustainable. Légionnaires with the appropriate training were delegated to their services accordingly. My EPMS qualification, by all the luck in the world, exempted me from these tasks. The regiment had a sports department, but they didn't require additional personnel, so I was lucky enough to be left alone to support Guard 24 if and when needed.

Because of my military driving qualification, I was quickly designated as a section driver. The 6-ton TRM 4000 trucks were loaded for our training programs, which involved weapons training and drills at the numerous ranges, plus inter-company training courses and jumps. With the company's recent intake of légionnaires from basic training, all four sections set off for the west coast of Corsica. It took me some time to get used to navigating the island's skinny roads hugging the rocky coastline, along with aggressive drivers, and I constantly fought the urge to look out to the sea with its mesmerizing and seemingly endless horizon.

1st Company on our way to jump. (*Credit:* Joel Struthers)

Our destination was an abandoned hotel that had been partially destroyed by an FLNC bomb some years ago. It would be our main staging area for the four-week combat locality course, also referred to as urban warfare or fighting in built-up areas (FIBUA). It covered every aspect of urban warfare, such as exhaustively clearing buildings or protecting them from the attacking force.

During the final week, we drove to a mock village with a combined shooting range. We trained day and night, and then returned to Calvi for the standard end-of-course TAP tests. This quickly tied into a regimental exercise initiated with a night jump onto a drop zone in northeastern Corsica. I fell out of the aircraft with my gaine—fell, since I was carrying the section radio set and blank ammunition, which added an extra 20 kilograms to my kit—and shot to the ground like a meteorite.

After regrouping, we marched up the mountains overlooking the town of Borgo. Fighting through dense maquis, the only bush that fights back, we passed the 2nd Section. Seeing them carrying their LLR 81mm mortars broken down into three components—tube, base plate, and bipod—none of which were practical to carry and weighed 45.2 kilos in total, I realized I could have had it a lot worse. A few hours later, we finally arrived in the St-Florent Valley and set up camp. As planned, the dawn attack on our position led to an exfiltration under 50-calibre heavy machine gun–covering fire. We then spent hours crawling through maquis, once again dead tired and cursing life. A nice maquis-based sauce on a steak, however, is quite delicious.

As winter slowly set in and the island's vacationers left, our company departed for Les Rouses, mainland France on the Franco-Swiss border, and a centres d'entraînement commando (CEC) 23e RI (Régiment d'infanterie). The company boarded a C-130 Hercules at the Calvi airport and flew to a French Air Force base near the French Alps, finishing the journey by truck. We arrived at the 1848 Fort des Rousses, suitably frozen for our stage d'entraînement commando (winter warfare course). With the company weapons secured in the regiment's armoury, we were shown to our barrack blocks. Sections were then called down to the stores to be fitted for boots and telemark skis, poles, sealskins, Gore-Tex winter gear, survival beacons, first-aid equipment and sleds, avalanche rescue tools, and other ancillary winter kit.

Over the next three weeks, we would learn how to both telemark and downhill ski, with winter-survival and alpine-battle drills culminating in a final exercise with live fire. Our French Chasseurs Alpins instructors, who wore oversized white berets, got to work introducing us to telemark skiing in the forests surrounding the fort. We then joined tourists on the local hills for the downhill skiing component. We were quite the contrast on the slopes in our winter whites and green berets among civilians clad in their multicoloured ski apparel.

When our collective telemark skills improved, the instructors took us to higher altitudes and into the alpine. The instructors taught us how to build snow bricks and shelters by compacting the snow with our skis. We then constructed walls around the hole (using snow for bricks), laying our skis across the top and covering it all with a tarp and loose snow so that it would blend into the surroundings. This created a well-concealed and somewhat insulated shelter for three, which we then burrowed into with our weapons and backpacks, creating a cold-air trench and entrance. This was home for two nights. We spent our days trekking up and across the alpine with our backpacks and weapons, using the telemark skis with seal skins attached to their underside for adherence to the snow. In the evenings we returned, organized guard duty, set inert anti-personnel mines around our perimeters, and deployed night patrols.

Since I could already ski, everything came easily enough to me. But one day I made a soldier's mistake—a serious one. While inside my shelter after a patrol, I had removed the magazine from my FAMAS, but I forgot to clear it and check prior to releasing its action. And bang! An accidental discharge (AD), albeit with a blank round. Regardless, Lieutenant De Mesmay wasn't impressed. I explained my mistake, and he gave me the look of parental disappointment. To my surprise, nothing more was said about the incident.

That error weighed heavily on my mind. An AD with a live round is a cardinal sin. In basic, Jock had shared his experience in Northern Ireland, where a soldier returning from patrol made the same mistake I did, but with a live round. It killed Jock's friend, who was sleeping in his barrack bed.

On Saturday afternoon, we were given permission to ski the local hill, and a troop truck was available to take us there, leaving the fort's gates at 1400 hours. Several of us from the 1st Section decided to leave on foot at 1200 hours in order to get in some extra time skiing. On our way downstairs, we ran into the company NCO, a hardened Frenchman with a hundred years' service. He asked us where we were going, and promptly sent us back upstairs, saying we would take the truck at 1400 hours like everyone else.

Back in our barrack room, I was mid-complaint about this rude disruption to my life when the NCO walked past within earshot. He marched into our barrack room, and I paid for my bellyaching with a head-butt to the mouth. Not a word was said. In reaction, I automatically brought up my guard, to which the NCO responded by grabbing a metal stool from the corner, strongly suggesting I don't bother taking it any further. I didn't; I had just reacted in defence mode. He then ordered me to go clean the hallway and washrooms. After a stop at the fort's infirmary to stitch up my bleeding lip, and the hallway mopped, Lieutenant De Mesmay passed by and told me I could skip the washrooms and go skiing. He suggested I stay clear of the NCO.

The course passed without further incident, and the final exercise was upon us. We loaded up the trucks with five days' worth of provisions and made our way on skis to an explosive range. Here, we detonated our explosive charges, exfiltrating up into the alpine using the skills we learned over the past weeks, finishing with live fire on a shooting range and a ski descent off the mountain.

It was time for graduation, and two other regular French military companies on course attended the ceremony. Regimental songs were sung, and commando brevets were awarded. When I compared the regular companies' singing with that of our own company, there was no contest. The French regulars sang at a much faster tempo, to match the pace at which they marched, and it just didn't sound right to me. I still had several stitches in my swollen lip, so I refrained from singing. It made the head-butt worthwhile.

Back in Calvi, we squared away our kit and went straight back into the company routine. An entry-level company sniper course was scheduled, and I was informed that I was one of two légionnaires chosen from our section to attend, joining nine other légionnaires and caporals.

The 4th Section's Lieutenant Bourban was running the course, and two 4th Company NCOs and caporals made up his training staff. All were qualified snipers. With trucks loaded, we made our way to the Cap Corse by the resort town of Saint Florent situated in a bay on the island's northern peninsula. Its sixteenth-century Genoese tower near Punta Mortella was built on the hillside overlooking the Mediterranean, a vantage point for spotting Barbary pirates. We spent a week at the range here, learning how to master the French military 7.62 FR F2 sniper rifle. My shooting was consistent, but with room for much improvement. The rifle is a right-hand shot, and as a left-hander I had to make the switch and learn how to adapt.

We then moved into other aspects of sniping, infiltrating, building observation posts (OP), and shooting from them. After our technical training, we would crawl into our OPs looking downrange in our designated arc of fire. We'd wait for a target to appear and make the shot before it disappeared again. The training caporals verified the results and passed these on to Lieutenant Bourbon via walkie-talkie; he would point to the shooter whose success rate sucked. Then he'd point toward a well-worn trail up a hillside. These punishments or runs didn't improve anyone's marksmanship, but it did wonders for our cardio.

For the infiltration exercise, we were teamed in pairs, binômes— I was partnered with a German légionnaire, Zurell, from the 3rd Section—and dropped off on the coast by truck. Our goal was to navigate Saint Florent's rolling hills and deep maquis-filled valleys, avoiding roads while our training staff on vehicle patrol would look for us. The pressure was on to be the quickest binôme back to its individual shooters' OP and make a shot. Everyone, regardless of where they went, fought the maquis. Each team arrived within an hour of one another. It had taken four hours on average, and we were all exhausted. When the last team finally arrived, and a few of us had made the shot in the early hours of the day, the lieutenant had us all return to the range blockhouse used as our sleeping quarters. We were duly informed that word from the training staff was that someone was seen using a road during the infiltration, and we were all told to get back in the truck for a second attempt. This time it would be a daylight solo infiltration without weapon.

The fact of the matter was that we all used a road at some point. Options were limited. We climbed into the TRM, and the tarp was closed so we couldn't see outside. A training caporal sat with us to ensure no one looked outside, and he laughed at our predicament. Gutted, we drove off. The truck suddenly stopped with a jolt, waking most of us up. One by one, our names were called, and when I heard "Struthers," I jumped out. Lieutenant Bourban was standing there with a grin on his face, pointing to a roadside café. Nice one. *Pains au chocolat*, charcuterie with fresh bread, black coffee, and a cold beer made for the perfect breakfast on April 1, 1996.

I respected the lieutenant, who was likely the same age as I was. He was capable, demanding, and didn't let people get away with shit. But he had a good sense of humour when it suited him. He would also shoot when he could, do the 8-kilometre runs with us, and he didn't ask of us what he couldn't do himself.

The next exercise involved a longer-distance march. Paired up in the same binômes, we set off with a set of coordinates that would lead us to an orange flag somewhere on our maps, where we would find our next set of coordinates to follow. During the exercise, or prior perhaps, I drank water from a local stream. Diarrhea set in, slowing my progress. Soon I felt like death. Quitting wasn't an option. If I didn't complete the exercise, I wouldn't qualify for the brevet. Zurell took over map-reading, and we eventually made it back to our OPs. Exhausted, I fell asleep on my rifle right away. Zurell's shot woke me up abruptly soon after.

The final phase of our course involved a jump with the FR F2, along with the ubiquitous TAP tests back in Calvi. I counted on scoring maximum TAP points to place well within the overall course ranking. Several of the guys were better shots on the final evaluation but scored lower on the TAP. In the end, this allowed me to finish first. The following day on the 1st Company parade square, Capitaine Gomart presented us with our brevets, a pin with an FR F2 over a target.

With our kit squared away, titre de permissions filled out, and dress uniforms on with our new brevets, we were ready to head into town. That evening, we followed Lieutenant Bourban and the training staff into Calvi for a meal and to a bar afterwards. Sadly, Calvi was quiet since the summer vacationers were long gone.

Section training continued for nearly ten months, during which I notched thirty-six jumps. Soldier well, hold your own physically, and you're left alone by the caporals, NCOs, and officers. This wasn't overly complicated. One morning during the run, our head NCO said that in light of my general performance, I should consider volunteering for the Groupe des commandos parachutistes (GCP) selection process. I wasn't aware that one could just volunteer, but I took his advice and passed before Lieutenant De Mesmay and asked for his approval to volunteer for GCP pre-selection, which he duly approved. The 1st Company capitaine then authorized my request with the 1st Section's lieutenant's recommendation.

Two of the regiment's companies were due to leave for Bosnia as part of the UN/NATO force, and the 1st Company was heading to Gabon, West Africa. Unfortunately, my pre-selection approval meant that I wouldn't be going with the 1st Company. I had mixed emotions about that. I was missing my first opportunity to go on tour, but I was also thrilled at the idea of making it to the GCP. Hopefully, it would lead to bigger and better opportunities.

Returning from Calvi late one Sunday afternoon after a few glasses of pastis with Rake and some of the Russians I knew from basic, I noticed my name on the section order sheet. I was the designated toilet cleaner? At this stage, numerous légionnaires fresh from basic training had joined the section, with a group arriving every two to three months. Caporal Nagisa was our duty caporal that week. He was Japanese, and his French was less than stellar. I approached him in the hallway and asked why I was supposed to be cleaning toilets.

He took exception to me questioning his directive, and after a short back and forth gave me a push, saying, "It's an order." Nagisa was shorter than me, but stocky. I was pissed off at being told to clean toilets after ten months in the section. "Fuck that," I thought. The push pissed me off too. An unwritten rule exists within the lower ranks that in a confrontation that's perhaps more personal, you can suggest the higher rank remove his rank. Which I did. Nagisa removed his rank and pushed me again, this time harder. I responded with a left to the side of his face. He dropped to the floor, then curled up into the fetal position, holding his right cheek. I immediately felt bad and concerned. What had just happened was a huge mistake on my part.

The following morning, I was summoned to the lieutenant's office. I was nervous as hell. Nagisa was at the medical *infermerie*, and I was asked to answer for my part in that. The lieutenant didn't really say much, but he told me to put on my dress uniform and make my way to Capitaine Gomart's office.

Capitaine Gomart was straight to the point. "Who do you think you are?" he demanded. My saving grace, however, was that Nagisa had corroborated my story, saying he had removed his rank and pushed me. Capitaine Gomart finished by telling me to watch my step and that I wasn't in the clear yet, as the incident was on the regiment commanding officer's desk for a decision as to what would happen to me next.

As I cleaned the section toilets, Caporal Marius van Loon, a 100-foot-tall Dutchman new to the section, warned me that this type of behaviour wouldn't happen again, or all the caporals would intervene. Fair enough. A few days later, I was summoned to the lieutenant's office again. To my surprise, I was told to pack my bags and make my way to the Laveran military hospital in Marseille for my GCP pre-selection medical exams.

The next day, Caporal Pavil Holcik, a Czech from the 4th Section, and I made our way from Bastia, a port town located at the base of the Cap Corse, to Marseille by ferry. On our second day of tests at the military hospital, I was sitting in the hallway waiting for my next exam when a cold feeling came over me. Two nurses walked by with Nagisa in tow, his face bandaged.

Fuck! This was not good. Nagisa wasn't a bad guy, really. My emotions had gotten the better of me, and over something that wasn't a big deal at all. The capitaine was right. Who did I think I was? This was the type of thing that had gotten me into trouble before the Legion, and I needed to stop making these kinds of stupid mistakes.

When our medical tests were completed, Caporal Holcik and I returned to Calvi and presented ourselves to the 1st Company duty office. By then, most of the company had left for Gabon. The duty NCO handed us both a two-week leave slip, noting that GCP pre-selection would start the day after our return. I was taken aback, and stuttered something. The NCO asked if I had a problem. I was about to open my mouth again when he asked if I wanted to give the leave pass back to him. His comment was accompanied with a look that clearly said to shut the fuck up. Which I did. He then added that the company capitaine and our section lieutenants wished us luck, and asked that we do the 1st Company proud.

CHAPTER ELEVEN

Pre-Selection

Before anyone could retract my leave, I was out of the regiment's gates and onto a plane to mainland France. With the European Union's open borders and my military identification, it only made sense to spend my time exploring Europe. I made my way to Barcelona, Spain, on a train via Nice and rented a small apartment on La Rambla with a view of Christopher Columbus's ship, the *Santa Maria*. But more importantly, I was ready to mingle in my newly acquired civilian clothing. It was August, and Barcelona's vacationers were enjoying themselves. I would try my best to do the same.

Contrary to some people's idea of a vacation, I ran twice a day through the city's Olympic Park and along its waterfront. I found a spot to do my sit-ups, push-ups, and chin-ups, all in preparation for the GCP pre-selection. During the afternoons, I hit the beach, generally the location where I had noticed the most attractive female sunbathers during my last run. I had a French infantry training manual with me to study, but more interesting distractions took over.

I met an American girl, Laura, who was on holiday with her sister. She was a university student who had grown up on a ranch in Montana. Laura put some effort into getting me to talk, and in time I started to act like a normal civilian. I was somewhat out of practice in the art of casual conversation, especially with an attractive woman. Laura had long brown hair, brown eyes, a nice laugh, and she was worldly from her travels. She also had a very nice bum.

When the sun started to set, we said our goodbyes, and then met that evening for a meal on La Rambla, not far from my apartment. We sat, drinking Spanish red wine and talking, and Laura asked what brought me to Barcelona. I wasn't really sure how to explain this without alarming her. Who joins the French Foreign Legion? It almost comes across as bullshit. I told her I was with the military, and that bored her enough to move on to a new subject. Perhaps me inhaling my meal before she was done with her appetizer was proof enough that I wasn't a regular civilian on holiday.

With a bottle of red wine in hand, we moved the conversation to my apartment balcony and then into the bedroom. Lying in bed with her, I thought of the major downside to the Legion: not enough sex. Laura helped ease my short transition back into civilian life. The fact of the matter was that after enduring the Legion, relaxing was a challenge. Even the concierge at my apartment asked me why I was always in such a rush to be everywhere. My leave flew by, and although I felt ready to return to Calvi, I was somewhat anxious about what lay ahead.

On my return to Calvi, I mentally prepared myself for what was to follow and presented myself to the Compagnie d'éclairage et d'appui (CEA). Eleven caporals and three première-classe légion-naires were listed on the order sheet posted on the wall, along with room allocations and timings for the next morning's pre-selection program. In my designated barrack room, I noticed Holcik was already organizing his kit. Everyone kept to themselves somewhat, either organizing kit or trying to get some sleep in anticipation of the next day's physical efforts.

Standing next to my bed was a première-classe légionnaire whom I recognized from the 3rd Company in Castel. We quickly intro-duced ourselves. Chris, a Brit, was a medic with the CEA Milan Sec-tion. He was tall and on the lanky side. Back in Castel, he had been in the course ahead of me, and I remembered that he spoke excellent French for a Johnny (Legion slang for a Brit). Chris explained that he had grown up in France. His sense of humour was on point, and after a few laughs we realized that a few of the caporals with three to five years of service seemed annoyed. Was it the noise, or our rank? Service was everything in the Legion, and anyone viewed as circumventing tradition wasn't popular. I wasn't overly bothered. It was their issue, not mine. I was young in service, but I had gotten myself to pre-selection.

Monday morning, the CEA parade was like all others. The pre-selection stood two steps to the left of the GCP section. As per our orders, we were dressed in our combats without berets or belts. After the company was released to its section, the GCP NCO, Sergent-Chef Bariat, in charge of pre-selection, directed us to the GCP section's one-level building close to the regiment headquarters for a briefing.

In the classroom, we were introduced to the 11e Division Parachutiste, Groupement de Commandos Parachutistes (GCP), teams qualified in high-altitude free fall and other skills that fall outside the remit of the combat companies. Nineteen teams from the division's nine regiments formed the Groupement, attached to the Commandement des opérations spéciales (COS), France's Special Operations Command.

The REP's GCP was unique in that the team's NCOs and junior ranks are all légionnaires. Two teams of ten qualified members are commanded by a capitaine and a lieutenant (second-in-command). This thirty-strong unit allowed members to be on courses or other assignments and still maintain two operational teams. The GCP section was split into operational cells:

- Command: officers, head NCO, and two qualified vehicle mechanics
- Communications: Morse code and radio communications
- Training (TME–tire (shooting), mines, explosives): tasked with team training
- Intelligence: surveillance and intelligence gathering
- Medical: medical support, including a chief medic and two junior NCO medics
- Technical Operations (TO): covert infiltration and exfiltration, and operations.

After this introduction, we were told what would follow over the next few weeks and then dismissed. Sergeant-Chef Bariat met us at the regiment's gym for the usual TAP tests. That afternoon, we started a series of written tests covering subjects taught on the caporal course. Since I hadn't done my caporal's course, I'm sure I didn't impress anyone with those results.

The next day, we were asked to assemble and then disassemble several types of weapons: a FAMAS, FN Minimi, HKMP5-SD6, AK-47, and the .50-calibre Browning heavy-machine gun. Aside from the FAMAS, I wasn't familiar with any of these weapons. We then did the same with the 9mm Beretta 92 sidearm. Again, my knowledge was lacking. Weapons expertise is subjective, and it's dependent on your section's specialty. It wasn't just a case of drawing a weapon from the company armoury and then learning how to strip and reassemble it. We were given two chances to disassemble and assemble each weapon while a GCP NCO watched and evaluated. When the evaluation was complete, we were then asked to watch slides in the classroom showing NATO and Eastern-bloc military equipment and write down what they were, or more so, what we thought they were.

On day three, our swimming test was held at the regiment's amphibious centre, followed by a hand-to-hand combat evaluation. With the TAP and physical evaluations completed, and basic infantry knowledge tested, we were then split into groups and tested on our specific company specialties.

The following day, we were properly introduced to the section's Heckler & Koch MP5 submachine gun and 9mm Beretta 92 pistol. First, we were shown how to disassemble and reassemble the weapons, and then we were individually blindfolded and told to do same. This was followed by the section's house-clearing techniques, culminating in live fire drills at the regiment's 50-metre outdoor range.

After our evening meal, we set off separately on a night map-and-compass orienteering exercise. It wasn't long before all of us were grouped next to a roadside culvert. The set of coordinates provided to us, with a specific description or clue to its location, had been mixed up. An NCO from the section pulled up in a P4 and started shouting at us, then paused as he realized the error. He quickly sent us on our way to the next set of correct coordinates.

We all ended up marching as a group until we found the final set of coordinates, which we soon realized corresponded to Punta Bianca, the regiment's shooting range on the coast. We staggered in around first light, completing the 30-kilometre distance. Here, we were each issued a FAMAS and told to engage our individual target. We lay on the cold ground focused on our individual silhouettes 300 metres downrange.

The FAMASs issued weren't ours, and they weren't sighted. I was left-handed, and the odds were that the FAMAS handed to me was sighted for a right-hand shot. At 300 metres, even a small sighting difference adds up. Excuses or not, my first few rounds were not on target and a significant correction—a guess—did the trick luckily. My close-up range work was better, but I was somewhat concerned. Once our shooting was completed, we returned to the section building, where we were stood down and told to eat and rest.

At 0430 hours the following day, a Saturday, we gathered outside the Calvi Supermarket in full combat kit, with backpack, helmet, and FAMAS. Our backpacks were weighted to 20 kilos. We were ready to start the 30-kilometre TAP run, which had to be completed in less than five hours to meet the GCP requirement. However, anything over three and a half hours was considered a poor effort within the section. The section record of two hours and twenty-eight minutes was held by a former 1st Company South African.

We set off, grouped together. As we left Calvi, we passed the Acapulco Nightclub, off limits to légionnaires in uniform, with its loud music and late-night revellers spilling out into the early-morning air. We continued running toward the airport.

About forty-five minutes in, once we passed the Calvi airport, the pack started to spread out. Everyone started to find their own pace. At the 10-kilometre mark, Hetny, a Pole, and I ran together in the lead, stopping at the 20-kilometre mark to eat an orange and have a drink of water. We set off again before the cramps could hit. My legs and feet were already aching, but mentally, I thought I had the three-hour finish mark beat.

The sun was now making its slow appearance, rising over the horizon, and the temperature started to climb with it. I could also see the long, twisting road ahead of us, which snaked up to the highest point of the run. By this time, carrying the FAMAS had become increasingly awkward. Head down, I slogged upward, finally reaching the apex, and immediately began the equally punishing descent into the village of Mondale. My legs felt like Jell-O, and the bottoms of my feet were burning from the constant friction. At this point Hetny picked up the pace, but I slowly fell behind.

With the sun completely visible over the horizon now, I could see the regiment's orange-tiled rooftops and water tower far off in the distance. This boosted my morale a little. At the 29-kilometre mark, I ran past another nightclub and was treated to girls in short skirts wandering out of the club to their parked car on the road. "Où allez-vous, soldat?" "Where are you going, soldier?" one called out. Mentally, it was the hardest part of the whole run. Don't stop, I told myself.

The last leg was through the main gate to get to the regiment's running track for two final laps. I knew I had to dig deep if I had any chance to close the gap with Hetny. We ran two laps around the regiment's track, but I couldn't catch up to him. I finished in two hours and fifty minutes, a minute behind Hetny. It was an excellent run on his part, and I was happy with my effort. Everyone arrived within forty-five minutes of one another, and then our bags were weighed to ensure no one had dropped weight during the run.

We were dismissed until Monday morning. Walking back to the barracks was hell. My legs wanted nothing to do with it. Back in barracks, I quickly removed the surgical tape from my shoulders, back, and feet, which had been applied to stop friction burns, before showering and changing into the next uniform.

It was the weekend, and the Corsican summer was in full swing, and Calvi was a playground for the rich and famous, with their yachts anchored in Calvi Bay. The beaches were also full of European tourists soaking up the Corsican sun. Several of us made our way to the beach in our approved regimental beach attire: white Legion shorts, a white golf shirt with Legion insignia, sport socks with stripes in the Legion's three colours, and clean runners to finish off this summer fashion statement. The legion socks did the trick; I met an Italian girl. Michaela was a brunette, and her Italian accent had an immediate effect on me. Corsican beaches were topless, which had its added effects too.

Lying on the white sand reflecting on the past week, I felt like my efforts were paying off, and I was pleased with my progress. But then again, who could tell what the examiners were seeing, and what exactly they were looking for. From a physical standpoint, all our performances were somewhat close.

That evening, Michaela invited me and my friends back to their campsite. Thankfully, it was within the regiment's approved beach area, so we didn't have to change into our dress uniforms; we could stick with the Legion socks. We were introduced to Italian hospitality. Michaela and her friends made us spaghetti over the fire, and we provided the Corsican wine. We sat and drank, talking and laughing at one another. Then Michaela and I snuck away to her tent. As Corsica's renowned former resident—Napoléon Bonaparte—once said, "At twenty-two, many things are allowed which are no longer permitted past thirty."

But on Monday morning, it was back to Legion reality. We broke into four groups and made our way up into the Corsican mountains to hike the GR20, reputed to be one of the most picturesque hiking routes in Europe. I was partnered with Chris and GCP Caporal-Chef Laskowski, or Lasko as he was known by his teammates. Originally, I thought Lasko looked like he could have an attitude about him, but that wasn't true. Prior to the GCP, Lasko had served with the 2nd Company (Mountain Warfare). More interestingly his grandfather had been a Polish légionnaire and served in Indochina, and his grandmother was a Vietnamese national. Quite the mélange of Legion history there.

Lasko set a good pace for us as we passed through pine groves and clambered over rocks, summiting a steep incline above the town of Calenzana, with its small stone homes built on the rock hillside. Then we dropped down on the other side of a ridge, where we picked up a tarmac road paralleling the mountain. A car appeared. The Corsican driver stopped and asked if we wanted a ride. "Yes!" said Lasko. We stored our backpacks in the trunk of his Renault, and he drove us to a village at an impressive speed. Near a roadside café was a small clearing next to a narrow river. This was our designated rendezvous point, and we were the first to arrive. The remaining teams showed up after our midday naps, complaining about the hike. We nodded in agreement. It was hell.

The section's 2iC, Capitaine Desmeulles, joined us at this point. His English was excellent, and he spoke to us in a cordial manner, making light conversation. This threw Chris and me off at first, as

Groupe des commandos parachutistes (GCP) selection candidates rapelling into Punta Bianca weapons range. (*Credit:* 2ᵉ Régiment étranger de parachutistes)

we were not accustomed to such personable behaviour. Many officers in the Legion seemed to live by the rule that familiarity breeds contempt. Capitaine Desmeulles had served in the 2nd Company prior to the GCP. We set off in our respective groups, and up we went. Stopping at an *auberge* on the GR20 trail, Chris bought us fried eggs, and ham, and a Corsican Pietra beer. It was by far the best meal I'd had in ages, and the cold beer a welcome means of hydration, or carbs for that matter. Then teams arrived, ate, and rehydrated, and then we began the climb, following Capitaine Desmeulles up to the Monte Cinto mountain refuge.

At 2706 metres, Monte Cinto is Corsica's highest peak. It was a steady climb, and we followed a GR20 path that ran up and alongside a stream bed, racing each other and passing tourists camped out on the mountainside overlooking sheer drop-offs into the valley below. We reached the refuge just before sundown. Capitaine Desmeulles decided we would stay in the refuge rather than camp outside. After having something to eat, I slid into my sleeping bag on the shelf-like bunks and crashed out. I was asleep in no time, but in the early hours, we were all awoken by a massive thunderstorm, with the wind howling and rain lashing the refuge's walls and windows. The civilians who camped outside had made their way into the *auberge*, soaked.

At first light, we set off for the summit stepping over people's belongings spread across the mountainside. A hiker on the trail asked us where the summit was. Capitaine Desmeulles just pointed up. After several hours, we made it to the rocky summit strewn with hikers' garbage. What a damn shame. But the view was incredible. I could see from one side of Corsica to the other. Never had the island felt so small. We descended the mountain as a group, and returned to the regiment. The GR20 had felt like a timeout in the selection process more than anything.

Returning from fire and movement drills on the Punta Bianca range—something I enjoyed and where I felt I held my own—we stopped at the regiment's old jail, a Spanish fortification dating back to the 1800s. We were given thirty minutes to assess the ground and fort to formulate an attack plan. The ground rules: we had ten men and the weapons and support vehicles available within the regiment's armoury. Plan away! This was a new way of thinking for most of us. We submitted our plans to the NCO, who would submit them to the section capitaine.

At this point in the selection process, I could sense who my competition was, albeit none of us knew what the intake quota was. Holcik was always consistent, and got along well with the selection training staff. Dimitri, a French caporal from the 3rd Company, was also a solid competitor. Ursa, a Romanian caporal from the 3rd Company with five years' service, was fit and he invariably finished within the top five in all the physical tests. Selak, a Croatian and newly promoted caporal from the 2nd Company, finished well throughout. On the more intellectual side was Caporal Garcia, another Frenchman. He was a communications specialist who would be an obvious choice for the section's communications cell. Hetny, who could not only run but do push-ups like I've never seen, was struggling with the weapons drills on the firing range. The others didn't stand out.

The opportunity to watch the section jump was motivation enough for doing the pre-selection. We watched as team members kitted up and struggled into an SA 330 Puma helicopter parked at the regiment's free-fall drop zone. The Puma then climbed to 3500 metres. We could just make out the team's exits until their rectangular light-blue chutes opened at 1500 metres, followed by the characteristic crack in the sky. High above, they slowly formed a single-file spiral in a stepped formation and collectively made their way to the DZ, landing evenly staggered from one another in a 20-metre circle. Their landings were smooth and controlled. It was impressive, and a far cry from our combat company's automatic jumps.

The following day, we squeezed into the Puma for a live fire, rappelling into the range and working on the fire and movement drills taught to us over the past two weeks. With range work completed, we got back in the Puma and rappelled onto the roof of the regiment's old SEPP building, clearing it from top to bottom as we had learned. We were having a blast, but we were also being watched and evaluated on our ability to put into practice what we had been taught, as well as integrate within the team. Skill was important, but so was personality.

After the day's training, I was singled out, and told to wait outside the section's classroom. I was concerned. My name was called, and when I entered, Capitaine Raoul, the GCP commanding officer, motioned for me to sit down. "How do you think you're doing?" he asked. My instinct was that I was out—done. But I responded, "Trying my best, sir." He nodded, devoid of any facial expression, and then told me that pre-selection was not finished yet; however, I was being sent to Castel tomorrow. Castel? Capitaine Raoul then clarified that I would be doing my caporal's course, and when I returned I would join the section's Technical Operations (TO) cell. I had made the team. I hid my excitement and said, "Oui, mon capitaine."

CHAPTER TWELVE

Caporal

The idea of returning to the 4e RE for the Certificats militaires élémentaires (CME) F1 wasn't thrilling. In fact, I was gutted, albeit I realized this was just a requirement that would lead me back to Calvi and my new section, the GCP. October 1996, fourteen of us première-classe légionnaires from the regiment's various companies were headed to Castel for one long month. We took an SNCM (Société nationale maritime corse méditerranée) high-speed ferry from Calvi to Marseille, and then the train to Castel.

Together with a group of fifty première-classe légionnaires, we presented ourselves to the training company, and to Adjudant Madureira, one by one. The Portuguese NCO, whom I had been warned was a lunatic, made me enter his office and repeat my presentation three or four times, each time yelling at me to exit his office and start over. Once I finally got it right, he asked the junior NCO sitting next to his desk if my service record indicated that I was retarded.

The course began in earnest, and the two training *pelotons* (platoons) were shown to their barrack rooms, where we got ourselves organized. The training NCOs then briefed us on what to expect next. We would spend our first two weeks at the CME training farm called Bertrandou, located in the Pyrenees foothills close to the medieval town of Carcassonne. And we were off. The trucks were loaded with food and stores, and we drew our weapons from the armoury. Then we marched 35 kilometres *sac à dos* (with backpacks on) with Carnet des Chants, through the night to Bertrandou, arriving tired and wet the following morning.

Bertrandou was a larger building than the farm at Raissac where I had done my basic training. The adjacent field had a full-scale PC.

A wooded area surrounded the farm, and we wasted no time setting up our two-man tents in two straight, evenly spaced columns. It was fall and the weather was cold and wet. Madureira was temperamental from the very start. One minute he was calm and collected, and without warning he would flare up at the slightest transgression. Madureira was a short man, but he had a big voice and he seemed to be most at ease when yelling. We spent a lot of the day in the classroom with either Madureira or an NCO instructing. Three légionnaires were posted to the kitchen each day. Making meals was our responsibility, and if we didn't cook, we were made to eat rations instead.

Madureira had started his career at the 4ᵉ RE as a fut-fut, and he was a big fan of Legion songs. Great. We had so much in common already. After our evening meal, we were given a song or two to learn for the following morning. The NCOs would call it a day, and retreat to the warmth of a dry roof and wood fire in the main building, while the rest of us spent the night trying to learn a damn song or two in the rain. In the morning, Madureira would arrive and listen to our efforts. If the song faltered, and it always did, he'd immediately lose his shit, hollering, "Marche canard!"

Those long nights started to piss me off; the lack of sleep and fatigue were getting to me. At that point, my attitude was, "Fuck it. I can marche canard, do push-ups, and run the PC all day long, so I'm going to sleep instead." Sure, it was the wrong attitude. But if the others wanted to sing, they could go ahead.

One cold and rainy evening, the songs stopped. Construction, however, became the new thing. We spent the entire night building a large 4ᵉ RE insignia out of rocks. Madureira felt this would really improve our little tent camp. Another night, we built a covered eating area for the NCOs, so they had a dry spot to sit while we ate in the rain.

Another popular past-time was the ceremonial changing of the tents. There was no rhyme or reason as to when this swap would occur; we were simply ordered to pack up our tents and kit as fast as we could and then march off collectively in song. After belting out a few of Madureira's favourites—often in "Marche canard!"—we would usually return to our starting point and rebuild camp.

These were long days punctuated by classroom work, orienteering, the PC, and even longer nights in song or some other bullshit. We dug two-man fighting trenches, and spent a damp night watching for an NCO attempting to sneak through our lines. We needn't have worried. They were all fast asleep in their beds in the warm and dry main building.

That morning, Madureira arrived and reviewed our trenches. He yelled at us to immediately assemble, with our gloves on. We all stood at attention in the ranks, wearing our leather gloves. Madureira slowly walked the line and stopped at a fut-fut's feet. He was wearing a single glove. Madureira stood before him with an evil smile, wearing the other glove that he had found in a trench, and displaying some impressive hand movements with it in front of the fut-fut's face. We were ordered to wear our gloves the entire day and without fail.

Wearing gloves made the day's duty caporal's efforts a lot more challenging. Each day, a légionnaire would assume the role of the peloton's duty caporal, which entailed receiving Madureira's orders and ensuring they were respected. Orders were issued and the duty caporal would make two copies in the course ledger by hand in black ink, using a ruler to keep the lines straight, properly formatted, and without error. One copy was given to Madureira for marking; the other was posted on the order board for the peloton to read. The following morning the duty caporal's last responsibility was to present the peloton to Madureira, who would then inspect our uniforms, boots, and our personal hygiene efforts: shaving. Most of us at this stage looked somewhat dishevelled. Madureira would smile, his one tooth sticking out abnormally, and say, "Are you unhappy, légionnaire?" He also noted that the duty carporal's written orders submitted the night prior were complete shit and would have to be done again.

If things weren't to Madureira's satisfaction or done his way, the orders as an example, he would order the duty caporal to punish the section, in this case a new duty caporal taking over for the day. Additionally, if we had a lousy duty caporal who made loads of mistakes, the peloton would suffer. When this went on all day, tempers would flare. But the purpose was clear. We were only as good as our weakest link, and teamwork was needed to overcome our shortfalls.

After week two, we returned to Castel, where our comfortable barrack beds were well received. But routine continued: cleaning, duties and inspections, two rounds circling the company building in song prior to morning and afternoon parade, presentation to Madureira, and execution of the day's orders. By now, our peloton had become a lot more efficient, saving us a lot of grief.

Within the peloton, we had a wide variety of abilities and personalities. Some among us were support staff working for a regiment's Compagnie de commandement et des services (CCS): administration, communications specialists, medics, and mechanics. Others were from the regiment's combat companies: infantry, mechanized, or engineer. Length of service also varied. Many of those with higher years of service were from the REP. This meant that duties such as the daily toilet cleaning went to those with the least service. I saw fut-futs write their own names down to do the toilet cleaning—smart! It may seem arrogant, and although the REP were on equal standing, we were expected to outperform the others.

Time spent on the ranges involved a mix of drills, and Madureira losing his mind over some error, followed by the never-ending NCOs' weapons inspections. A Q-tip was used to check for residue, and if unsatisfied, the NCO would return in an hour for a re-inspection. This would go on late into the night. The idea was that we would learn where to look for residue when we were inspecting a légionnaire's weapon once we were back in our combat sections. We were being treated like raw recruits, a theme that repeated itself. Of course, this had its place. But for most of us, if not everyone, it was a little tiresome.

The CME peloton joined the rest of the 4ᵉ RE on an exercise in the Pyrenees, and we set up our tents in blizzard conditions. The duty caporal organized a guard duty for the night, and then we sang. Morning came and we dismantled the tents, then descended snow-covered slopes on foot to a valley. Preparations were quickly made for an ambush, and patrols were sent off with blank rounds to detect the exercise's acting enemy force. Madureira gave strict orders not to engage if we encountered the enemy.

I was partnered with a Norwegian from the REP's 3rd Company, and we made our way through dense woodland. As we progressed, we were suddenly shot at (blank rounds) from somewhere in front of us. Instinctively and unfortunately, we returned fire because that's what you do in a contact. Using fire and movement, we then retreated to proper cover. Madureira was clearly furious once we had returned to the rest of the peloton, and in his tirade he referred to our regiment's training as shit. At that moment, I had an accidental verbal discharge, replying, "The 4^e RE is shit." Well, a hard slap across my face followed. Madureira then ordered both of us to stand to attention. With his face inches from ours, yelling and spit flying everywhere, he charged us with insubordination and said that we were as good as off his course.

That night, the peloton marched to a new bivouac area, set up tents, lit a fire, and we were issued wine. And the singing started. Madureira later pulled me and the Norwegian aside and told us not to sweat the day's events. And as for me, he said I deserved a slap, so suck it up. "Oui, mon adjudant," I replied. This was a side of the Legion I respected. Issues were laid bare, and I knew where I stood.

I had to admit that Madureira had my respect. He had completed the Brazilian military's Manaus jungle commando course, renowned for its brutality and high failure rate. Students are required to pass a prisoner-of-war scenario, which has broken many a man. Sitting around the fire, we listened to his stories, and throughout our course he would have us all yell, "Selva!" or "Jungle!" in Portuguese.

When the exercise was over, we loaded the trucks and made our way to the Centre d'entraînement de l'infanterie au tir opérationnel (CEITO), the French Army's infantry shooting test range. It was located smack in the middle of the Roquefort region of France. The entire 4RE training company was present, and the GCP section was also at CEITO doing its annual Groupement GCP evaluations. While we were getting ourselves installed into the barrack blocks, I was told to go and present myself to Capitaine Raoul. The team was in accommodations across the camp mixed with other French regular GCP teams. I found them and presented myself to the capitaine and the section's head NCO, Adjudant Taikato, a Maori from New Zealand. I also presented myself to Adjudant Martin, another Kiwi, who was leaving the section, *fin de service*. I recognized some of the other section members I had met during pre-selection and said hello quickly. Seeing their set-up gave me the extra drive I needed to get this CME deal behind me.

Spending a week on the CEITO firing ranges during the day and night was enjoyable; the ranges were more varied than the ones we usually experienced. In the bitter wind and unrelenting rain typical of the region, plenty of ammunition was used, and a variety of weapons were available. We each shot the LRAC 89mm anti-tank rocket and AC 58 anti-personnel grenades. Those who were off the mark did the marche canard.

We ate at the mess hall in the evenings before heading back to barracks for a long night of weapons cleaning. During our final days at CEITO, we were used as support for the 4ᵉ RE training company's CME F2 sergent course. We were broken into sections using the VABs, four-by-four French armoured personnel carriers. A VAB with mounted .50-calibre heavy machine gun providing fire support would assault its target. Once the VAB came to a complete stop, légionnaires would dismount from the rear and take up firing positions in the range's slit trenches. Targets would appear and the student NCOs would be assessed on their fire orders and reactions to different scenarios.

With CEITO completed, we returned to Castel for the course's final evaluations. This comprised both written tests and infantry-related field tests. My least favourite evaluation was that of our drill commands. A dozen légionnaires on loan from basic training were at our disposal. A training NCO evaluated our drill orders as we went through the various commands used to get the légionnaires to march with FAMASs and bayonets in song on the company's parade square. I forgot to have them mount their bayonets before marching off in song, but I didn't do too badly.

The physical fitness tests were my best chance to gain maximum points and finish well within the course ranking. My former EPMS course NCO and the caporal-chef who had crashed the P4 were the physical fitness evaluators. I broke the 4ᵉ RE's caporal parcours du combattant course record, which I was proud of. Some of our peloton were satisfied with doing the minimum to pass. But then again, some of them were going back to desk jobs, and we all had different objectives.

Once our tests were completed, Madureira marched the peloton onto the regiment's main parade square for our presentation to the regiment's commanding officer. Results were read out, and the top finisher was made to step out of rank and present to the regiment's CO. One of the less enviable tasks of coming first was the responsibility of marching the peloton off the parade square, singing the course song. I took my place at the front of the peloton with the regiment CO, officers, Madureira, and guests watching. My drill command for a left turn should have been a right turn, and the course was now facing the wrong way. I could see smiles on my course-mates' faces. I didn't, however, see a smile on Madureira's face when I glanced his way. I quickly corrected my error, and we marched off in the proper direction only to hear Madureira scream from the sidelines, "HALTE!" I had forgotten the damn singing part.

The top finisher was also given the duty caporal responsibility for the final remaining hours. This meant organizing the weapons being returned to the armoury, cleaning the barracks, and returning the kit to stores. Cleaning the barracks was a handful, considering nobody could give a damn. Everyone was keen to leave Castel and return to their regiments, sections, and girlfriends—and most certainly not in that order.

I was the last man in the barracks. Madureira walked up the stairs to review them and then congratulated me, offering some final advice: "Open up a little, Première-Classe Struthers." I answered, "Oui, mon adjudant." It was an Oprah moment.

The CME course was an experience I wouldn't ever forget, thanks to Madureira. He was effective at his job, and he knew how to get people motivated even if they were resistant to the idea.

CHAPTER THIRTEEN

French Equatorial Africa

With the CME F1 behind me, I enjoyed watching the world go about its business on the train ride from Castel to Marseille, the beauty of the French countryside with its old villages, castles, and châteaux unfolding, and civilians getting on and off the train at different stops. I noticed how people were either well dressed and seemingly organized, or the complete opposite. Wearing our dress uniforms and kepis, I observed that civilians wouldn't sit beside a légionnaire unless seats were limited.

Arriving at the Gare de Marseille-Saint-Charles train station, we joined the city's crowds and made our way to the port to catch the ferry to Corsica. Back in Calvi, a small contingent of rearguard had been left behind to man the company while the CEA was in Gabon. I presented myself to the duty office, and was told I was going to the Central African Republic (CAR), tomorrow, to join the section. Bangui, the country's capital, was in turmoil after a military rebellion.

I moved into my GCP section barrack room (*chambre* 21) on the ground floor of the company building and introduced myself to its two occupants, Caporal Smith (Smithy) and Caporal Popov. Smithy, who was from Crossmolina in Ireland, was waiting to go on his level 2 (CTE1) communications course in Castel. Popov, an ex-Russian Military Spetsnaz, was leaving for Djibouti, Africa. He didn't have much to say. The room was the same size as those in the 1st Company, but the difference was that only three of us were using it. It was decorated, if that's the right word, with lounge chairs, a coffee table, TV, VCR, stereo, and a small fridge. Boots, webbing, and backpacks were scattered all over the room. This was a departure compared to the tidiness of the combat company barrack room.

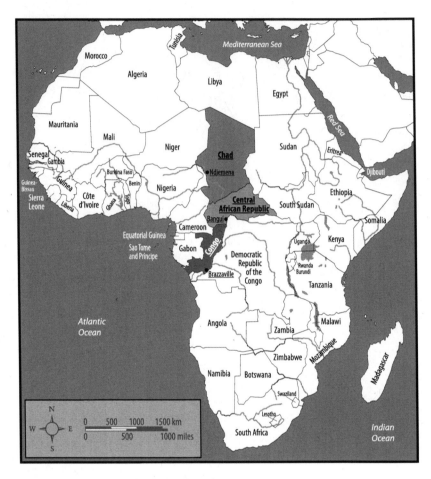

Map of Africa. (*Credit:* Mike Bechthold)

Later that evening, I made my way downtown to meet Michaela. We had been keeping in touch using this new and weird tool, email. She worked for Sony Records in Rome and had been mailing me CDs, notably the Oasis album, *(What's the Story) Morning Glory?* Michaela had timed her arrival in Calvi with mine, and we had planned to spend the weekend and weeknights together. My unexpected departure for Africa changed that. We ate dinner at a little restaurant overlooking the Calvi Bay, with Michaela putting on a brave face while I was thinking about the journey that lay ahead.

The following morning, I left her hotel room and caught the bus back to the regiment in time for the CEA's morning appel. Michaela was crying. I'm certain she sensed that a relationship with a légionnaire wasn't ideal, but we kept in touch and remained friends.

The Partition of Africa in the 1880s saw Belgium, Germany, and France compete against one another in order to control territory north of the Ubangi River. France named its new colony "Ubangi-Shari," later incorporating four other colonies (French Congo, Gabon, Chad, and French Cameroon) into one colonial federation known as French Equatorial Africa (AEF).[15]

During the Second World War, Central African soldiers formed part of the grand French colonial army, Troupes Coloniales,[16] and partook in the Liberation of Paris. Soon after the war, France adopted a new constitution and granted full French citizenship to residents of Ubangi-Shari. Ubangi-Shari obtained independence from France in 1960 and changed its name to the Central African Republic.

Due to widespread repression, human rights abuses, and allegations of cannibalism, France later removed Emperor Bokassa from power in 1979 during Operation Barracuda. France had maintained a presence in the CAR, but at the time all I knew was that I was about to travel to Africa and join the section.

Operation code-name Almandin II, France had deployed elements of the 1er Régiment de parachutistes d'infanterie de marine (1er RPIMa) its lead regiment in the Commandement des opérations spéciales (COS), with supporting roles from Régiment de parachutistes d'infanterie de marine (RPIMa), and the 2e REP's 3rd and 4th companies, including the section.

On November 21, 1996, I joined a dozen légionnaires and NCOs from the 2nd CIE who were on their way to Chad. The French Air Force C-160 Transall left the Calvi airport for the Istres-Le Tubé Air Base west of Marseille. The next leg was the following day, so we were billeted at the base. I took the opportunity to go for a run along the base's flight line, which took me back to my days living on Canadian Air Force bases. It also reminded me that I needed to call home and let my parents know that I was headed to the African continent.

The following day, a mix of légionnaires and regular military boarded an Air Force DC-8 loaded with cargo. I felt restless on the

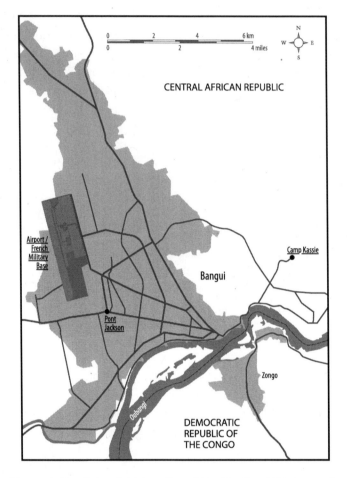

Map of Bangui city, Central African Republic. (*Credit:* 2ᵉ Régiment étranger de parachutistes; Mike Bechthold)

flight; I had no idea what was to follow. Africa, the section, and entering a conflict zone were all obviously very new to me. My focus would be on doing my job professionally, while trying to avoid standing out for the wrong reasons. I couldn't sleep, and I watched the continents change outside my window. Hours later, a voice from the cockpit announced over the intercom, "Descent into Bangui."

It was dark outside, but as we touched down, I tried my best to see through my window what was outside. Coming to a stop, the DC-8's door opened, and warm, humid air wafted into the aircraft, accompanied by the stench of rotting vegetation and burning garbage. I then heard my name called. Capitaine Raoul was standing at the door. I jumped up, put on my kepi, grabbed my small backpack from the overhead compartment, and made my way to the door. I was the only légionnaire getting off the plane; the DC-8's other occupants were continuing to Chad.

Stepping out onto the stairway, the first thing I could see was the old airport terminal against the backdrop of the clear night sky. Initially, it seemed strange, but then I realized there was little artificial light that's normally associated with airports. A French VAB armed with 20mm cannon slowly circled the aircraft. I clambered down the stairway, grabbed my other backpack and duffle bag from the air force ground support staff, and followed Capitaine Raoul to the section's waiting VLRA. GCP teammates, wearing full combat kit, were in the back. I felt out of place sitting next to them in my summer dress uniform and kepi. Suddenly, a long burst of heavy-calibre red tracer lit up the sky over the airport terminal, followed by the low thud of a distant mortar impact. I felt a surge of adrenaline.

It was a short drive to the French-controlled side of the airport, and taking in my new surroundings was pushing the limits of my situational awareness. Everything was new. The smell, the people, and the atmosphere of tension that hung in the air. French Jaguar fighter jets were parked in a hangar as we passed, and three C-160 Transalls were lined up further down the tarmac alongside a lone Dassault Atlantique maritime patrol aircraft. Several Puma helicopters were also parked around the base. The French airbase was also HQ and the command post for the regiment's 3rd and 4th companies, along with a French marine reconnaissance company armed with 90mm Sagaie light-armoured tanks. We stopped outside the section's two large tents—my new home.

Capitaine Raoul pulled me aside and told me that as I wasn't a qualified section member yet, I was to watch and learn from the others. He then quickly briefed me on the situation. The army of CAR-elected President Ange-Félix Patassé was divided, and the rebels who opposed him had taken the Petevo district on the southwestern edge of the city. The rebels consisted of army officers, as well as soldiers who were well armed and capable. What I didn't know was that conflict wasn't new to the rebels, and there were undesirables within the mix. Locals were being robbed and raped, and there were rumours of summary executions.

The French had an additional garrison consisting of the 1er RPIMa close to the parliament and presidential palace. We were some nine-hundred-strong French military in the country, and the French ambassador had remained with a section of légionnaires protecting his residence. Our section had been patrolling on foot and by vehicle over the past few weeks. Recently, however, rebels had been pillaging the homes of high-ranking politicians, government officials, and the military command—anyone with money, basically. Their criminal activity was becoming more frequent, and we were on standby to deal with such behaviour.

I was issued my FAMAS, Beretta, ammunition and anti-personnel vehicle grenades, Kevlar vest, and chest webbing. I was told to find myself a bed and square away my kit. There were twelve of us inside the tent and Caporal Brook, a Brit with the TME cell, helped make sure I had the appropriate communications gear. Brook seemed out of place with his posh Brit accent, but from what I saw during pre-selection, he was a fit and a capable soldier. I then dismantled my FAMAS; it was already set up for a left-hand shot, which was a stroke of luck. Sergent Rich Maguire, a Scotsman from the TO cell, was also helpful and answered my questions. It was somewhat of a relief to be there. Finally, the unknown was no longer.

But my relief was temporary. I was in the shit already. I hadn't presented myself to the section's NCOs, and the French Sergent-Chef Cuvillier was quick to check my mistake. In the NCOs' eyes, this was lack of proper respect. I was read the riot act, and then I presented to every NCO. In my defence, it doesn't really happen this way in a combat company, so I was learning on the fly.

My introduction to Bangui began that evening when we were alerted of a situation in an expatriate neighbourhood. As everyone was getting on their kit, I noticed guys wore military boots of their own choice, acquired on the civilian market. My military issue "rangers," as they were known, sported a solid rubber sole with high leather boot, and closed with laces and two buckles. Not only were they uncomfortable, noisy, and hard to put on and take off, they didn't keep the water out. Instead, they kept it in! Our issued combats weren't much better. They were made of low-quality cotton and were tight-fitting and totally impractical.

Luckily, my newly issued chest webbing for carrying ammunition and grenades was a vast improvement from the 1st CIE. In addition to my FAMAS, I carried a 9mm Beretta pistol with leg holster; it was impractical to wear it higher as the ballistic vest and chest webbing prevented you from drawing your weapon. Within the team, two carried the FN Minimi Para machine gun; the sniper, the FR F2. We all wore the voice-activated Motorola radio (VOX) for inter-team communications. We left the camp in the VLRA wearing our green berets, our Kevlar helmets at our feet, if needed.

Bangui was an eye-opener. Light smoke drifting from the wood stoves used for cooking was pervasive, giving off an acrid smell. I also caught whiffs of meat cooking, along with the stench of sewage. Sodium street lights—those that were still working, anyway—were swarmed with all manner of insects and groups of children trying to catch them. Locals sat out on the front porches of shops and houses in the cooler night air, watching us with their big eyes as we drove past. The kids yelled "Barracuda!" at us, a reference to Operation Barracuda.

The city was primarily made up of shantytowns, single-storey homes, and some old abandoned colonial villas. All were in a state of semi-ruin. As we drove along, I saw larger colonial villas and signs of real conflict. Large-calibre impacts and scorch marks scarred their walls. Mortar rounds had left small craters in the roads. We approached the CAR government and presidential neighbourhood, which was also the location of hotels popular with international business travellers. The Sofitel hotel located on the banks of the River Bangui hadn't been spared; it sported some impressive impact marks.

As we approached the expatriate neighbourhood where shots had been reported, my new teammates flicked off their FAMAS safeties. I did the same. This was my first time with a live weapon outside of a supervised shoot. The VLRA rolled to a stop. We jumped out and started searching the neighbourhood's main road and smaller adjoining alleyways. I was partnered with Lasko and followed his lead. As I walked down the road, weapon at the ready, the locals glared at me, or ran away. With nothing to see, we got back in the VLRA and made our way to PK Zero. This wide avenue was lined with large irrigation ditches and a mix of fields and homes, all of which were either abandoned or derelict. Everything seemed eerily quiet to me.

We returned to camp, debriefed, and I got into my sleeping bag. As I lay there, I revelled in my new surroundings before falling asleep. Africa was clearly new, but also no one was barking orders at me, and there was no appel or parade in the morning. The only requirement was to be ready for 0900 hours.

Before breakfast, most of the guys ran the track inside the base's perimeter, or hit the gym to avoid the day's heat. I joined Caporal Gilles, a Frenchman I had been teamed with for an exercise during pre-selection, for a run. As we ran, Gilles mentioned he had left the French regular paras to join the Legion, specifically the REP. He was somewhat new to the section, having recently finished his qualifying commando course and SOGH (free fall) course and gave me some good pointers on what to expect. He included a few tips on dealing with our section NCOs' personality traits, all the while keeping our pace at an impressive rate.

In the afternoon, we made our way toward Camp Kassie, a rebel-held military camp outside the city limits with a dirt road and jungle covering its approach. The VLRA stopped on the roadside well short of the camp, and we disembarked. I was partnered with Cuvillier, the French NCO who had read me the riot act the day before, given point, and told to follow the well-worn path through the tall elephant grass. Using section operational procedures I had learned in pre-selection, we progressed, sweating in the African sun. With my safety off, and finger resting on the trigger guard, I was acutely aware of my surroundings and the risk of running into an armed rebel. After all, we were not far from Camp Kassie. It wasn't long when from the rear of our patrol Capitaine Raoul gave us the order to stop. We reversed course, returning to the VLRA. I felt that was a test.

As the newcomer, I was quickly designated as the VLRA driver and Capitaine Raoul's P4 chauffeur, if needed. As section CO, he answered to the regiment CO, Colonel Puga, who was in command of French military operations in Bangui. Capitaine Raoul had a reputation for taking initiative. If the regiment was tasked with an interesting mission, the section would be summoned. But the 1er RPIMa was in town, so any premier jobs would go to them. Capitaine Raoul seemed like a fair man to me; he just got on with the job and expected us to do the same. But we knew he was the boss. I certainly felt like he treated me fairly, and as the days passed, he gave me the room I needed to learn my trade.

Within the week, the fighting between the rebels and the CAR army increased. The city's streets and markets were abandoned. Firefights were brief, but still deadly for the local population, who bore the brunt of mortar or AK rounds or poorly sighted RPGs.

In response, the section was broken into smaller teams, and our job was to identify expatriates' homes listed by the French Embassy as Bangui residents. We did this in preparation for an eventual evacuation, if warranted. Brits, Canadians, and other foreign nationals living in the city were advised of the plan. While some were happy to see us, others weren't so receptive. We were perceived by some as an extension of France's colonial past and aggravating or even provoking the situation. While driving through the neighbourhoods pinpointing certain residences, I noticed the Canadian Consulate. I asked the NCO if we could stop. I entered the small building in full combat kit, introduced myself to the consular, and enquired, half-jokingly, on the Canadian passport application process. The consular seemed quite uncomfortable, but I ensured he had our contact details in case he needed assistance.

Within that first week, Capitaine Raoul was summoned to HQ. An undisclosed number of rebels were pillaging the home of a high-ranking CAR official. On his return, we each grabbed our night-vision goggles (NVGs), FAMAS, or the HK MP5 equipped with passive laser sight, then jumped into the VLRA and P4, and sped off. We quickly cut across the runway, the shortest distance to our target. In proximity to the neighbourhood in question, we crawled to a stop, cutting our lights. Then we disembarked and continued on foot. Evenly spread out in pairs, each with a FAMAS or the MP5, we approached the target slowly and deliberately. An SUV was parked outside a white colonial house framed by large trees and thick elephant grass. We could see movement inside the residence. Over the VOX, Capitaine Raoul ordered the two leads to approach the target more closely, while the rest of us formed a defensive semicircle.

The stillness of the night was quickly shattered by a burst of AK-47 fire. At close range, it certainly had my undivided attention. The first rounds landed at the feet of our two teammates approaching the target, Lasko and Caporal-Chef Prigent, a French Tahitian. They immediately returned fire. Tracer rounds cut through the darkness and some hit the ground and trees surrounding us. Instinctively, those of us with a line of sight on the rebels returned fire. But it was difficult to tell exactly where the rounds were coming from, and who was who.

"Cease fire!" Capitaine Raoul shouted. We were told to secure our perimeter. This was my first firefight. I kept my focus despite the chaotic atmosphere, where everyone was trying to gauge the situation, do as they were told, and look out for the bad guy.

The house was cleared and its external floodlights were turned on. Unfortunately, our night vision then became useless. This, in turn, did wonders for my natural night vision. Although I could see the surrounding wooded area, my eyesight was off. Everything was out of focus. Kneeling by a tree for cover, with my FAMAS shouldered at the ready and watching my arc, I caught a slight movement in my peripheral vision. The motion came from a dark area within the taller trees. What was it? My blood was racing from the intensity of the firefight, and my eyes were still adjusting. Was what I saw actually anything? Looking over the barrel of my weapon, I stood up and took three steps toward a more pronounced treeline. The only sound was the faint crunch of dead grass underfoot and my heartbeat, steadily thumping in my ears.

Then I saw it again, a movement near a tree. Now it was clear to me: the silhouette of a man crouching. Taking up the slack on the trigger as I made my approach, my concern was twofold. Was this a rebel or a teammate? And if he was a rebel and I opened fire, what would be my teammates' response close to my arc of fire? As

Lasko in front (AC 58 anti-personnel grenade in hand) and El Wahidi and Capitaine Raoul in the background to the left. City of Bangui. (*Credit:* 2ᵉ Régiment étranger de parachutistes)

I approached, it became obvious that the silhouette was a rebel bent over his weapon, with his head down. At this range, approximately 3 metres, I knew I had the upper hand.

This all unfolded within a minute or two of our initial contact with the rebels, all of which had been chaotic. I approached the rebel from the side at a faster pace, pointing my weapon at his midsection and spitting out the words "Bouge pas!" "Don't move!" Most Central Africans speak some French, and he twitched his head slightly to the side as if to acknowledge my presence and the command. He seemed stiff and afraid to move.

Keeping my eyes and FAMAS pointed at the rebel, I shouted to Capitaine Raoul, asking him to come to my position. He was visibly shocked to see that I had captured a rebel. Capitaine Raoul immediately kicked the AK-47 from the rebel's grip, grabbed the man, threw him to the ground, and kicked him in the back of his head, driving his face into the hard dirt. We then secured his arms and legs using the tie straps attached to my webbing. The rebel, wearing his CAR army uniform, looked up at me. I could see fear in his eyes.

The team searched the surrounding area. Once it was cleared, we loaded our captive into the VLRA. Lasko and I followed behind in the SUV we recovered from the rebels. Since rebels were treated as common criminals, we handed the guy over at the local police station, then made our way back to the section's tent and parked the SUV beside Colonel Puga's command tent. Colonel Puga thanked the section for a job well done. Capitaine Raoul's debrief was short and to the point. It was a close call, and could have easily gone bad. It was a good lesson for all of us.

As an aside, Capitaine Raoul told me that my reaction could have been a lot better. He was right. I should have dealt with the rebel more aggressively. True, I had been in a good position to engage the rebel, but the situation didn't necessarily require deadly force.

Having to make a life-or-death decision was new to me. Shooting or killing a fellow human being isn't a natural act or a first reaction for a kid from Canada. It's a conscious and considered act. After all, that's what separates professional soldiers from others. Our work would continue to provide me with opportunities to refine my new profession.

The following day, two rebels were found dead in the tall elephant grass. The rebel whose life I had spared? The police executed him. It was a quick and brutal justice, and one all too familiar in this part of the world.

CHAPTER FOURTEEN

Soldiering

Several days later while patrolling in our vehicles outside the city limits, we came to a stop face to face with a rebel patrol some 25 metres away. They were using four-by-four flatbed trucks, four in total, one with a supporting 14.5mm Dushka machine gun. These dark-skinned men, some with hatred in their shining eyes, often wore a mishmash of military uniforms, such as combat pants, or just shorts with combat jackets and berets. Some were tall and lanky. Others were heavy-set, but overall, they were youthful. The rebel soldiers disembarked and ran for cover. We did the same.

I positioned myself directly behind one of the VLRA's front tires with my FAMAS pointed at the Dushka's trigger man, who was still at his weapon. Looking to my side, I noticed my teammates in the ditch with their rifle-launched AC 58 anti-personnel grenades at the ready. The surrounding shantytown was soon devoid of locals. I wasn't exactly well protected, and I felt a little exposed behind the tire. Taking cover to the rear, Capitaine Raoul yelled, "No one shoot!" He got up and walked forward — a brave move. The rebels' leader then met him halfway.

Three of our teammates slipped behind a building with the aim of semi-flanking the rebel vehicles if called on. Capitaine Raoul soon returned to the VLRA and made a call to command. HQ said the rebels could turn around and leave the area. We watched as they sped off, leaving billows of red dirt swirling behind. The whole thing seemed surreal.

The situation in Bangui intensified. Embassies and foreign-national neighbourhoods were placed under permanent guard, and French military checkpoints were established along the city's main arteries and roads leading to the international airport. The airport terminal was secured by légionnaires and French d'Infanterie de marine.

Against the backdrop of increasing violence, we drove to a range roughly an hour outside the city limits to work on our fire and manoeuvre drills. This also meant I could properly sight my weapon—finally. I was on a steep learning curve, and I spent a lot of time practising with the high-explosive AC 58 anti-tank grenade, which can pierce armour up to 350mm thick and destroy a four-by-four truck.

Rebels had been firing RPG-7 rockets and mortar rounds from their side of PK Zero into pro-government neighbourhoods, and locals were being killed. Our new task was to deter this behaviour. After a briefing, Brook, Caporal-Chef Ciocarlan (a Romanian), the section's IT guru, and I piled into a P4. We drove to within a block of PK Zero, parked the P4, and made our way on foot in the darkness, following narrow paths that threaded among shanty homes and derelict buildings surrounded by garbage, flies, and fierce-looking stray dogs.

Our objective was to find a good vantage point and neutralize anyone with a weapon either on PK Zero or the other side. We found a suitable site behind a small but sufficient retaining wall and agreed on arcs of fire. Within minutes, bullets cracked overhead. The shots were off target, but they were clearly aimed at our position. Seconds later, I saw a figure standing in a small opening between buildings. He let out a short, reckless burst of fire in our general direction before disappearing. The distance and lack of light made it hard to see, but the AK sound was definitive. I waited. Sure enough, the stupid fucker fired at us again. My response was quick. I fired a succession of single-action shots at the target. Did I hit my mark? I wouldn't have been far off, that I knew. He didn't step out again.

Ciocarlan had radioed the section on standby after the first incoming rounds, and they soon came running down the path to our position. We then moved a short distance away and sought better cover. The plan was to cross PK Zero and clear the buildings and general area from where we had been targeted. As we were receiving our orders, a teammate suddenly disappeared, seemingly swallowed up by the ground. He had fallen into an abandoned sewage hole. A hand reached up from below. We quickly extracted him, and the smell was overpowering! Everyone burst out laughing, even as rounds knocked chunks of cinder block out of the large wall we were using as cover.

We put down effective covering fire, shooting through gaps in the wall directly at our target. Two well-placed AC 58 anti-personnel grenades flew straight, hitting their mark. The enemy fire ceased. Half our section then made the short sprint across PK Zero under the other half's covering fire. Then the remainder crossed. We waited in the dark. No shots. No rebels to be seen. Nothing. Putting on our night-vision goggles, we made our way down a dark embankment into taller elephant grass leading to a large open field. Without warning, a high-pitched scream stopped us in our tracks. Our lead had surprised a local with his pants down relieving himself. Daylight was approaching, and we checked the area to make sure he hadn't thrown a weapon into the grass. Then we called it a night and returned to our sleeping bags.

I was still wired and thought about how the evening's events had played out. At this stage, and a month into the tour, I felt like things were starting to solidify. I was comfortable with the environment and the job. I wasn't being treated like the new guy anymore. Perhaps it was a sign that I was pulling my weight.

In my downtime, I took the opportunity to write to my maternal grandfather, detailing my experiences. My service in the regiment was changing his understanding of the Legion. He hadn't liked the idea of "mercenaries," as he put it, tarnishing an old and honourable profession. It's true that as a foreigner I wasn't fighting for my country, but I would argue that France and Canada have historical connections and common values that can't be dismissed. A légionnaire is a member of the French military, whose discipline, training, and governance is under military and French law. I can't speak for others, but I can certainly vouch for my teammates' professionalism, integrity, and accountability for their actions. I never considered myself a mercenary; I was a soldier. And the word *soldier* derives from the Anglo-French *soudeer* or *soudeour*, meaning *mercenary*. *Mercenary* is defined as "a soldier hired into Foreign Service."

While lying on my bed writing and sweating in the Central African heat, increased radio chatter from the command tent got my attention. It wasn't long before an NCO stuck his head into our tent and said, "Let's go."

With the VLRA loaded, we drove at speed to where a 3rd Company section had ventured too close to Camp Kassie and came under heavy-calibre fire. Passing the 3rd's VAB, we disembarked and made our way through the bush to the high ground, where the rebel fire had originated. I heard the distinct double tap of a FAMAS up ahead. As I arrived on scene, Brook and Prigent were standing next to a four-by-four pickup truck with a .50-calibre machine gun mounted in its bed. A rebel fighter was lying face down in a ditch. He was still alive, but suffering the effects of Brook's double tap. The other rebels had disappeared into the bush. The 3rd Company VAB drove up to secure our location and recover the pickup.

A few days later, the 3rd Company came under fire in the same place. Once again, we deployed. The 3rd had cut down a rebel with their VAB-mounted .50 calibre. He was lying on the road, clearly dead. The .50-calibre round had done serious damage, ripping half his chest away. It wasn't a pretty sight. In single file, we followed Adjudant El Wahidi, who was Moroccan-French, leading the way into a cemetery past grave markers and uphill through tall elephant grass. The midday sun burned overhead. As the gradient increased, sweat trickled down my face, stinging my eyes. Then two mortar rounds, one after the other, impacted the hillside to our left with a loud crump. They were far off their mark, but the mortars made one hell of a bang. Any closer and I might have shit myself.

El Wahidi suddenly let out a burst of automatic fire from his FAMAS, yelling that a rebel was to his front. The rebel had immediately turned and fled into the elephant grass and trees. Rather than chase him into the unknown, we regrouped and walked in an extended staggered line, hoping to flush him out or the others. The long grass waved in the breeze, masking any movement, and it was almost impossible to see farther than a few metres ahead. It wasn't long before we came to a large clearing with a number of straw-roofed huts. I was partnered with Sergent-Chef Lawson, a tall and lanky Brit NCO, who provided cover as I cleared several huts.

After clearing a hut, I stepped out to the sound of RPG-7 rockets flying directly over our position, exploding well behind us. We took cover, at the same time trying to pinpoint their origin. Quickly regrouping, we continued our advance, using fire and movement drills, one covering the other in short bounds. But as we progressed, the shout "Grenade!" sent everyone diving. I threw myself on the ground, covering my head in a natural and time-honoured fashion. A friendly high-explosive AC 58 anti-personnel grenade detonated on the ground, sending dirt and shrapnel flying in all directions. In the heat of battle, the AC 58 had mistakenly been fired vertically by one of our team. I lay still for a few seconds, and after everyone confirmed they were OK, we resumed our advance.

Eventually, we were told to halt our progress as we were dangerously close to the rebel stronghold, Camp Kassie, and that wasn't our objective. We returned to the road and took up defensive positions while we waited for the 3rd Company VAB. When the 3rd arrived, I immediately recognized my former Romanian training caporal, now Sergent Accante, from basic training. We chatted briefly, and one of his légionnaires handed me a bottle of water, which I damn appreciated. I'd easily sweated away my body weight running up that hill!

Back at camp, we sat through Capitaine Raoul's debriefing, where the AC 58 incident was obviously topic number one. He was not impressed. We were extremely lucky no one was injured or, worse, killed. I was just relieved it wasn't my error. The next topic was an observation position (OP) the section was to man over Christmas to monitor a rebel-held checkpoint.

The OP was set up in an abandoned two-storey building on PK Zero with a direct view of Pont Jackson and its rebel checkpoint and bunker site. To me, this was a win-win scenario. Not only did we have a new objective, we were spared garrison activities over Christmas, which suited me just fine. On Christmas Eve and New Year's Eve, coolers arrived containing a variety of food from the quartermaster, including lobster and a bottle of champagne. We ate our meals listening to the calls to prayer from mosques echoing into the warm night. On New Year's Eve, tracer rounds from the

Central African government troops and rebels crisscrossed above us, announcing the arrival of a new year, 1997.

OP life was a little boring, but this soon changed. Lawson had been positioned some distance from our OP as sniper overwatch, and he was discovered, no doubt, due to local informants. Targeted by rebel small-arms fire, the REP's 4th Company was called to provide support while we extracted him. I was tasked with driving the VLRA. Following the direction of an NCO riding shotgun, we inadvertently drove directly into an ongoing firefight. Gilles and Ciocarlan were in the back of the VLRA providing support. The 4th Company légionnaires, in body armour and helmets, stared up at us from their firing positions as we drove through their line. The look on their faces said it all: WTF?! AK rounds zipped by, but we quickly extracted Lawson and made our way to a secure staging area to support the 4th Company if assistance was needed.

A new element added itself to current events. Emboldened, the locals held demonstrations against the French troops. Their presence, which was motivated and agitated by the rebels, was more and more frequent. Large crowds of protesters would approach French military checkpoints, and the French troops would respond by firing warning shots and tear gas to disperse them. Typically, this would suffice, but today was different. The size of the protest had visibly increased, and someone was shooting at the French Marines' checkpoint. We were sent in proximity to the checkpoint, wearing body armour and in our vehicles at the ready.

The Marines had responded by firing a VAB 20mm cannon shot over the crowd to disperse them and to make a point. Even I, the rookie, could sense the atmosphere in the air was different. Soon, a long burst of AK-47 fire, followed by frantic radio chatter, proved that something was up.

Capitaine Raoul immediately instructed me to drive down the wide avenue toward the commotion. As I tried to get a grasp on the situation, I could just start to make out what looked like a car in the ditch and people standing around. As we approached and slowed down, I could see that the two occupants in the French military staff car were deceased. Another was lying in the grass, motionless, being looked after by French medics.

A 4th Company VAB immediately passed us at speed. Its VAB .50 calibre then began engaging or laying down covering fire down-range. Capitaine Raoul yelled at me to follow the VAB, which I did, stopping behind it at a Total gas station. Several rebels were lying on the road, dead. Disembarking from the P4, we proceeded to clear the buildings, assisting the 4th Section in securing the general area. In the confusion of the moment, one of the NCOs quickly briefed us on what had just happened. A French military delegation had met with rebel commanders at the gas station to discuss certain terms, and it didn't go well. As the French staff car left, the rebels had opened fire. 1er RPIMa (COS) snipers positioned in an apartment complex covering the meeting had reacted appropriately. The dead rebels at our feet were the result of their effective marksmanship. It wasn't long before two rebel commanders and their subordinates returned to the scene, apparently under an agreed truce. Our photo ops cell NCO, Sergent-Chef Testaniere, was instructed to take pictures for future reference.

Later that evening, we gathered in our OP, and we could all sense that things had changed. Capitaine Raoul gave his orders. A COS Super Puma armed with a 20mm cannon would engage the city's main power station in the early hours of the morning; it was our signal to assault the Pont Jackson bunker site and adjacent buildings. Once that objective was achieved, we would venture deeper into rebel-held territory.

My initial responsibility in all this was to drive the P4 behind our team's VAB and use it as cover. Once the VAB had smashed through the makeshift barricade of burned-out cars on the bridge, I was to break left and assault the building adjacent to the rebel bunker. The second P4 following behind us would stop short of the bunker. My second responsibility, once I brought the P4 to a stop, was to dismount and fire an AC 58 anti-personnel grenade into the building's left window. Another teammate, El Wahidi, would do the same to the right window, and then we would clear the building. The VAB would stop and unload its personnel to clear the second target building to the right of the main road and then, if needed, provide close-fire support for the team with its .50 calibre.

We discussed our fallback positions, dealing with trauma, and other details or scenarios. Once the briefing was completed, we were told to go and kit up. With the P4 positioned behind the VAB, I dropped the hinged windshield forward, flat onto the hood.

The call to prayer rang out, reverberating off in the distance. I found myself considering my current situation. Having joined the French Foreign Legion only two years ago, I was about to assault a rebel-held position in Central Africa with the regiment's GCP. I was full of emotions: nervousness, uncertainty, and excitement at what lay ahead. Fear was a factor, too. I wasn't afraid of dying per se, but I didn't want to screw up. We were all being counted on. We were, after all, a team.

The four of us sat silently waiting in the P4, with El Wahidi sitting shotgun. I made sure my FAMAS was properly stored beside the P4's gearshift and that the AC 58 was ready. Our two teammates in the back would provide the initial covering fire. Making my mark on a small target from 50 metres at night with an AC 58 was going to be a challenge. The FAMAS has a special sight for the grenade, but it's virtually useless at night. That said, because the grenade was a shaped charge designed to penetrate armour, it would punch through the building's cinder-block wall if my aim was off.

As I sat there visualizing a walkthrough of the plan, I detected a sound. I listened again carefully to make sure. My adrenaline kicked in, and I was certain I could hear the quiet thud of a Puma helicopter's rotor blades in the distance. Here we go.

Word came over the radio to start our engines. We looked at one another and smiled. The OP gates were opened, and the VAB pulled out, with its distinctive turbo diesel engine whistling as it kicked in, and accelerated down PK Zero. At almost 14 tons, once this vehicle was on the move, it was hard to stop. And that was the plan, at least in this case. I followed the VAB as closely as I could, tailgating it and praying to the gods that the driver didn't hit the brakes too suddenly.

The VAB then made its right turn onto the dirt road that led to Pont Jackson. Its .50 calibre opened up, the sound of the initial burst drowning out everything else. Shell casings bounced off the road, hitting the hood of the P4, and the pungent smell of gunpowder flooded our nostrils. The VAB then hit the bridge's barricade, sending the wrecked cars flying. Driving over the bridge, I felt a blow to our right side. The impact hit hard enough that I had to fight to keep the vehicle straight. I managed to make the hard left turn, then slammed on the brakes. A yawning second of silence followed as the P4 came to a complete stop in a whirlwind of red dust.

We were now at our most vulnerable, no longer covered by the VAB and right on top of the target. Testaniere, on our P4's rear-mounted 7.62mm machine gun (MAS AAT 52), laid down covering fire, and El Wahidi jumped out of the P4. I picked up my FAMAS, but in the heat of the moment, I took the wrong one—a spare carried up front. Everything seemed to be happening in slow motion. Noticing my error, I grabbed the correct FAMAS with the AC 58 loaded on the muzzle. Taking a step forward as El Wahidi's AC 58 left his weapon, I located my target and fired. Then I reconfigured the FAMAS. I was farther away than planned, but the AC 58 flew straight and hit the window's lower corner, exploding and sending shards of cinder block, concrete, wood, and glass onto the road. I quickly rechecked my magazine, nodded to El Wahidi that we were good to go, and we advanced to the building's main entrance using fire and movement. We reached the door, and I kicked it as hard as I could—three or four times—until it finally gave way. This wasn't ideal, but it was reality, not a Hollywood movie. We then cleared the building room by room.

Afterwards, we joined our two teammates outside. They had detained three adolescent boys, who were kneeling on the ground, hands on their heads, visibly scared. Children were used by the rebels as errand boys or whatever was needed. These kids, smartly, had hidden when we launched the assault and the rebels fled. After being searched, they were told to clear out. The boys ran off and disappeared into the darkness. Theirs was childhood worlds apart from what I had experienced growing up.

Our team regrouped; however, I noticed my P4 had a nice little flat tire. As the section continued up the road, I was left behind with Ciocarlan to cover as I changed the tire. The COS Puma flew a loose orbit overhead, hammering rebel positions in the distance with its 20mm cannon.

With the tire replaced, Ciocarlan and I drove up the road to rejoin the section waiting some 500 metres away. Driving through a smaller crossroads, we came under fire from a heavy calibre-type round. Thank the gods their aim was off. I watched a red tracer round cut past our front. A Marine VAB 20mm at another intersection had mistaken us for a rebel vehicle. This potentially fatal error didn't really sink in right away, and we both laughed nervously once we were clear of the danger.

Regrouped with our section, we waited at the intersection, and it wasn't long before the early-morning light brought with it civilian casualties caught in the crossfire and family members asking for help. We radioed for assistance and a French military ambulance arrived. As the evening's adrenaline wore off and we sat idle watching, it hit home that these people, some seriously injured, were innocent victims.

We were soon replaced by a section from the 4th Company and made our way back to the Jackson bunker site, where we were put on standby for a few hours. On a further search of the bunker and buildings, several weapons and small-ammunition caches were recovered. Afterwards, I sat in the driver seat of my P4 drinking coffee as two teammates used the Peugeot's rear hold to clear the recovered weapons. Suddenly, a loud shot rang out. An old French MAS36 (1936) bolt-action rifle had accidentally been discharged. Capitaine Raoul had a lot to say about that error. Personally, I was also unimpressed. I had coffee all over my combat vest, pants, and webbing.

We eventually returned to our own beds, and I slept like the dead. Adrenaline affects people in different ways, but this adrenaline dump took it to a whole new level. After we had time to rest, we were debriefed. The operation had achieved its objective. The rebels had fled Bangui, with their commanders retreating to their native villages. The 1er RPIMa, the Marines, and the REP didn't suffer any losses, although two crew members in a Sagaie armoured vehicle were injured due to a friendly fire incident with the Puma overhead. The rebels suffered losses.

Being left alone for a few days with ample time for sports, sleep, general recovery, and a beer or two at the camp's foyer was a much-needed reprieve. But it wasn't long before we were briefed on our next task. We left Bangui under the cover of darkness, equipped

Team briefing before our night infiltration. (*Credit:* 2ᵉ Régiment étranger de parachutistes)

with state-of-the-art night-vision goggles, known as LUCIEs, from the GCP quartermaster. The new NVGs were light, compact, and improved depth perception. Following the main road out of the city, we eventually turned off to navigate a narrow dirt trail lined with trees and thick vegetation. We stopped short of our objective and continued on foot. A local informant met us at a predetermined spot to help pinpoint the location of a rebel commander's home in a small jungle village.

As the section progressed through the village, embers from the locals' cooking fires flashed in our NVGs. A blend of foreign smells drifted in the air. Approaching our target—a home better built than the others—we waited outside its entrance until signalled to enter. As we broke through the door, it was obvious that our target wasn't there. But his family was, and they were terrified. The younger children were shaken to the bone, and the mom and an older sister were trying to comfort the kids to no effect. Who could blame them? Here we were, a bunch of foreign soldiers with weird equipment on our heads, bursting into their simple life. We left the family with bottles of water, and some wise advice for the woman's husband.

Our efforts continued, and we set ambushes on remote trails leading to rebels' villages. Hiding in the bush through the night, cradling my weapon and wearing NVGs, my eyes started to play tricks. Shadows on the trail began to look like rebels slowly sneaking up on me, not to mention the bugs relentlessly buzzing around and crawling on me. These were long nights, and all in vain.

Our stay in the CAR was coming to an end, and the REP was going to be relieved by another French regiment. Ammunition that would soon expire needed to be spent, so we dedicated an entire day to working on our contact drills, firing as many rounds as we could. Capitaine Raoul arrived later in the day and I was duly summoned, with an order to stand to attention. I was promoted to caporal. He removed the Velcro première-classe patch from my combat vest and replaced it with the caporal rank, accompanied with a solid punch to the chest so it stuck properly.

As we drove through a small village when returning to Bangui, I saw an older gentleman standing at the roadside waving. He was wearing his Troupes Coloniales uniform with medals. We stopped, and I watched closely as he approached. I wasn't totally aware of what or who I was looking at, but I listened as he introduced himself to our head NCO, El Wahidi. He mentioned that every month the French government sends him his military pension. I was impressed with his uniform, which was well looked after and still fit him perfectly. I was looking at an example of the Central African Republic's history and its hard-earned freedom.

We spent our last few days in the CAR at Camp De Zimba, a jungle-training facility on the banks of the Bangui River. The exoticism of the riverboat trip to and from the camp was a highlight. Dense jungle framed the river's shorelines, and fishing villages were piled along its banks. I found this side of Africa enchanting. Its scenery, smells, wildlife, and people all drew me in.

There was basically nothing to Camp De Zimba. Just a few small buildings surrounding a dirt parade square in the jungle. We were left on our own. I ran the jungle trails, and that was about it. We drank beer at night around the fire and bought food from the locals.

The author shooting his FAMAS at the range outside Bangui city's limits, and soon to be promoted to caporal. (*Credit:* Joel Struthers)

It was a peaceful existence after a busy few months. I think this was supposed to be our R&R prior to leaving the CAR. One evening, the 1er RPIMa arrived in a plume of helicopter downwash and dirt, rappelling into the camp. The ten-man team then left by *grappe*, attached to a cord slung under the helicopter, churning up the jungle's red earth even more for us to taste. Show-offs.

Our military A310 Airbus left Bangui Airport on a sunny and sweltering morning, the norm in these parts, as I listened to the *Throwing Copper* album by Live, with its hit song, "Shit Towne." In a way, its lyrics were somewhat fitting. I watched the continent and countryside below change once again, seeing a less naive image of Africa three months after I had arrived. We landed back at the Istres-Le Tubé Air Base with several hours to spare before our C-160 flight to Calvi. Gilles's fiancée Stéphanie met him at the base's front gate. She didn't live far away, and Gilles invited a few of us to enjoy her delicious chicken sandwiches. Stéphanie was very nice, a happy person, always smiling, and the fresh food and hospitality were much appreciated.

CHAPTER FIFTEEN

Mont-Louis

Back in Calvi, everyone was given leave. Except for *moi*. Selak, Garcia, both fresh off leave, and I were going to the Centre national d'entraînement commando (CNEC). We passed the "pre" entrance exams consisting of a timed relay with sprints, push-ups, sit-ups, chin-ups, and the obligatory rope climb at the regiment gym. We then left for Marseille by overnight ferry via the town of L'Île-Rousse (L'Isula) and onward to Toulouse by train early March 1997.

Based in Mont-Louis in the French Pyrenees, the Centre national d'entraînement commando is run by the 1er Regiment de Choc; however, it's divided between the two training centres. The 2e Niveau (Commando Course) starts in Collioure, a coastal village near the Spanish border. Our course was for the members of the Commandement des opérations spéciales (COS), France's Special Operations Command. Present were new members of the: 1er RPIMa, 13e RDP, Marine Commandos, Air Force forward operators, and the Groupe d'intervention de la gendarmerie nationale (GIGN), and second-tier Groupement GCP (1er RCP, 3 and 8 RPIMa, 1er RHP, 35e RAP, 17e RGP, 1er RTP, 11e CCTP, and the 2e Régiment étranger de parachutistes).

During our many runs, I had grilled Gilles on what to expect, so I had an idea of what I was getting into. Preparation was half the battle.

Selak, Garcia, and I got along fine; however, I just couldn't quite figure out Garcia. He'd completed a year at the Saint-Cyr military preparation school, then decided to join the Legion. We arrived in Toulouse and presented ourselves to the operational support base and met some of our course-mates. Ranks varied from caporal to sergent-chef. Yet here we met French regular force NCOs in their mid-twenties, which was a rarity in the Legion. As a result, more mature and experienced soldiers reach the NCO rank in the Legion. Regardless, everyone was polite, but I sensed some of these guys were a little unsure of what to make of légionnaires.

They struggled with my and Selak's accents and Legion speech patterns. "Legion French," as it is known, is laced with expletives, often in the native language of the légionnaires. It's spoken in short sentences in halting French. To the untrained ear (anyone who isn't a légionnaire) it sounds aggressive, even if that's not the intent. The funny thing is, most of us soon realized this, often after our first discussions with French civilians. Afterwards, we made the effort to speak properly.

Our bus didn't leave for Collioure until the next morning, so Selak and I took advantage of our newfound freedom. Garcia decided to play it safe. The city of Toulouse is known for the 1814 Battle of Toulouse, one of the final battles of the Napoleonic Wars. It's also home to Airbus Industries and numerous universities, so there were plenty of young people, both French and British, to socialize with. After three months in the CAR, I experienced a little bit of culture shock. The following morning, suffering somewhat from a late night out, I began my first course with French regulars. The long bus ride to Collioure was a perfect opportunity to catch up on my sleep.

The trip lasted the better part of the morning, and on arrival at the coastal fortification, we joined others on an adjacent soccer field for the physical entry test. Two guys didn't even make it up the rope in the required time. The GIGN member on the course was quicker on the timed circuit than the three REP men, but we owned the rope.

Twenty-two of us were shown to our barracks, a portable in the fort's large grass-bottomed moat. Names were posted on the doors, splitting the course in two teams. We each grabbed a bunk and a locker since we had only ten minutes before we had to be in the course classroom. Here, we were introduced to our commanding officer, the second-in-command, and our instructors, who had their level 3 commando instructor qualifications. They were on second-ment from various regiments. We were then briefed on the safety procedures and told that if we didn't respect the rules, a strike-two policy would result in a fail. More importantly, the commanding officer mentioned that, depending on when we finished, we were free from duty Saturday afternoon to Sunday at 2100 hours. He then warned us—looking pointedly, in my perspective, at us légionnaires—that disciplinary issues wouldn't be tolerated. We were dismissed with a parting "Bonne chance."

Our kit was issued from the CNEC stores: wetsuit, flippers, mask, snorkel, safety harness and helmet, rope, and an old MAT-49 submachine gun. Two Cold War–era PP13 hand-held radios were issued, one per team. We signed up for our individual kit and were told not to lose anything. This was said twice, with an emphasis on "anything" for those hard of hearing. Back in our barracks, we organized our backpacks and created the radio-listening rota. Each team had been issued a colour call sign. Once we heard our colour on the radio, we were to follow the instructions, and we had five minutes to make a designated rendezvous point.

At 2200 hours, the message "Red and blue rendezvous classroom" came over the PP13s. The 2iC proceeded to deliver a lesson on CNEC safety rules and regulations, French theory of commando warfare, and a course breakdown with its scoring criteria. The classroom's heat was purposely cranked up, and an internal battle ensued in trying to stay awake. Many of the guys spent the time in the class standing. A bucket of cold water sat on the instructor's desk for those struggling to keep their eyes open.

The CNEC fort's walls supported numerous obstacle courses to test us physically and technically. Early the next morning, our first lesson involved the use of proper safety techniques. Our personal safety harnesses consisted of two lanyards with carabiners to ensure we were attached to the various safety cables. Click on, then click off. Failing to respect the safety procedure sounds simple enough, but after a couple of weeks, feeling fatigued and trying to maximize your speed leads to errors.

We learned the proper techniques for the various types of obstacles, culminating with a timed effort. Throughout the training, we were marked on our time consistency, so slowing down later in the

2ᵉ Niveau, Centre national d'entraînement commando (CNEC). (*Credit:*
Joel Struthers)

course would affect our overall outcome. As always, technique was
key. The easier we were on our bodies, the less chance of injury.
Efficiency equalled endurance, which equalled longevity.

We worked in pairs on hand-to-hand combat lessons, and I partnered with Selak. For the amphibious training, we put on our wetsuits and flippers and fought the Mediterranean's swells. The distances we swam were always increasing, and those who had good technique and speed were grouped together. The farther out we went into the waves, the more the motion sickness caused us to throw up in our snorkels.

A Navy Whaler and six-man Zodiacs were introduced into the training. We sat in the craft's lower deck, and guys got seasick from the surging swells. At times this made vomiting contagious. Finally, never soon enough, the boat's alarm would sound, and we would make our way onto the deck in teams of six. Zodiacs were thrown overboard at speed, and we followed, jumping into the sea wearing our wetsuits. The Zodiacs were deliberately flipped upside down, and we waited beneath them, our bodies shaking and teeth chattering uncontrollably from the cold. Peeing in one's wetsuit, which did wonders as far as temperature is concerned, was considered a personal problem. Instructors would signal for us to right the Zodiacs, and this led to a rush to get back onboard. If we were too slow, the instructors would keep us in the water for longer periods of time. And one could only pee so much.

As a team, we mastered paddling our Zodiac and the plastic-hulled two-man kayaks, which we manoeuvred using foot pedals that controlled the rudder. The trick was to ride the wave onto the beach and avoid letting the kayak's nose drift off course too much, otherwise you'd flip and your face would act as a brake on the sea's sandy bottom. We wore runners for the water training, which were invariably wet and full of sand after a beach landing. Soon, we figured out that an instructor would be waiting for us onshore, and that once we had left our kayaks with training staff, off we'd go for a run. Another lesson learned: to quickly rinse my shoes and socks before starting the run.

My least favourite training experience by far was "Swerve on my fucking nerve." Jammed inside the tarp-covered truck with our backpacks, the vehicle would speed off, and then we were ordered to put on our wetsuits in the dark, cramped, and moving space. The driver purposely swerved violently back and forth, sending us crashing to the sides or piling to the front as he braked hard. The tactic was that half the group would make themselves as small as possible in the corners or sides of the truck so the guys on the inside could change. Then we'd switch out. Tempers flared, but we got it done.

This training culminated in a final swim. With our wetsuits on, backpacks and MAS49s in their dry bags and flippers in hand, we exited the truck in the evening's darkness and swam to the Navy Whaler anchored off in the distance. Once inside the craft, we removed our weapons and backpacks. Then we waited for the Whaler to speed off, and the alarm signalling us to make our way on deck and drop our Zodiacs. We then paddled as a unit to a small castle ruin on the Mediterranean coastline, assaulted the castle, recovered the hostage, and rowed back to the Whaler.

The Collioure individual tests involved descending by zip line from the cliffs into the water and tackling a floating obstacle course. Then we'd do a cliff jump wearing our backpacks and with our MAS49s attached to our sides to avoid knocking out our teeth, followed by a 50-metre swim to the dock. It was timed, so one had to get it done, but it was good fun, to be honest.

On our final evening in Collioure, we were broken into smaller groups for a map and compass exercise. Selak, Garcia, and I were teamed up with two French regular NCOs, and we set off into the local foothills. A few hours in, we stopped for fifteen minutes of sleep before a climb. After about ten minutes of climbing, Garcia suddenly swore, then mumbled "MAS" and ran back down the hill to retrieve his weapon. Once the exercise was complete, we returned to the fort to sleep on the moat's cold ground. The only one of us who slept well that night was the GIGN guy, since his kit was quality civilian gear, designed for the temperatures we were experiencing. The military-issue sleeping bags were complete shit. Different unit, different mentality, different budget.

At first light, our radio message sent us running to the fort's obstacle course for the final time trial. The average times to complete it ranged from between fifteen and twenty minutes. Selak, an 8 RPIMa (Régiment de parachutistes d'infanterie de marine) NCO, and I battled for the top time, each taking the lead at times throughout the course.

Afterwards, we boarded our bus for the Pyrenees, arriving through the gates of Mont-Louis Fort, a fortification designed by King Louis XIV's French military engineer, Vauban, in 1679. Among ten other military sites and fortifications in France, it was part of the king's "iron belt" of fortifications and defences to protect the French-Spanish border. Here, we were issued our mountain kit and shown to our rooms. After lunch, staff informed us that we were free until Sunday evening.

Selak and I waved down a taxi. We were in our civilian clothes: no leave slip needed, no uniform checks, and no MPs to worry about. The local ski hills weren't open yet, so the town would be quiet. Regardless, we left our dirty laundry with our hotel's reception desk and set off to buy provisions. But it wasn't long before my hotel bed was calling. That evening, I met up with Selak for a meal. We asked the restaurant's waitress where to go to meet girls in town. As a proud grandmother and the restaurant owner, she didn't really have much advice for us. We figured it out. After a proper meal and a few drinks at the empty local nightclub, all I could think about was that soft, comfortable mattress and heated hotel room.

As we left the nightclub, I noticed a guy kicking the door of a parked Volkswagen Golf with someone inside, while two others stood by watching. I told the guy doing the door kicking, a French-Arab, to lay off, and he and his friends then turned on us. Safety in numbers I guess. Selak and I felt otherwise, and it wasn't long before they ran off with their tails between their legs. It was a short skirmish, and the young woman inside the car rolled her car window down slightly, thanked us nervously, and drove away.

Back in barracks on Sunday evening, all our course-mates had returned from visiting their families or girlfriends. Most légionnaires didn't get to go home on the weekends; Croatia was a bit far for Selak, as was Canada for me, so I wasn't that interested in listening to them. I was more concerned about my left hand, which was sore from hitting someone's face.

First thing on Monday morning, we took part in hand-to-hand combat drills to get us back on track, then went straight onto an obstacle course. Rock climbing was on the curriculum, with a fascinating lesson on knots, which we immediately forgot but would be tested on later. In the classroom, we worked on explosive-charge calculations and reviewed the explosive range safety rules.

The instructor had our undivided attention for those, which we put to the test on the explosives range. That evening, we were divided into small teams and waited for our turn to run to the steel beam, set our charge, and exfiltrate. We looked at our watches, waited for the explosion to see if our detonation cord was cut at the right length, and then returned to verify if our charge calculation did the job. Afterwards, live chickens were issued to us to kill, clean, and cook over an open fire for dinner. *Bon appétit les gars.*

The March nights were getting colder, especially at high altitude, and we slept on the empty moat's grass once again. What seemed like only minutes later, we were woken by the aggravated voice of an instructor yelling over the radio frequencies, "Wake up, idiots!" Panicked, we rushed to get our sleeping bags into our backpacks. No one really cared that our radio-watch had fallen asleep. It was inevitable. We were all tired and needed the sleep.

My competitiveness was getting the better of me on a timed obstacle course, and my hands were suffering; the weekend's events hadn't helped matters either. One obstacle, known as *la gouttière*, involved scaling a 50-metre steel drainpipe that ran up the fort's stone wall. If you climbed aggressively, your knuckles inevitably scraped against the stone wall. Mine were raw, and with an already sore left hand, I swore my way up *la gouttière* and as I tackled the other obstacles, to the instructor's amusement. He'd say, "Go légionnaire fucking." The translation doesn't really work, but whatever.

That evening, we were awoken by stun grenades and German shepherds barking in the barracks doorway. Instructors in balaclavas dragged us outside and covered our heads with potato sacks. The trucks had their high beams directed at us, and we were put in stress positions, with dogs barking in our faces. Our personal belongings, such as a compass, knife, and flashlight or lighter, were taken.

This was the prisoner-of-war phase of our training. Stress positions were quite annoying, which is the idea, and if an instructor noticed you slacking off, he would slap you upside the head and make you either correct the position or change to another one. The exaggerated push-up position, with your rear-end up as high as you could get it, was effective. The slaps were not overly hard; I certainly don't think any of us were close to quitting. We knew this was coming.

We were driven outside the fort, pulled from the truck, and our blindfolds were removed. Then we were told to drop down a manhole into a dark drainage pipe. Crawling through the cold and a wet concrete tunnel filled with mud in complete darkness, I could hear the guy in front of me cursing. Arriving at a tight bend, I could manage only to worm my way forward, arms at my side. I had to control my urge to freak out, but I literally saw the light at the end of the tunnel and managed to hold it together. After we were dragged out of the pipe, we were sent to an abandoned farmhouse's cellar full of pig shit. With a potato sack over my head, I squatted, my back against the farmhouse's stone cellar wall, arms extended straight out. At first light, we were dragged outside, one by one.

Eventually, it was my turn, and it was a relief because the stress positions made for serious muscle discomfort. Maybe this wasn't that much fun anymore. The instructor launched me into a warm-up routine: push-ups, sit-ups, marche canard, run here, run there, climb that tree. Whatever got the blood flowing. Another instructor arrived in full protection gear, and I was given hand-to-hand drills to be executed over and over. When the instructor felt I had reached my physical limit, two course-mates in similar gear set on me. The idea was to continue fighting and not give up. This got imaginative, as our own guys were more ruthless. Frozen cow dung stuffed into the mouths, or the more savoury alpine grass with a hint of cow piss and frozen dirt did the trick. After we were done being attacked, it was our turn to put on the protective gear and get our revenge on the next guy.

We returned to Mont-Louis later that morning for a hot breakfast, followed by an even hotter shower. Prior to being released, we were reminded that on Monday we would undertake the hand-to-hand evaluation, then sit for our written test, which was followed by a final timed obstacle course. Oh, and have a good weekend.

Selak, Garcia, and I took a taxi to the village of El Pas de la Casa, in Andorra on the France-Spain border. The long taxi ride cost us a small fortune, but we had big plans. Because of Andorra's tax-free status, Pas de la Casa's streets were lined with stores selling everything from electronics and clothing to music and cheap liquor. Naturally, there were restaurants, bars, and numerous nightclubs filled with women, which we had been told were worth the trip. We found ourselves hotel rooms and agreed to meet up later that evening for a big night on the Pas de la Casa. Things, however, didn't work out as planned. Each of us slept straight through the night and had just enough time the next day to find some much-needed cold-weather gear, new sleeping bags, and provisions for the final exercise before taking our taxi back to Mont-Louis.

On Monday morning, the examining officers sitting behind a table on the moat's grass ordered us to execute individual hand-to-hand combat techniques. Selak and I partnered up once again and obliged. We had agreed on vigorous application of technique, and were slow to get up at times. The smirk on the examiners' faces suggested they were satisfied with our efforts. Next, we sat for the written exams. Initially, we were left alone so we shared answers, but after a few minutes the regiment CO turned up and all discussions stopped dead.

That night, we were treated to a large pasta dinner and at 0300 hours we were issued our weapons, blank ammunition, inert mines, training grenades, radio batteries, and three days' rations. Then we were marched out the fort's gates for our final exercise.

Trudging single file through intermittent pockets of snow in the bitter cold, up we went through a mountain pass to ambush some unknown enemy force. We laid our mines, designated arcs of fire, and waited. A P4 soon came into view. We detonated mines, lobbed grenades, and spent blank rounds, then exfilled through the woods for an 8-kilometre run in the dark before regrouping in high ground and forming a defensive perimeter as first light appeared. After organizing a perimeter guard shift, we took turns getting a few hours of sleep.

From our vantage point overlooking a communications tower, we were briefed on our next assault. Explosive charges were set, and we exfilled, marching up into the Pyrenees, which were partially covered with snow. At the cliff's base, we removed our harnesses, ropes, carabiners, and helmets from our backpacks, made a night ascent, and then rappelled down the steeper back side. Descending into the adjacent valley, we came to a road. New instructors were there to join us, fresh and keen.

Two of our larger course-mates were told to go retrieve jerry cans of water stashed roadside. A detonation of white powder followed, simulating two casualties. Using our combat vests and metal poles provided for stretchers, we extracted for what I assume was several kilometres. At some point, I could see headlights in the dark down the road. As we arrived, I realized it was a military TRM. The instructors then casually told us that we were done. Confused, I asked the instructor if he was sure. We were exhausted.

Once our kit was accounted for and handed to the instructors, we were driven to a nearby town and debriefed by the course CO. This was followed by that most French of traditions, a drink. We entered a local café in the early morning, drank coffee and beer, and ate its stock of fresh pastries. The CO individually congratulated us. He seemed to appreciate légionnaires and chatted with us for quite a while. His brother had been a capitaine at the regiment's 2nd company.

In a decidedly unglamorous town parking lot, the course was presented to the CNEC commanding officer. Our course results were read out and commando badges were awarded. The REP finished in second, third, and fourth. Completing the Commando Brevet was physically challenging. And that was something I liked—having a feeling of being pushed to my limits.

CHAPTER SIXTEEN

The Ultimate Sacrifice

The section had its share of free-fall enthusiasts. They spent their time off in the United States, France, or Spain mastering free fly, which is basically a head-down free fall. That wasn't me, but I did want to master this military specialty. Capitaine Desmeulles informed me that I was going to join Dimitri for our Certificat d'aptitude au SOGH (Saut opérationnel à grande hauteur) at L'École des troupes aéroportées (ÉTAP) on the outskirts of the town of Pau, southwestern France.

The actual course designation was Certificat d'aptitude au saut operationnel à ouverture commande retardée à grand hauteur.

This was good news, but only a limited number of SOGH slots were offered to each regiment. Since Dimitri had finished our preselection first overall and I had finished second, I was going along as a replacement candidate in case someone failed the course's entrance exams.

Dimitri and I were issued our jumpsuits, ancillaries, and administrative files to hand over to the ÉTAP. We took a civilian flight to Marseille and then a train to the town of Pau, finishing with a short taxi ride to the ÉTAP's front gate, where we were directed to the course's NCO single-occupancy barrack rooms. My initial view of the ÉTAP was that it was more relaxed. At Calvi you could almost feel the weight of discipline and the attention to detail. When I opened the door to my room at ÉTAP, I thought, "Well, this is the lap of damn luxury!" It was a great start to the course.

The following morning, at the un-Legion time of 0900 hours, Dimitri and I joined the newcomers to the COS and a Belgian para officer outside the school's main auditorium. We introduced ourselves, shaking everyone's hands before heading inside and meeting our course commanding officer and instructors. We were briefed on the curriculum and requirements to achieve our SOGH wings. We were then released for the course medical visit. At lunch, I sat at a table in the NCO mess being served by junior ranks—my rank. That was weird. During the entire meal, I was expecting someone to notice and order me outside, yelling. Dimitri seemed to feel a lot more at home than I did.

After the lunch break, we all met at the gymnasium for the start of the course's entry physical exams, beginning with the usual push-ups, sit-ups, chin-ups, and squats, followed by a 90-metre sprint with a 20-kilogram duffel bag. Everyone passed, which wasn't a surprise, but we weren't finished yet. The 8-kilometre TAP run, or at least the 30-kilometre one, would be a potential problem for someone, I hoped. We were dismissed for the day and told to be back in the morning.

The next morning, we completed the TAP 1500-metre sprint and 8-kilometre run with a 10-kilogram backpack, followed by the rope-climbing test. Everyone passed. All that remained was the 30-kilometre run. The following morning, I crossed the finish line in two hours, thirty-six minutes. First place. The last runner actually walked over the line virtually on the five-hour time limit that the ÉTAP allowed.

It wasn't that long before I was summoned to the course CO's office. As expected, he thanked me for my effort and told me that, unfortunately, it was in vain. But I would be back soon enough, he added, and bid me safe travels returning to Calvi. I packed my kit and wished Dimitri good luck.

When I arrived in Calvi, I found out that the section had been deployed to Gabon, Africa, with the 1st Company, and I would be taking a six-week-long Certificat technique élémentaire (CTE) 12 medic's course. I felt sick. I assumed this meant a return to Castel, and I wasn't ready for that yet. The CTE 12 is usually done in Castel, but thankfully this particular course was being run from the regiment in Calvi. The course was composed of a mix of caporals and première-classe légionnaires from differing companies billeted in a 1st Company annex barrack block. Mornings involved some form of physical exercise, with an emphasis on the medical aspect; for instance, a TAP run or PC with course-mates on a stretcher. This was followed by classroom lessons on the human anatomy, first aid, and later, combat-related trauma care. We then delved into infirmary-type duties, of which I had zero interest. But I figured the expertise would help my cause as a soldier and as a person.

Part of the course in Castel involved secondment to the large military hospitals. In our case, we would assist the regiment's smaller infirmary. All my course-mates were from combat companies, and if they completed the course successfully, they would support the infirmary when their companies were on regimental service. The lessons on how to assist doctors or nurses in various non-emergency services, like administering vaccinations and taking blood, didn't really inspire me. On Saturday morning, we sat for an exam on the week's curriculum, and those who didn't pass were restricted to barracks for the weekend to study and re-sit the test on Monday morning. That was enough motivation for me to pay attention and make the grade. I think this was true for most considering it was mid-June, and Calvi's beaches and bars were starting to fill with vacationers.

I was given the role of course duty caporal during the first week's rotation. Initially, I was enthusiastic, but this new responsibility wore thin fast. On my first morning, I said to the légionnaires, "Look, we're all on course together. I don't need to be telling you to polish your boots or empty the barrack room garbage cans before parade. Take the initiative." The truth was that I didn't want to babysit, and I thought a Napoleonic address would do the trick.

How naive. From the get-go, certain guys didn't do shit, and that came to a head on a morning run. A German légionnaire named Müller, for whatever reason, rubbed me the wrong way. Müller was always being called out on something. He was a continuous pain in the ass. While running, I got tired of listening to him give our Arab-French course-mate a hard time. As I ran up beside him, I said, "Would you shut up!" and shoulder-checked him—hard—into a wet drainage ditch.

That evening, after the day's classroom work back in barracks, Müller approached me and asked, "What's the problem?" I simply told him that he had two options: shut up, like I had said, or we could take it outside and resolve the issue. He opted for the latter. At my request, a French caporal, Domigo, on course from the 2nd Company, joined us as a witness, and we stepped into the night. I took off my caporal rank. Circling, I gave Müller the first swing. He was taller and bigger than I was, but his swing was slow and telegraphed, which I avoided and delivered a straight to his *boche* chin. That wobbled Müller, and I then kicked his feet out from under him. I stood over him, ready to finish. "Enough," he said.

Domigo, who agreed Müller deserved a lesson, accompanied him to the infirmary and used the opportunity to administer his first set of stitches. Training well spent. The next morning, our chief instructor questioned me as to why a légionnaire needed stitches. I explained, and nothing more was said. Domigo took the duty role the following day, and in combat-company style, he had légionnaires scrubbing our barracks all night. Müller cleaned all the toilets with his toothbrush while wearing a headlamp.

We quickly moved on to better things, like jumping on the Calvi drop zone with medical equipment pallets. We were briefed on the exercise and shown how to palletize our equipment. Two teams would exit the C-160 Transall, complete with gaine, FAMAS, and the pallets. A lot could go wrong. The pallet followed the last jumper out. It was heavy, and being taken out by a pallet was not on anyone's to-do list. We were then to make our way to the neighbouring village of Montemaggiore, locate the two casualties, and then exfil with them to the coastline.

Jumping from the Transall, we all hit the deck like dead weight and immediately set about stripping down our gaines, then the pallets, accessing our supplies, and setting off on foot to Montemaggiore. Like most mountainside villages, it looked deceptively close, but the trek took us two hours. Finally, we located our casualties (légionnaires volunteered from another combat company) who had simulated gunshot wounds. We administered oxygen treatment, IV drips, bandages, and immobilization, all under an instructor's review, and transferred the "victims" to stretchers for a race back to the regiment's infirmary. After reaching the coastline, we loaded our two casualties onto 3rd Company Zodiacs for transportation to the regiment's amphibious centre. Back on stable land, it was a final dash to the infirmary. The casualties got a rough ride, but bragging rights were taken seriously.

The medical training continued. We stuck catheters into one another, usually in the leg, and worked in the infirmary taking blood and giving injections. Two course-mates were tasked with staying at the infirmary each night, and my night fell on a Friday evening when a légionnaire from the 3rd Company was shot by a Corsican separatist in Calvi outside a bar. The on-call medical officer pronounced the légionnaire lying on the medical table, with bullet entry and exit wounds, deceased soon after his arrival at the infirmary. Another légionnaire who witnessed the shooting had put his fist through a store window in frustration. The medical officer gave him a good verbal lashing for his stupidity before stitching up his forearm without anaesthetic. The légionnaire's blood-alcohol level was sufficient.

A few days later, I was summoned to the CEA company building, and I presented myself to the duty NCO sitting behind his desk. He ordered me to go get Gilles's dress uniform and kepi from his locker. It was an unusual request. I asked, "Why, what's going on?" Without even looking up from his paperwork, the NCO replied casually, "He's dead."

I was stunned. That shock was compounded by the cavalier, even callous, way the NCO had broken the news. I was angry, but I controlled my feelings and went to Gilles's room. I recovered his uniform and kepi from his locker. Inside were photos of his fiancée, Stéphanie.

I quickly networked with others to find out what the hell had happened. News eventually trickled back to the regiment. The CEA, 1st Company, and section had been deployed to Brazzaville, in the Republic of the Congo. Fighting between government troops and militiamen loyal to the former leader had escalated, requiring evacuation of some six thousand expatriates caught up in the civil war. Gilles had been killed during expatriation efforts.

His body was due to arrive in Calvi from Africa the next evening, and caporals from the CEA's rearguard would man his honour guard while he lay at rest in the regimental chapel. Six of us were designated to carry his coffin onto the parade square for the regimental ceremony scheduled for the following day.

I was excused from course to get my uniform ready and assist in the preparations. A small private ceremony for Gilles's family and Stéphanie was held before the regimental parade, where all companies not on tour were present in full parade uniform. Gilles's coffin was moved from the chapel to the centre of the parade square. The French minister of defence awarded Gilles the posthumous Croix de la Valeur Militaire, and Médaille Militaire. Then the regiment sang our regimental song. You could have heard a pin drop when it was over. It was a moving moment.

Capitaine Raoul indicated that I was to attend a dinner that evening in Calvi for Gilles's and Stéphanie's families. Stéphanie seemed to be taking everything in stride, but I'm sure she was doing her best to put up a strong front. I could see that Gilles's family was hurting. Everyone was. I wasn't really sure what to say or how to act.

I was back on course the following day, but my head wasn't into it. An examiner from the local fire rescue service arrived that final week, and we were tested on a variety of first aid skills. We were also tested in the infirmary and wrote a final exam. Then we ran the usual TAP tests. The top finish overall on course went to Première-Classe Légionnaire Gambier, a tall Frenchman. He was athletic and smart, with the right attitude. We had run the 8-kilometre TAP together, and he asked about the GCP. I just told him that it was in his best interest to try out.

When the section eventually returned from Brazzaville, I could sense that the team was rattled, but little information was being shared. Smithy was there the evening Gilles was killed and he described how the events unfolded:

The day, June 7, 1997, had started with an intelligence brief on the situation, and the section had then been tasked with the rescue of French and other expatriates who had called the French embassy for assistance due to an escalation in fighting between different factions within Brazzaville. A 1st Company section (roughly thirty men) was sent to assist the team by securing the neighbourhood, while

Smithy, in Brazzaville, listening to the REP's gradual withdrawal to the airport. (*Credit:* 2ᵉ Régiment étranger de parachutistes)

we accounted for the foreign nationals. A Congolese army liaison officer also joined us and the 1st Company to help navigate through the city and communicate with friendly pro-government forces. Different warring factions had assumed control of various parts of the city, so it was hazardous. You could easily drive into an area under rebel control. Also at the time, many of Brazzaville's main streets and avenues had temporary barricades manned by Congolese soldiers or pro-government militia. The section progressed to Avenue de Djoue, which was situated in a district known as the Quartier Bas Congo, stopping periodically to check the road for danger. At one Congolese military checkpoint, due to concern over friendly fire and because the situation was so tense in the city, the convoy stopped 100 metres short with some of the section disembarking from their vehicles and positioning themselves in the tree line along the avenue, just to observe the road ahead.

Drivers remained with the vehicles while the rest of the section found a suitable place to cover their firing arcs. The Congolese liaison officer made his way to the checkpoint, and after a few minutes, he gave the all clear. We embarked once more and progressed slowly down the road. After only a few hundred metres, automatic gunfire from the left side of the road peppered the roof of the vehicle just above our heads, spraying us with shards of metal. Our driver accelerated, and the vehicle lurched forward. The team immediately returned fire, aiming for the source of the AK-47 tracer rounds coming out of the bush.

Our driver brought the vehicle to a sudden and abrupt halt at which point we dismounted and took up firing positions. We made our way toward where we could hear the shooting to support the 1st Company, whom we soon found at their firing positions at the roadside. A message on the radio had mentioned there were casualties, so we knew they were in bad shape. Upon hearing this, our team's chief medic, Adjudant Karine, along with Gilles, made their way toward the source of the more sustained gunfire where elements of the 1st Company were still pinned down close to the initial kill zone. At this point, the 1st Company was returning fire using a combination of automatic fire and shoulder-launched rockets and grenades, pounding the Congolese positions for a good thirty minutes.

A Congolese officer then appeared, walking up the avenue toward our position with his hands in the air asking for a ceasefire. The shooting ceased; however, the situation remained tense and the guys were uneasy. We continued to watch our angles in anticipation of follow-up action by the Congolese. At this point we heard over the radio that Gilles was KIA, and that several others had been seriously injured. Minutes later, the remainder of the 1st Company reinforcements arrived to secure the area and facilitate the recovery of the casualties. The convoy made its way back to the staging area with its casualties. Then the medics went to work and assisted the injured. Among them was one of their own who had been shot while travelling in an ambulance. A 1st Company driver had taken a bullet through the ankle and two légionnaires were injured; one with a round through the jaw, the other a round to the head. Brook, Smithy, and Garcia helped Karine record Gilles's injuries and prepared his body for return to Calvi. From what Karine had said, he and Gilles were running to assist the 1st Company's injured when Gilles just collapsed.

Gilles, who was a good man, a good soldier, and like the many other légionnaires before him, had made the ultimate sacrifice.

CHAPTER SEVENTEEN

Marseille

The team members from Brazzaville were given leave, and the remainder of the section continued with training. Once the section was complete again, we were told that the section's qualified medics were heading to Marseille to spend a week with the city's *sapeurs-pompiers* (military firefighters) as paramedics. Under the French Ministry of Defence umbrella, both the city of Marseille and Paris have military sapeurs-pompiers. Adjudant Karine, our head medic, along with Brook, Dimitri, Selak, Ursa, and I, took the ferry from Île Rousse to Marseille.

Once the initial administrative requirements were completed at the sapeurs-pompiers' main fire hall, we were issued our blue overalls and sent to the city's satellite fire halls. I was assigned to the city's east side with Karine. Karine was a steady figure within the section, one you needed to prove yourself to, which could easily go one way or the other. On arrival, I was introduced to my new ambulance crew: an NCO, driver, and two junior-rank paramedics. They were from Marseille and spoke with its accompanying thick accent. Everyone was cordial and seemed interested in the idea that a légionnaire was joining them. Each hall had four ambulances in total, and I stood at morning parade with my ambulance crew. Parade was very much like ours. The main difference was that the sapeurs-pompiers wore blue uniforms and their distinctive F1 silver helmets.

Marseille's firefighters were renowned for their professionalism, of which I was aware, so I was keen to see how everything really worked. After parade, the NCO walked me through the next steps. My role was to assist the ambulances' paramedics—watch, learn, and help as requested. This would include cleaning the ambulance, restocking shelves, and ensuring the oxygen bottles were refilled after each return to the fire hall. I was then shown to an area adjacent to the ambulance bay where we could sleep between calls. Our ambulance was on standby, and if the hall was alerted by the Service d'aide médicale urgente (SAMU) dispatch, the ambulance bay's siren would sound. That meant we had to be at the ambulance ASAP. We'd find out our destination as we left. Once on scene, the NCO would assess the situation and, via radio communications, inform the SAMU dispatch if a doctor was needed. SAMU doctors were mobile in their Peugeot hatchback sedans, roaming their designated areas and supporting efforts as required.

As I put my kit away, I had to admit that I was looking forward to the experience. Marseille is a big old city, and a tough city at that. For that reason, I could only assume that I would experience its numerous charms one way or another. It wasn't long before the bay's alarm rang. I ran to our ambulance and jumped into the back with the two paramedics, and we raced to our first call, sirens wailing.

The Mercedes had a window accessible to the driver's cab, so I could see the road ahead as I did my best to hang on. I immediately noticed our driver's skill as we raced past parked cars on both sides of the city's narrow roads. Intermittent blasts of the siren, along with our NCO yelling profanities from the passenger window at drivers who were in our way, helped us to negotiate the congested intersections.

On that first call, we arrived at an apartment building and climbed the stairs to the fourth floor. From behind a locked door, an elderly woman's frail voice informed us that she had fallen and couldn't get up. The NCO then asked if she was well clear of the front door, which was locked. "Oui," she replied. One good swing of a sledgehammer did the trick, smashing the door—and missing the woman's head by mere inches. I could tell the NCO was annoyed by this near miss. We took the elderly woman to the closest hospital after some basic first aid.

Our next call was to assist a young boy who hadn't been able to reach his grandfather. We met the nine-year-old outside his grandfather's large apartment building, which was in one of the city's tougher housing projects. Where his parents were, I had no idea, but it wasn't my place to ask, really. We took the elevator to one of the upper floors and knocked at his grandfather's door. Nothing. We knocked again several times. Still nothing. The NCO checked the handle. The door was unlocked. Calling inside, he took two steps through the doorway and then turned around, ordering one of the paramedics to take the boy back to the elevators and wait with him there.

The NCO indicated that I enter the apartment saying, "Don't touch anything." I immediately recognized the smell. As I walked inside, I noticed a plastic shotgun casing on the floor, then two legs partially obscured behind a corner. When I looked around the corner, the grandfather's body was lying there. The upper part of his skull was missing. Blood and brain matter covered the walls and the balcony's glass sliding door. A shotgun lay next to him. I then realized I was standing on some of his teeth. It was a graphic and sickening sight, and the last thing I had expected when riding up the elevator.

The NCO knocked on the neighbour's door and a young couple answered. He asked them if they had spoken to their neighbour recently, or heard anything from his apartment. When they answered no and asked why, he told them to look inside. The woman did, and she rushed out of the apartment, shocked. I don't know why the NCO did that. Maybe to make a statement about modern life where one can live in a building with hundreds of people, but no one pays attention to their neighbours. The boy was told that his grandfather was dead, an apparent suicide, and the police were called. This was now a crime scene. As the first responders, our work was done.

The experience was sad. However, another incident made an even bigger impression on me. A young girl, maybe seven or eight years of age, couldn't wake up her mother. The SAMU doctor pronounced the mother deceased as the girl stood in the doorway, watching. An empty bottle of pills was recovered from her mother's bedside.

Most of our calls involved elderly people, who at times just wanted company, or had minor medical issues that didn't require

SAMU's assistance. We also had a lot of calls from middle-aged people suffering from anxiety.

Dealing with the city's street people was also something new to me. Quite often, these were the same individuals day after day, night after night. The homeless, drug addicts, drunks, or people suffering from mental illness—most likely all four. It was an eye-opener. I watched a male patient in his late forties unravel as we tried to administer first aid to his self-inflicted knife wound. The paramedics' actions and attitudes were always professional. Here was a guy who had just urinated, defecated, and cut himself, yet the paramedics remained polite and firm with him while trying to help. The NCO was tougher, more direct. I guess you had to be in his type of role.

Between calls as we drove around the city, we often returned to a particular street corner so the NCO could stop and talk to its sex-trade workers. A social visit between professionals working the same beat, perhaps. One day, we even drove to the NCO's home, and I met his girlfriend and parents; these were quick visits between calls. I was learning plenty. I got in on each call, trying to help where I could. The SAMU doctors were always willing to show me new skills or let me try new things. I gave CPR on a regular basis, which I discovered is rarely successful. I broke some ribs on an elderly man after he was declared deceased. It may seem wrong, but it was a way to learn the proper technique on a real body, which might help save the next patient.

From time to time, I ran into my teammates at the city's various hospitals. It was a chance to share our experiences. Selak was the unlucky one tasked with cleaning up the remains of a young child hit by a high-speed train. I'm glad I missed that one.

My week working on the ambulance was a blur of alarms, sirens, bursts of sleep, and speeding through the city. My last call was at an elementary school to attend to a teacher experiencing chest pains. As we entered the school courtyard at recess, the kids started surrounding us and shouting, "Les pompiers! Les pompiers!" (Firemen! Firemen!) It was a hero's welcome for Marseille's best.

By the week's end I certainly saw the city of Marseille differently, both the good and the bad, and I felt more at home there.

On our return to Calvi from Marseille, we were given leave, and I spent mine early season snowboarding in the French Alps, Tigne (Espace Killy), to be exact. I then made my way to Dimitri's hometown of Épinal in northeastern France for the last few days of leave before returning to Corsica. Dimitri's father and his sister, Manon, welcomed me into their home. Manon, who was studying to be a teacher, was tall, blonde, and very attractive. I hadn't expected this when walking into Dimitri's family home. Dimitri was in full girlfriend mode, which worked in my favour; Manon offered to show me the town, which I happily accepted.

We found ourselves in the local nightclub that first evening, and I was obviously on my best behaviour, as bro code dictates. Our conversations switched from English to French, and I think as it got later into the evening, her English improved and my French worsened. Regardless, my last memory of the evening was slow dancing with Manon after last call. Maybe even a kiss or two. I woke up the next morning in the spare room, in my underwear and socks, my pants and shirt nicely folded over the chair. She had put me to bed! Women from northern France can drink. At some point, I walked downstairs, where everyone was having breakfast, talking, and laughing.

Dimitri then gave me a look of utter disappointment, to which I felt like saying, "I didn't do anything!" As best I could remember, that is. After breakfast, which I didn't touch, he said to me, "Manon thought you were a nice guy. You missed your opportunity, Joel." Apparently, French bro code isn't the same as Canadian bro code.

CHAPTER EIGHTEEN

Jesus Christ Pose

Everyone agreed regimental service sucked the big one, and that's what was waiting for us in Calvi during the later months of 1997. No one joined the French Foreign Legion to cut potatoes or be a lifeguard, but these are the practicalities of military life. Fortunately, the GCP was left alone, or at the most tasked with guarding the regiment's amphibious centre. This was the least involved service task, and it was done in combats devoid of any formal inspection.

Life in the regiment for a GCP caporal was as good as it got, really. We were left alone and exempt from company morning roll call, and our NCOs didn't bother us unless they were dropping in for a social coffee before parade. We were treated as equals. Well, those who were SOGH-qualified were treated as equals. I wasn't there yet. Rank, however, was always respected, but we mixed socially more than in a combat company, which they didn't do at all.

GCP caporals were generally past the five-year service mark, so they didn't need to wear their uniforms outside the regiment. This was problematic during the summer months for those of us with less service, since all the popular nightclubs were off limits to légionnaires in uniform. I was still far from the five-year service mark, so I was missing out. Following Lasko's suggestion, I started leaving the regiment through one of the side gates used to access the NCOs' accommodations buildings in my civilian clothing.

The légionnaires on guard didn't question me; they just assumed I was an NCO. However, if caught, I risked jail time, but at that age some things are a priority. For instance, Calvi's Acapulco Nightclub. My teammates were talking about something in the club, but my focus was on the blonde go-go dancer up onstage. Her dance moves, short skirt, and fit body had my attention. Later, I noticed her walking among the club's crowd, and I introduced myself. She was Polish, and we spoke briefly in English until she was due back onstage. Later in the evening, she came and sat with me.

At some point in that discussion, she grabbed my hand and led me outside to the parking lot. Loud electronica music from the nightclub was thumping. She sat on the hood of someone's car, pulled me close, right into her legs. I looked around at the club-goers milling in and out of the parking lot, then gave her a look that asked, "What? Right here?"

My plan to remain low key and not bring attention to myself was out the door at that point. I don't think people even noticed what we were doing, or would care. The music changed and that was her— gone. It was her cue to get back onstage.

I made my way back to the bar and joined the others, a little shell-shocked. Soon after, I felt a light tap on my shoulder. I turned to see Capitaine Desmeulles standing there. "I hadn't realized you were over the five-year service mark, Struthers," he said casually. I didn't have an answer, and I'm sure one wasn't expected. "Come see me on Monday morning to discuss it." I was in Capitaine Desmeulles's office first thing Monday, and he gave me a generous verbal warning. That was the end of me pushing limits. No more Acapulco. C'est la vie.

The summer months passed, and the tourists left. The island's mountain peaks were soon covered in snow, and winter had transformed the Mediterranean's turquoise water to a darker blue. Routine set in, and during the mornings we were generally left on our own to do whatever athletic activity we wanted. If I didn't go for a run with Ursa, Smithy, and Brook, or ride the sports bureau's mountain bikes, I would run to the Rocher Beach. The Rocher was a small but popular beach in the summertime, frequented more by locals than tourists. A narrow dirt path ran along the coastline, cutting through maquis and rocks to the beach. Not far away were the ruins of a Genoese tower, and large boulders shaped by centuries of crashing waves dotted the bay's coastline. After a sweat pushing the pace, diving into the Med's cold water was a shock to the system but always welcomed. Tasting the sea's salt, and looking across the bay to Calvi's citadel, Corsica was making its mark on me.

During the rest of our time, we frequented the ranges or jumped. Christmas arrived, and team members from Operation Almandin II were awarded the Croix de la Valeur Militaire, avec étoile de Bronze (Military Valour with Bronze Star). It was an honour having a medal pinned on my uniform. Christmas dinner was held in the regiment's vehicle parking area, a large open-air hangar. The regiment's CO with entourage passed by each company and gave a Christmas speech, followed by the collective singing of the regimental and company song. Soon, the company comedy skits began, and the regimental and company gifts were handed out. The company ended up eating, drinking, and singing late into the Corsican night. A perfect Christmas—not.

I snuck away as soon as the singing started. I wasn't alone. Others from the section followed: Smithy, Selak, Holcik, and some NCOs, including recently promoted sergents Maguire, Lasko, and Brook. Drinks were had in *chambre* 21. Music from Soundgarden, Pearl Jam, the Matthew Good Band, and the Red Hot Chili Peppers was cranked, and our spirits were high because the following morning we were all on two weeks' leave—the regiment's Christmas gift.

I was out the regiment's gates at the earliest opportunity. I sat at the Calvi airport for hours before my flight to Nice; I didn't care. Back on mainland France, I caught the train to Viviers-du-Lac, home to a civilian parachute jump club at the Aéroport de Chambéry. I was there to get my *brevet de parachutisme sportif,* a civilian qualification, to make sure I was comfortable with free fall before my SOGH course scheduled after leave. It wasn't a requirement, and it was a cost out of my pocket. However, a few of my teammates had done the course and suggested the idea. Plus, I wanted every advantage I could possibly get, and this was my opportunity.

The regiment assisted by calling the military casern in Albertville, approximately 60 kilometres from the club, securing me a bunk space for a week. The French military free-fall team happened to be training at the club at the same time. When they noticed me looking a little out of place and understood my reason for being in Viviers-du-Lac, they kindly offered me a place in their minivan for the daily drive to and from the club.

That first morning, I sat in the back of their van listening to jump talk among the half dozen women and men who were training for the Military World Parachuting Championships. I didn't say much. At the club, I met my instructor, and we went over everything in detail, including what was to be done on my first jump. Then I was issued a parachute and all the ancillaries, and along with several other jumpers, we walked over to the PC-6 Pilatus.

The climb to altitude was one of anticipation: my first step into the void. Well, somewhat; I wasn't doing actual free fall just yet. I first had to step out from the Pilatus and simulate releasing the *petite voile*, or small parachute, which would release the main chute. However, I'd be attached to a tether cord that would open my chute manually; that way I wouldn't be a liability to the school. If the instructor was happy with my first simulation, the following jump would be actual free fall.

I watched the others go out the door, and my heart rate increased a little more with each exit. Then it was just the pilot, the instructor, and me. I made my way to the door, gave the instructor a thumbs-up, and stepped out. He was happy with my simulation, and my jumps were then used to work on a stable free fall as I descended through the cold air, watching my altimeter for that designated altitude from which to deploy my main chute.

I felt the thrilling sensation of going from a confined and noisy space to wide open and blissful quiet. Freedom. Flying the parachute under canopy was simple enough. But back on earth, the proper parachute-folding technique was my stumbling ground. In my defence, several female "free fly" (head down) pro skydivers wearing fashionable tight shorts and skimpy shirts were doing a photo session, folding their parachutes next to me, quickly and without effort. Not only was I surrounded by experienced, highly skilled military jumpers, but also civilian jumpers with some amazing derrières. But I focused and finally figured it out, and within a few days, attained my qualification with a week left over to snowboard in the Alps before returning to Calvi.

Back in Calvi, I was informed that the regiment required a minimum commitment of two years once I was SOGH-qualified. So before I left for my SOGH course, I signed on for the additional year needed to make the commitment. Capitaine Desmeulles wished me luck, reminding me that I was representing the regiment, the company, and the section—so I should behave myself, but also have fun.

After being reissued an olive-green jumpsuit, jump helmet, goggles, altimeter, gloves, jacket, boots, and a civilian airline ticket to Nice, I was ready to leave for L'École des troupes aéroportées (ÉTAP), this time with a secured spot on the course. Dimitri was back from his SOGH course by then, and he told me that I would have the time of my life. He even gave me the phone number of his friend, well, ex-girlfriend, whom he met on his course and lived in Pau. Once again, I was confused about what bro code meant in such a scenario.

In February 1998, I made my way to the ÉTAP, familiar with what would follow. Arno arrived at the ÉTAP accommodations block at the same time. Arno was a junior NCO with Commando Hubert, the French Navy's commando program, which is similar to the British Special Boat Service or the much larger US Navy SEALs program. Arno seemed like a character, and we got along fine from the get-go. Next door was a regular force GCP NCO I had done the commando course with. Once settled, we all jumped into Arno's white VW and headed to downtown Pau for a meal. Two other members from Hubert joined us later. During the discussions back and forth, my franglophone accent and Legion vocabulary had its effect on the guys. After I'd spoken, Martin, the taller of the three Huberts, would say to the others, "Qu'est-ce qu'il a dit?" What's he saying? I think they could all sense that this constant need for clarification, which became a running joke, bugged me.

On Monday morning, we all gathered in the classroom for our SOGH course briefing and introduction to the training staff. There were nine candidates, including three NCOs from Commando Hubert, several NCOs from the regular GCP teams, and me. The course had been broken into two separate phases: the first, CASOGHI (Certificat d'aptitude au saut opérationnel à grande hauteur en individuel), using the military CPE12 chute, which is very much like a civilian free-fall chute; the second, CASOGHE (Certificat d'aptitude au saut opérationnel à grande hauteur en équipe), involved the much larger GQ 360 chute and gaine. Candidates with prior military free-fall experience would join us for the second phase. To qualify for our SOGH wings, we needed to complete twenty-five team jumps with GQ 360, gaine, and FAMAS.

Once the briefing was complete, we made our way to the Section d'entretien et de pliage des parachutes (SEPP) for an introduction to the tools of the trade, the CPE12 parachute and its safety features. The proper procedures for folding our chutes was shown, along with the technique for untangling it. Nine of us stood with a CPE12 deployed behind our backs and a SEPP technician created an issue. Then we had five minutes to get the parachute untangled.

This was an extremely easy test to screw up if you didn't use the procedure taught. We had spent the last few hours practising, during which I managed to tangle my parachute so badly it had to be dismantled at its harness by the SEPP. Next, we worked on our free-fall body positioning, emergency procedures, and finished practising our exits from a mock airplane door inside the SEPP building.

In class, emergencies were discussed in detail. The main chute not deploying or a partial deployment required us to release the main chute from its harness by pulling the appropriate handle, which also opened the secondary chute, referred to as the reserve. Once we moved on to the larger GQ 360 operational parachute (James Gregory and Raymond Quilter—GQ Parachute Company Ltd.) on the next phase, however, we would have to open the reserve chute manually. The biggest factor is how the parachute is folded. If it's done incorrectly, problems will occur. For this reason, the reserve parachute is folded by the SEPP, and as a matter of safety, opened and refolded every six months.

The following day airside, an air force single-engine PC-6 Pilatus arrived. Its distinctive turbine sound immediately made my pulse start racing. Our first jumps involved using a tether cord attached to the main chute so that it deployed automatically, the same idea as my *civvy* jumps in the Alps. Our drop zone was Wright Field, named for the Wright brothers, who had been invited to Pau to train two French pilots in 1912. We exited the Pilatus at 2500 metres over the DZ, facing the instructor in the doorway to demonstrate the action required to open our main chute. The next jump allowed us ten seconds of free fall.

Our helmets were equipped with radios that let the instructors correct our errors while they watched with binoculars below from Wright Field's small control tower. Our target was a circular bull's eye made of small rocks in a field adjacent to a large wind sock. After landing and packing up our chute, we would present ourselves to our instructors for a debrief and push-ups if we had missed our mark or done something stupid.

The next objective was correcting a bad exit induced by our instructor as we left the Pilatus. At 3500 metres, we were either pushed out the door headfirst, tumbling uncontrollably, or shoved out backwards to the same effect. We had five seconds to stabilize. Our goal was a stable exit, then to perform a 360-degree turn to the left, then to the right, followed by forward summersault and cork-screw spin, finishing with a ten-second *derive* (an aggressive dart-like dive away) before opening our chute at the minimum altitude: 1000 metres. Fall past the minimum and the parachute's barometric deployment system would kick in and automatically release the main chute. But you didn't want that to happen. Failure to respect the minimum ceiling twice resulted in a course fail and return to unit. We had two weeks to progress with an undisclosed number of jumps in which to do so.

Safety was paramount. The risk of mid-air collision was high and unforgiving. Our instructors were always reinforcing the need for us to pay attention to the small details. We also wore an orange training helmet and orange ankle wraps for improved visibility, both in free fall and from the ground.

Our exits were increased to 4000 metres, and we jumped with an instructor to work on lateral movement. The instructor exited first and we followed, trying our best to touch hands and then correct for any change in rate of descent or lateral movement he induced. The focus was on our ability to control the free fall. When we were close to our opening altitude, my instructor grabbed me by the chest straps and purposely threw me into a spin as the minimum altitude was fast approaching.

We all qualified for the CASOGHI phase, and when we were at the SEPP handing in our parachutes, an instructor arrived and asked if we wanted to jump from a C-130 Hercules. Fuck, did I! Sitting at the front of the C-130, once it had dropped its automatic jumpers, we climbed to 4000 metres and the side door was opened for us.

When the instructor's verifications were done, we used the C130's inner door handle and swung ourselves out into the airstream as instructed, facing the nose of the aircraft in an upright stance, arms at our sides. Then we spread our legs shoulder-width apart and our arms out in a "Jesus Christ" pose. If done properly, you are taken for a good ride and gradually fall into a stable free-fall position. Done incorrectly, you spin out of control. Jumping out of that C-130 was the coolest thing I had done at that point. Watching the Hercules fly away, the noise of its turbines and smell of jet fuel were replaced by calm and the wind in my ears. I was free falling above the Pyrenees mountains, and that was a good place to be.

CHAPTER NINETEEN

GQ

The CASOGHE (Certificat d'aptitude au saut opérationnel à grande hauteur en équipe) wasn't scheduled to start for another week. Our course CO agreed it didn't make sense for me to return to Calvi; the trip back and forth would take four days. So the commanding officer called Calvi and it was agreed that I could remain at the ÉTAP. The jump gods were looking over me.

It was easy to get used to a leisurely breakfast at the NCO mess before my bus ride flightside at the civilized time of 0900 hours. Flightside, I sat patiently with my parachute, waiting for a chance to jump. PUMA SA330, C-130, C-160, PC-6, left door, right door—whatever was offered to me. Instructors would jump with me from time to time so I could improve my skills.

In the evenings, Dimitri's ex-girlfriend Clara met me at the front gate, and we would drive into Pau to meet her girlfriends. I got along well with Aceline, an elementary schoolteacher, and she started to pick me up in her rough-looking Peugeot 25. Aceline was a tall, athletic type with short hair. She even laughed at my jokes. Or perhaps it was my French vocabulary that amused her. It didn't matter. We did the things consenting adults do, luxuries a légionnaire certainly appreciates more than most others.

The CASOGHE began with twenty candidates. In addition to my CASOGHI course mates were two NCOs from the Mont-Fort Commando, two members from the 1er RPIMa (COS), two from the 13e Régiment de dragons parachutistes (13e RDP), an air force forward air controller, a few regular GCPs, a member of the Groupe d'intervention de la gendarmerie nationale (GIGN), and a German

Army captain on exchange. He didn't speak a word of French; however, he spoke a little English, so I was quickly designated his interpreter.

The course entry exams were reduced to the 1500-metre and 8-kilometre TAP runs, push-ups, sit-ups, squats, rope climb, and swim test. These were accompanied by a signed document from our respective regiments stating that we had completed the 30-kilometre run in the required time. A regular force GCP lieutenant won the 8-kilometre run, cranking up the pace at the last moment as we ran it together. I could sense that at first the lieutenant wasn't too sure about what légionnaires represent, but I think my pushing the pace eased any concerns he may have had.

The next morning, we all passed the qualification jump. Back at our NCO barracks that evening, a course cocktail president was chosen. This was apparently a French military tradition. Philippe Mollet, an NCO with 13ᵉ RDP, a regiment trained in covert espionage, was chosen. He would be responsible for organizing weekly or semi-weekly cocktail parties. A course president was also picked, but a lot less thought and consideration went into that one. Everyone took cocktails a lot more seriously. The regular force GCP lieutenant, the highest ranking of us all, was duly chosen. Our course was set and we were ready to go.

The following morning, our first task involved familiarization with the larger British-made operational GQ360 parachute. It was big and heavy with two identical chutes, the reserve being the same as the main. The obligatory folding and untangling tests were carried out, after which we were each issued two GQs. The following day, we jumped from a C-160 at 3500 metres, performing the same entry test done previously.

Our exits were changed for the succeeding jumps. Now we'd jump headfirst out the side door, facing the plane's tail. This was trickier. Our instructors followed us, and we worked on our lateral movement. The day arrived when we left the C-160 via the rear ramp, a simple yet thrilling walk off the edge. I had been waiting for that one. Seeing the Pyrenees in full view made them only more impressive. But with any exit, we had limited time to work on skills,

Pre-jump verification, Saut opérationnel à grande hauteur course (SOGH) ÉTAP, in Pau, France. (*Credit:* Joel Struthers)

so the pressure was on to execute a stable exit, get to our instructor, and start the session. Naturally, we all knew our instructor nailed his exit, and that he was out there waiting for us.

Night jumps were introduced. Free fall in the dark is an altogether different sensation and challenge. The lack of horizon means you can't determine the rate of descent, and judging lateral movement is difficult. This is why so much effort was spent on minimizing lateral movement or drift. During a night jump, if we were above a team-mate when he opened his main chute, we were both dead.

A back-lit altimeter was the tool that would enable us to gauge the right altitude in which to open our chutes. Our bull's eye on Wright Field was marked with red lights placed in an arrowhead formation, with the tip of the arrow indicating an approach into wind. A single light extending from the tip indicates light winds; two or three lights indicates increased wind conditions.

The 25-kilogram gaine was introduced to our jumps, attached by two buckles located at the waist and releasable straps behind our legs. You had to be careful not to catch the gaine on the way out the door as this would knock you into a spin. But despite being heavy and cumbersome, the gaine makes for a more stable free fall. It's virtually unnoticeable in flight unless a side buckle releases, which can throw you into a spin in a matter of seconds if you don't com-pensate for it. Once under canopy, the gaine is released and hangs from a cord just below your feet, which you step over as you land.

As our individual proficiencies improved and our instructors felt we were ready, we began jumping in small groups with the FAMAS strapped to the side of the GQ's harness. It wasn't long before ten-man teams were jumping; the instructors would initially join us to complete the numbers. We exited the aircraft in single file, spaced a second apart to ensure a gap between jumpers. When exiting, the procedure was to count to three, then turn into the wind (the direc-tion—turn right or left—was provided by flight deck) to minimize drift in free fall and ensure everyone was subject to the same drift.

Team leaders were chosen based on ability, and prior to jump-ing, the team leader provided a pre-jump brief. This detailed jump height, order of exit, type of exit, the anticipated right or left turn into the wind (to be confirmed in the air), with a recap on emer-gency drills. A few of us who were given the opportunity to do so exited first, leading the team under canopy to the designated DZ. An equally skilled jumper was placed in the number two position, as he needed to gauge the leader's landing and then correct for any errors so the rest of the team was given the best possible approach. During my pre-jump brief, generally done on the bus ride to airside or pre-boarding the aircraft, someone would eventually say, "Qu'est-ce qu'il a dit?"

It was advantageous to have heavier jumpers at the front and the lighter ones at the rear to ensure a well-staggered team under canopy. The team leaders would open at 1200 metres and the last jumper at 1500 metres. Once under canopy, the leader would turn and make his way back toward the furthest jumper to regroup the team. For instructional purposes, team leaders wore coloured armbands so jumpers could see them. In a perfect scenario, a team deploys its canopies well grouped, which allows maximum altitude to reach an intended DZ. The leader will then judge wind conditions and act accordingly. If he realizes his team, or more so the last jumpers, won't make the intended DZ, he will immediately find a suitable replacement DZ. The unofficial SOGH motto was "Better lost and grouped than alone on target."

As we became more skilled, we were given smaller DZs. We were landing on the ÉTAP's soccer field by the course's end. Night exits were staggered a little more, and each jumper left the aircraft with a small light strapped to his ankle. The leader wore a strobe light on his ankle so he could quickly be pinpointed both in free fall and under canopy.

The temperature in western France was dropping. The colder mornings meant that runny snot got into your eyes, but they were also remedies for the inevitable hangovers after our course cocktail parties. These parties were held on Thursday evening after night jumps. Coincidentally, that was student night in Pau's downtown core, known as Le Triangle, a triangular street intersection lined with popular bars. Aceline and her friends mingled with us, and I mingled in my *Gentlemen's Quarterly*–style jeans, new brown leather shoes, and a dress shirt, usually topped with a blue or grey sweater. It was basically the same outfit everyone from the ÉTAP or anyone in the military wore outside the perimeter in the evening. The officers in our group wore better-quality shoes and sweaters, obviously. My overenthusiastic mingling eventually led to Aceline's slap across my face, which would have made Madureira proud. Friday mornings were rough, and pre-jump our instructors would check us for bloodshot eyes before inspecting our equipment. It wasn't uncommon for someone to run off to the side and throw up.

I was enjoying this new life. On the weekends, most of the course went home to their families, wives, or girlfriends. But both Arno and Philippe were always keen to take road trips, notably to San Sebastián, Spain, to explore its tapas bars filled with Spanish girls. In fact, it wasn't long before our CO noticed my civilian acclimatization and suggested I get a much-needed haircut. After all, I wasn't a Navy commando or a French military spy, he said. Roger.

We all eventually completed the twenty-five team jumps needed to graduate. With the ÉTAP CO, course CO, and guests watching, we made our final jump on Wright Field, April 17, 1998. Both teams landed short due to high winds, and we walked the last 500 metres with our parachutes, FAMASs, and gaines. The coveted first-place finish went to our GIGN course-mate, and deservedly so. Some years prior, as a fresh rookie on the team, he had taken part in the GIGN's assault of the hijacked Air France flight by Algerian terrorists at the Marseille Provence Airport. I think he got tired of my questions on the subject. I managed a fourth-place finish and was the proud owner of my new SOGH wings, numbered 2003.

Parachutes were returned to the SEPP, and I thanked the course commanding officer and instructors for how well they had treated me. I left a brand-new légionnaire's kepi with a Canadian flag inside it at the ÉTAP instructors' bar. I said my goodbyes to my coursemates and then caught a ride back to the Commando Hubert base at the Toulon naval shipyard where France's new aircraft carrier, the *Charles de Gaulle*, was docked.

Hubert's base was off on its own in a wooded area, hidden away from the rest of the naval yard. I had a look at its miniature submarines and high-speed Zodiacs, all impressive state-of-the-art equipment. What really caught my attention was a US nuclear-attack submarine docked at the long jetty below Hubert's main building. A US SEAL team was in town to cross-train with them. I was envious to say the least.

But I had no time for envy. I needed to mentally prepare for returning to the Legion way of doing things. It's a fact that in a bid to set itself apart from the rest, the Legion maintains iron discipline and places heavy restrictions on personal freedoms. Although this works as a short-term solution, it results in a high turnover. I also needed to get a proper haircut before making my way back to Calvi.

CHAPTER TWENTY

Part of the Team

Two large MPs were standing inside of the Calvi airport terminal watching for légionnaires coming and going. Both were Polish capo-rals on secondment from the 2nd Company. They were not smiling. I saluted as I walked past. Back in the section, Capitaine Desmeulles politely congratulated me on getting my wings and told me to pres-ent myself to Capitaine Raoul, who was now the 3rd Company's CO, and also to the section's SOGH-qualified members.

I was finally a qualified GCP team member, and I could jump with the section. And it wasn't long before there was an opportu-nity for two jumps onto the Calvi DZ and a night jump into the village of Borgo. On my first jump with the team, Karine walked me to the edge of the C-160's ramp, pushing me over and hanging on. We spun out of control, and then he did his best to release me into an uncontrollable spin, but I was confident in my abilities and stabilized right away. However, my arrogance would change soon enough.

That evening, the C-160 climbed to altitude. Inside, a red light cast an ominous glow. Then the ramp lowered. I edged closer to the ramp, taking in the view of Bastia, a long sliver of yellow and white lights far below. This was my first night jump with the team, and I would be number three off the ramp. As I did my pre-jump checks, the white illumination light on my altimeter flickered. Not a good sign. Was the battery dying? If it was, I should step to the side. No jump.

The light continued to flicker slowly. But it wasn't out yet. On the Transall's green light, the two men ahead of me jumped in quick succession. I followed, stepping off the ramp, pitched head down. I quickly stabilized, then made my turn into the wind and started

Team jump, C-160 Transall, Calvi, Corsica. (*Credit:* 2ᵉ Régiment étranger de parachutistes)

looking for the leader's flashing strobe. Bastia's lights made it diffi-cult to locate the leader's strobe light. I quickly glanced at my altim-eter. Blackness. It was dead. I lifted my arm with the altimeter as close to my eyes as possible, thinking that might allow me to see something. Instead, the movement only induced an immediate air-flow instability. As a result, I was being buffeted by the unequal flow around me, and quite aggressively. Keeping that position was pointless and damn uncomfortable.

My only solution was to listen for the sound of the leader's main chute being deployed, a distinct crack. In the worst-case scenario, I would hear number two's main chute deploying. Unless I had drifted, he should be closer to me. I still couldn't see him, which was very unsettling. I felt I had been in free fall for the right amount of time, and I should hear their openings pretty damn soon. But then again, this was a new predicament. Was my sense of timing off? I also didn't want to open too high, or too low and look like a fucking idiot on my first team night jump.

Then I heard it. Crack! Then another. Both chutes opened in succession, and that was my cue to pull my main. I yanked on the handle, and I immediately felt the parachute leaving the harness, followed by its crack as it opened. I was pulled to an immediate and somewhat violent stop. Then I safely stored the handle in my combat vest (lose that and you pay for it in one way or another), landing without incident. No one was the wiser, but the risk I had taken set me straight. In the future, I would make damn certain my night altimeter battery was properly charged. As ever, the devil is in the details, and it's the small things that can ruin your day—or night.

An 11th Parachute Brigade exercise was to take place in Corsica, and preparations were in the works. Our team was tasked to secure a DZ for the brigade's airborne insertion onto the island. Equipped with weapons and gaines, we boarded the Navy Super Frelon helicopter at the Calvi hangar in the late morning. My gaine weighed more than 30 kilos alone, plus there was my 12-kilo parachute, FAMAS, sidearm, webbing, and ammunition. However, the Super Frelon had a lot more room than the Puma and a rear ramp for an easier exit.

The Super Frelon made its way down the southwestern coast, which was covered in woodland, fringing the island's idyllic sandy beaches. The helicopter climbed to 4000 metres, and we exited over Roccapina Beach. Opening our chutes at 2500 metres, we covered some distance under canopy, our light blue parachutes drifting their way through the sky and landing on a picture-postcard Corsican beach.

We threw our parachutes into the section's waiting VLRA. Garcia was the driver, and he was still waiting to do his SOGH. I knew exactly how he felt not being able to take part. The rest of us set off on a 15-kilometre hike to the Figari Airport, which was comparable in many ways to those we had seen in Africa, so it made for a somewhat realistic training exercise. Arriving at our destination, we set up OPs so we had eyes on our target, and our communications operators sent their coded messages to brigade command.

The proposed DZ was a large field that ran alongside Figari's main runway. The remainder of the team secured the DZ, setting markers in place for the approaching C-130s and C-160s with wind direction updates to their flight crews. At 300 metres above ground, two regiments of men and equipment, including several small support vehicles, were dropped on Figari. As this was happening, the

Group exit, C-160 Transall. (*Credit:* 2ᵉ Régiment étranger de parachutistes)

remaining GCP assaulted and cleared the airport's main terminal, rappelling in from three Puma helicopters.

Phase two involved an assault of the citadel of Bonifacio (Bunifaziu), with its chalky limestone cliffs and abandoned Legion garrison, which was home to the Groupement opérationnel de la Légion étrangère until 1977. A small annex building was manned by a French regular communications company acting as an enemy force for the exercise. The GCP was to assault the building and secure the town's "mayor," a volunteer hostage. That evening, our team took off from Figari Airport in a Puma helicopter and jumped over the island's southernmost coastline, its luminescent waves crashing onshore. We linked up with 3rd Company Zodiacs for the amphibious insertion and secured the high ground covering the parking lot next to the old garrison. Two regular force GCP teams then rappelled in from a Puma, with our team providing cover as tourists watched, and we cleared the complex together. The mayor of Bonifacio was secured. A digital photo of him was taken and sent to command for facial recognition. With confirmation received, a Super Frelon landed and transported the mayor back to the Figari Airport. Exercise accomplished.

I finally felt part of the team, able to perform the needed skills to get the job done, albeit still very junior and lacking in experience. Some of my teammates on this exercise were part of the section's raid on a Mujahedeen camp in Bosnia in 1996, Opération faucon noir. Under the command of a British Special Forces officer, the raid using a US Military Blackhawk helicopter was a success. I always had questions about that raid, but I never felt right about asking. At least today I could perform my role in the team. Before that, I was just a légionnaire in waiting.

CHAPTER TWENTY-ONE

Paris

The trailer for the movie *Saving Private Ryan* often showing on the TV in chambre 21 was awesome. I couldn't wait to see it, but sadly, we didn't have a proper movie theatre in Calvi. Anyway, more pressing news arrived. A combined peloton from the 1st Company and the CEA were chosen to represent the regiment and the Legion at the July 14, 1998, Bastille Day military parade, or *défilé*, in Paris. Several of us from the section were included.

Bastille Day commemorates the storming of the Bastille fortress in Paris, a defining moment of the 1789 French Revolution. To mark the event, various military units from the French army march down the Champs-Élysées, starting at the Arc de Triomphe on Place Charles de Gaulle (historically and perhaps more commonly known as Place de l'Étoile) and ending at the Place de la Concorde in front of the presidential tribune.

Because of our much slower marching pace, the Legion is typically one of the last in succession. Leading the Legion are the pioneers—sporting beards, axes, and leather aprons, a tradition dating back to Napoleonic times—closely followed by the Legion's band, known as La Musique principale. Preparations prior to the day involved hours and hours of marching up and down the Calvi airport's main runway in the early morning. Being among the 1st Company once again, I recognized a lot of faces, but others were missing. Some guys had been promoted to NCO. Others, like Schubert from the Aide moniteur éducation physique militaire et sportive (EPMS) course, had deserted. I also recognized the combat company's way of doing business, with NCOs yelling and légionnaires running around traumatized.

We landed at the Paris–Le Bourget Airport in a C-160 and hopped on buses to the Legion's Fort de Nogent. Built in the late 1800s, the fort had been under siege by the Prussians in 1870, and it was the scene of bitter fighting during the Second World War between the occupying German army and the French Resistance. In the 1960s, it was a makeshift prison for two hundred French officers involved in the Algerian putsch. Today it's a Legion recruitment centre. We settled into our barrack rooms and got our lockers organized and uniforms ready for the next day's training.

Next morning, dressed in our parade uniforms with medals, epaulettes, kepis, and FAMASs, we boarded several buses for the drive to an air force base to perfect our march spacing and timing on the taxiways. Lieutenants would arrange the rank and file, instructing a légionnaire to take a step forward or back, chin up or chin down, FAMAS up or FAMAS down, all the way down the line. This took time, and it was painful, usually leading to a comment or two from the ranks. The same orders and constant corrections in spacing were barked from the sidelines as we marched.

When it was time for a break, we left our weapons on their bipods and broke rank. NCOs would designate several légionnaires to ensure every FAMAS was evenly spaced laterally and horizontally, down to the centimetre. Orders to move a FAMAS to the left or right or back and forth lasted until we were called back to the ranks. This obsession with perfection seems a bit over the top, but attention to detail is what it's all about.

Another detail that was annoying involved the inevitable oil stain on your shirt that resulted from having the FAMAS strapped to your chest all day. This meant that once back at Fort de Nogent, we all had to wash and properly iron our shirts to get them ready for the next day's inspection. Thankfully, we all had a brand-new shirt, an extra pair of pants, and new kepi in our lockers for the Bastille Day parade.

But it wasn't all about marching and ironing. France was hosting the FIFA World Cup, and the final match between France and Brazil was being held at Stade de France on the 12th. We were each given a titre de permission for that evening. Wearing our short-sleeved summer dress uniforms and kepis, Dimitri, Smithy, Chris, and I took a taxi to the Champs-Élysées and walked into Chesterfields Pub. Several other légionnaires from the 1st and CEA arrived soon after, joining the lively crowd. One of the female bartenders was offering to paint the French flag on people's cheeks, and a French légionnaire asked if the cheek was the only option available. No, it wasn't. Soon, his johnson was red, white, and blue.

Like a man on a mission, Chris didn't lose time getting into the beer, and he quickly became chatty with a very nice, full-figured French girl who also enjoyed her beer. Here, I met Amy, an American girl studying archaeology in Paris. She had short brown hair, which I liked for some reason. Not every girl can pull off short hair. We all had fun watching the game, and after France beat Brazil 3–0, everyone made their way to the Champs to celebrate the victory. Amy and I jumped into a taxi before it was impossible to find one, and drove to her university dorm. Sitting in the backseat of the car, I watched the city go by. The light-adorned Eiffel Tower seemed to follow us, and I caught glimpses of the iconic symbol of Paris between the crowded avenues and boulevards.

In the morning, I woke up to my watch alarm in Amy's dorm room. When I pulled her close, a female voice said, "Nope. Wrong person." Amy's roommate was sleeping in the bed? I had no idea when or how she joined us. Under those circumstances, most men would say, "Forget the alarm and work. Let's see where this goes." But then again, most men wouldn't have to potentially clean Fort de Nogent's toilets. I hopped into a taxi and headed back.

It was still dark on the morning of the défilé when we boarded buses headed for the Champs-Élysées. Here, we joined the long procession of military vehicles, tanks, artillery, personnel carriers, and Paris-Marseille fire trucks. We then formed up on the Champs' old cobblestones. The order to stand at attention was given, then to present arms several times in order to warm us up and help us find our collective timings. We were then stood down. While waiting on the sidewalk for daylight to break, we distracted ourselves by watching girls walking home from the Champs' numerous nightclubs.

As the sun rose and the crowds started to arrive, a military-looking type in civilian clothes, with lady friend in tow, approached a few of us standing in a small cluster. He introduced himself as a

Saint-Cyr officer cadet, mentioning his sous-lieutenant rank. Then he asked, in a smart-assed tone, "Doesn't a légionnaire wear his kepi outside?" In stereo, Smithy and I said, "What? Get lost." He was right, however. We should have been wearing our kepis, but we had REP officers and NCOs who could make that observation. He left with his girlfriend, clearly flustered.

A crowd of onlookers had gathered on the sidewalks. Over the loudspeakers lining the Champs, we were told to form up. Trumpets sounded and the collective command "Gardez-vous!" was given, followed by "Presentez armes!" The loud crack of several hundred hands hitting their FAMASs resonated down the Champs, making the hair on the back of my neck stand up. It was damn cool. The presidential guard, on horseback with blaring trumpets, made their way down the Champs in their impressive uniforms, with helmets and swords at their sides, just as they would have done for Napoléon centuries before. The presidential motorcade followed behind, with President Jacques Chirac standing atop a VLRA saluting each of the unit's commanding officers.

An air force flyover at low altitude followed, and we all watched. The noise was impressive. Then the vehicles started to make their way down the Champs. With the lingering smell of horse manure and diesel drifting through the air, once all the vehicles had passed, the French regulars opened the march and we prepared ourselves.

To my side, a caporal asked his section lieutenant, "Mon lieutenant, do you know why the Champs is lined with trees?" The lieutenant replied "No, why?" The German caporal answered, "Because my grandfather liked marching in the shade." We all laughed.

It was now our turn to march. The heavy thud of the bass drum set our pace, and the 1st Company capitaine gave the order "En avant marche!" The heels of our left boots collectively hit the cobblestones, medals jangled, and our bayonet sheaths hit our thighs in unison. Crowds cheered, "Vive la Légion!" As we approached Place de la Concorde, we wheeled left toward Rue Royale, and the 1st Company capitaine saluted President Chirac, who was surrounded by French and foreign politicians, military personnel, and dignitaries.

The parade was over. Names were quickly yelled out. Mine was one of the them. Along with fourteen other légionnaires, NCOs, and a few officers, I would be going to Paris's Hôtel de Ville, or town hall, for lunch with the mayor of Paris, Jean Tiberi. I handed my FAMAS to a fellow légionnaire, and we then made our way toward our designated bus. But in true military fashion, it had already left on time. We followed the 1st Company capitaine to the Concorde metro station.

Lunch was held in the Hôtel de Ville's main ballroom. Huge paintings wrapped its walls, and light flooded through massive stained-glass windows, which provided views of the inner courtyard. Similar groups representing the various arms of the French military on parade that day joined us. Mayor Tiberi and his guests were seated at the head table and welcomed everyone with a few short speeches. Our tables were covered in white linen, fine cutlery, crystal glasses, and ample bottles of wine and water. A menu was set at each place, along with a gift—a watch—from the city of Paris. The meal was excellent, and we ate while quietly talking among ourselves. But then it began—the singing.

While still seated, a Saint-Cyr officer cadet class started with a class song. Then the 1st Company capitaine stood up mid-song and cut them off with his low tone intro to our regimental song. We all immediately stood to attention and joined in. No one sang after that, not because we were impeccable singers, but due to the regiment's history. The capitaine was visibly impressed with himself.

After lunch, we returned to Fort de Nogent by bus. Once we had packed all our belongings and cleaned the barracks, we made our way back to Calvi. The regiment was on summer leave. Months before, Smithy, Chris, and I had agreed to request leave in Canada. Smithy and Chris had never been to Canada, so why not? It was the perfect opportunity. We followed the appropriate protocol, requesting company and regimental approval. Both my and Smithy's leaves were approved, but Chris's wasn't. We had options, though. One of Smithy's contacts in the regiment's B2 was willing to liberate Chris's passport in exchange for a bottle of vodka. Done. We stashed his passport in my locker. Unlike the rest of the company, we weren't subject to random MP searches. The plan was simple. We would meet Chris at the Calvi airport for our flight to Amsterdam via Paris and hand him his passport prior to check-in. What could go wrong?

After a good familiarization of Amsterdam's nightclubs and zero sleep that night, the following morning we met my father at Schiphol Airport and flew on his scheduled flight back to Vancouver. My dad had set us up with middle seats in the front row, and the French-Canadian flight attendants fed us free drinks. Chris started speaking with a Dutch accent, which annoyed Smithy to no end. I fell in love with one of the flight attendants, a couple of them actually; it was hard to focus. Chris and Ken remained focused, each landing a spot in the cockpit jump seat to experience a landing in Keflavik, Iceland, and our final destination, YVR.

Smithy and Chris hung out with my friends doing what guys do when on leave from the French Foreign Legion, going for a run before most people are up, and renting a car and exploring the province of British Columbia. I went to Vancouver Island to visit my grandparents for a weekend. When we were all back at my family's home in Fort Langley, Philippe Mollet called. He was in Seattle, Washington, visiting his brother, who apparently worked for Boeing. Philippe drove across the border and met us for a night out, and we introduced him to the Shark Club sports bar experience in Langley! It wasn't exactly San Sebastián, Spain, but he met a Canadian girl, so his drive north wasn't a total waste. When I asked Philippe if his visit was work or pleasure—that is, was he spying on us—he just laughed. A textbook spy response.

Our two weeks' leave was quickly over, and we flew back to France feeling depressed. While waiting for our bags at Paris's Charles de Gaulle Airport, Smithy looked concerned after checking his cellphone messages. The section had been trying to contact all of us. Chris immediately called home, and he too confirmed the CEA had tried contacting him. Smithy called the section and informed them that we were inbound. When we entered the Calvi airport terminal, the military police were waiting for légionnaires caught out. They took Chris back to the regiment.

Smithy and I took a taxi back to the regiment, and El Wahidi informed us that the section had been put on alert. Everyone on leave was required to return to Calvi. He said he had tried calling my home phone number several times with no success. Unable to reach us, he gave up. Three of us had been caught out. Holcik was the third. The alert had been stood down days later, but it didn't matter. We were considered AWOL. We passed in front of Capitaine Desmeulles and then the CEA company capitaine. When asked where I was on leave, I replied, "Where I had asked to go, sir: Canada." The three of us from the section were each given seven days in jail.

The alert caught out many in the regiment. Consequently, the jail was full. Smithy, Holcik, and I were confined to the barracks, which was pretty cushy. The company duty NCO had us paint the odd white rock a little bit whiter and pick weeds from the company grounds, but we mostly watched *Friends* on TV, in French, in chambre 21.

We later learned that the charge was serious enough that we wouldn't be eligible to extend our service contracts. Smithy was quite irritated at the situation. He was closing on eight years' service. My home phone number was on the paperwork submitted for our approval to travel to Canada, but maybe the country code was missing a zero and the person calling didn't think to ask the operator for assistance. The whole thing seemed like overkill to me, but then again, I had gotten away with it once before so perhaps karma was doing its thing.

The charge against us was later reduced to a lesser one, meaning we could re-sign if we were given the option. Spending seven days in my room wasn't a big deal. Chris passed in front of the regiment CO and he was given thirty days' in the regiment's jail. After he served his time, Chris didn't have much sympathy for our groans over how the situation was handled.

CHAPTER TWENTY-TWO

Chad

A photo from the July 14 défilé was going around the company, and I was clearly the only one in the peloton's front row not properly aligned. WTF?! It was September 1998, and somehow months had already flown by since Bastille Day. The 2nd and 4th companies were headed to Chad, Africa, for a four-month tour in support of Opération Épervier. Its objective was to prevent Libya from destabilizing Chad and threatening France's interests.

In the novel *Beau Geste*, the title character fictitiously helped the French fight against the warlord Rabih az-Zubayr to control territory in the 1900s. But the history is accurate. Any territory the French gained was incorporated as a colony under the federation of French Equatorial Africa. In 1944, Chadians took part in the fighting for the liberation of Paris. Chad was granted independence in 1960, but France remained its most important foreign donor and patron for three decades. Eventually, official attitudes changed, and France's election of a socialist government in 1981 occurred simultaneously with civil war in Chad. France's ideological outlook against high-profile intervention in Africa would eventually evolve over the years. In the 1990s, France increased its military presence and activity in Africa up to the present day.

The fourteen section members going to Chad (a smaller team with Capitaine Desmeulles would travel to the Central African Republic to support the United Nations observers overseeing the CAR's elections) included the section's second-in-command, and newly promoted Capitaine Martin, plus NCOs El Wahidi, Lawson, Lecorre, Poux, Gazdik, and Prigent. I was part of the junior ranks going too, as well as Votte, Ciocarlan, Gehrke, Smithy, Holcik, and

Map of Chad, Africa. (*Credit*: Mike Bechthold)

Dimitri. For most, this was a second or fourth time in Chad. I, however, was looking forward to a new adventure.

Weapons, parachutes, and all equipment were loaded into shipping crates. Dimitri and I were designated as team medics, so he and I ensured we were equipped for all potential scenarios on the ground. If supporting one another, our webbing was organized so that we could find exactly what was needed. Both were identical.

We stored IV fluids in our backpacks and chest webbing. A tourniquet and two individual IV kits with plasma-glucose solutions went in the webbing side pockets. Central magazine pouches were designated for our FAMAS magazines. A grab bag for additional magazines would do the trick. Dressings, splints, stethoscope, and shears were stored in a backpack with medication for dehydration and diarrhea, along with creams for everything from sunburns to fungal infections. In addition, each team member was issued a small medical kit, which contained morphine to control shock and pain. A larger medic case was equipped with a portable stretcher, oxygen bottles, and the team's medical files. Prior to leaving, all members' vaccinations were current, and medical files were ready to be handed over to the French medical staff in Chad.

We boarded an Airbus A300 on September 12, 1998, at the Base aérienne 126 Solenzara (Air Force base built by the US Air Force during the Second World War) on the east coast of Corsica, flew over the mountains of North Africa, and across the rusty dunes of the Algerian Sahara into northern Chad. That evening, we arrived in N'Djamena, the capital. Looking out the plane's window at the view, my memories returned to my time in Bangui, as did the 40° Celsius heat that hit us when the doors were opened. In Chad, it was a dry desert air, which felt like opening an oven. I couldn't see much, since it was nighttime, but I looked forward to exploring the country's diverse landscapes, from its northern borders composed of arid mountainous terrain (part of the wider Saharan region) to the lush green savannah that blankets its southern reaches.

We boarded military TRM 2000s for the short drive to the French side of the airport, where we were shown to our barracks. The French military's fenced perimeters and guard towers were all well lit. Large berms ringed the camp, along with fencing rigged with razor wire and illumination mines.

Junior ranks shared a third-floor room with the regiment CO's radio operator, O'Connor, the very same O'Connor from my basic training. We claimed our beds and lockers, and squared away our kit. Toilets and showers were down the hall from us. Organized and hungry, we descended on the mess hall for a meal among a mix of French regular army and air force personnel. Then we made our way over to the camp's foyer for a cold beer to help us adapt to the oppressive Chadian heat. Three large ones did the trick. Later, we returned to our barracks and lifted O'Connor's bed vertically from the feet side up and watched him slide to the floor like a sack of shit. He didn't think this was funny at all, and moved rooms first thing the following day. It wasn't meant to be mean; we had different ideas about humour, I guess, three beers in.

The next morning, the photo cell briefed us on the current political atmosphere and the country's stability, including the local government's view on France's foreign policies and its interests in the region, which helped us understand our role. The political situation in Chad was assessed as stable, although we were all aware that this could change quickly. The local population's viewpoint on our presence was varied. In some situations, it was outright hostile.

Our primary objective was preparing for an evacuation of foreign nationals in the event it was required. We were issued a P4, two VLRAs, and a VAB. Holcik and I were designated VLRA drivers. One VLRA was set up as the personnel carrier, and the other was used for cargo transport. Those of us who hadn't driven the VAB before were given a crash course and drove the required kilometres around the city's outskirts to qualify for the endorsement.

This gave us time to get ourselves acclimatized. It wasn't long before we were airside boarding a C-130 Hercules and climbing to 5000 metres, the highest from which we could jump without using oxygen. I was lightheaded from the effort it took to attach my gaine and tighten my straps. I could make out the curvature of the earth as I left the Herc's ramp, jumping into the warm African air over the sand-coloured horizon.

Our DZ was situated next to a small shantytown guarded by a French military K9 section. Recently, French regular units who had jumped into the DZ had their gaine cords cut before landing. They had watched, helplessly suspended in midair, as the locals ran off

Team bivouac, Chad. (*Credit:* 2ᵉ Régiment étranger de parachutistes)

with their gear. The locals had also thrown rocks at the French units' trucks as they left the DZ.

Our 2nd and 4th companies had jumped before us. When we were loading the vehicles, the 2nd Company's head NCO briefed his légionnaires, saying that if one rock hit his trucks, they knew what to do. Sure enough, as we drove through town, some vehicles were pelted with stones. Our convoy came to an immediate stop and légionnaires dismounted. A handful of locals responsible for the rock-throwing were taught a lesson.

Next on the agenda was a three-day section training exercise. We loaded the VLRAs and started the three-hour drive east to a shooting range. The paved road soon turned to a dirt track, with large sun-baked ruts that had been carved out by larger transport trucks during the rainy season. It was a nightmare to drive on, and every bump reverberated in my back. We drove through flat and arid country, passing through small villages where smiling locals waved at us. Their lifestyle, with the most basic of amenities, was practically primitive compared to what I had seen before, even in Central

Africa. But they looked happy. These images stuck with me. I knew I had had opportunities in life well beyond what these people could even dream of.

We eventually arrived at our range, a simple dirt berm, and made bivouac around a large tree. We strung tarps between the vehicles and the tree for shade and dug a firepit for cooking. As the driver, my first responsibility was to fill the truck's fuel tanks from our jerry cans. Once that was done, my next task was equally important: dig a hole for our latrine. I walked downwind a distance into the vast expanse of savannah spread out over undulating terrain of mostly small shrubs and long dry grass. As I dug, a spider the size of my hand watched from a web it had spun in a shrub next to me.

Food was unloaded from the cargo VLRA, and the water tank towed behind it that was used for cleaning was unhitched. We had bottled water for personal consumption. Just as essential was our large cooler full of cold beer and sodas. The daily ration was two per person. Luckily, a few guys on the team enjoyed cooking, so they volunteered, making our first meal of pasta and chicken. Junior ranks generally did the food preparation and washing up afterwards. Focusing on good hygiene to avoid cross-contamination was critical. Bugs or stomach problems were prevalent in these regions, and an incident could bring down the whole team in a matter of hours.

In the evenings, a two-hour guard shift was organized. Our capitaine was included in the rotation; this is something unheard of in a combat company. The key was remembering where your replacement slept because waking up the wrong teammate in the middle of the night didn't go over well. The last shift started the morning fire and made the coffee.

Up early, we took our time getting organized, eating, and packing our kit. Everyone knew what needed to get done. We then zeroed our weapons and test-fired support weapons, transitioning to foot and vehicle contact drills. A Puma helicopter arrived later that afternoon in a cloud of dust. Sure enough, in the Pavlovian way, the sound got my adrenaline pumping. On board, with our parachutes, gaines, and FAMASs attached, we started climbing to 4000 metres. Sitting close to the flight deck for the day jump, I watched the pilots' movements on the flight controls. On the evening flight, I could make out the faint glow of small villages and their fires flickering in the darkness through the Puma's windows. That jump was particularly memorable. The lack of light pollution meant the stars were so much brighter than anywhere else I had seen. Free fall in the evening's warm air and landing in soft sand was undeniably a rush.

On our return to N'Djamena, the trucks were cleaned and fuelled, and the jerry cans and water tank were replenished. All the team equipment was cleaned, as well as weapons, which we returned to the armoury. This outing had been a test run for a longer trip that was planned in order to help identify potential problems and make the necessary adjustments. For example, particular tools were needed because the VLRAs inevitably gave us mechanical problems. The trip also helped us figure out what small things were essential, such as gloves for handling diesel-soaked jerry cans, or goggles for the dust, which was a big issue. We required covers for our weapons and a way to protect our ammunition magazines. A coating of dust was enough to jam a weapon. Black plastic garbage bags did the trick. Even though the "shower" consisted of a bucket of water in the field, having sand in your toes for the rest of the day sucks, so flip-flops solved that issue. Long johns helped ward off the cold of desert nights as our standard-issue military sleeping bags didn't do much. And last, but not least, we desperately needed padding for our asses. Those deeply rutted roads were enough to reduce any man to tears.

Something I found interesting and different was the camp's employment program, whereby local men, women, and teenagers, or "boys," as they were referred to, were hired to wash our clothing and clean our barrack rooms. They were paid a set wage controlled by the camp's administration. It was a good service and injected some much-needed money into the local economy. So, we hired Abbo. He worked hard, and we gave him any extras we had, or things we didn't really need that he could use.

On weekends, légionnaires could frequent the city's "authorized" bars and restaurants, all of which were within a small city block. On weeknights, we were confined to camp or the Rose des Vents, a local restaurant and bar with a dance floor—and working girls. This was new to me too. CFB Wainwright didn't have a Rose des Vents. In the age of AIDS awareness, the women were subject to medical checks by the French military hospital if they wanted to frequent the Rose. Sexual encounters were not advised, but it was a reality, so the French military exercised precautions. The women were ostensibly self-employed, and the military's only involvement was providing free medical visits. A lot of the woman were from Somalia and Ethiopia. Some were tall, elegant, and attractive, and they put in a lot of effort to dress the part.

Inevitably, it wasn't long before légionnaires were getting into trouble at the Rose des Vents. Making it back to camp by curfew was the main issue for some légionnaires. So the section was given a secondary Military Police (MP) tasking. Every evening, an NCO and junior rank wearing MP armbands were sent to the Rose to ensure someone was looking out for the légionnaires. This wasn't about ruining the fun, but more about making sure they didn't have *too much* fun. Clearing the bar at the 0130 hours became a challenge. Prigent and I concluded that a good dose of pepper spray would speed things up. It took less than two minutes for everyone to be outside. At 0129 hours, everyone inside knew we went chemical; however, some légionnaires took this as a direct challenge, making it a point to sit inside drinking their beers for as long as they could stand it. The girls were smart and always left on time or early.

One evening, the bartender at the Rose asked me if I wanted a drink. Since I was on duty and armed I said, "I can't drink alcohol, but I'll have a Coke, please." He replied, "OK, a Nigerian it is then." I reiterated, "I want a bottle of Coke." He smiled and returned with a bottle of Coke. After a sip, I realized the bottle was half-filled with whisky. This was a Nigerian. I figured, OK fine, one wouldn't do much harm. Weeks later, I overheard an NCO telling Capitaine Martin that "Nigerians make the Rose MP task a lot easier." The capitaine looked confused. I had to laugh. Very true.

CHAPTER TWENTY-THREE

Biltine

We loaded ten days of supplies into our VLRAs and headed east toward the town of Melfi. Our aim was to map GPS coordinates for certain locations, predominantly dirt landing strips, but the exercise was mostly a way to get out of camp and into the open savannah. We spent four days straight driving through the grassy plains, with the P4 and VLRAs spread out at distance to minimize dust. At times the vehicles had to slow down to a walking pace because driving the deeply rutted roads and washboard was not only uncomfortable, it could destroy a vehicle at speed. On the good portions we accelerated as best we could to make up for lost time. Finally, we arrived in the town of Bokoro, made up of old colonial and shanty homes, where we purchased fresh fruit, vegetables, local beer named Gala, and sodas. We decided to avoid the meat market, however. Everything was covered in flies. The vendors' vain attempts to brush flies away from their mouths, noses, and the meat made it even more nauseating. The smell didn't help either.

The road continued south to Melfi, passing an imposing hill shaped like a lion before eventually disappearing, thanks to neglect. A footpath winding through the high elephant grass was all that remained. The GPS gave us the direction to follow, and we drove at walking pace in the long grass. Progress was slow. The smell of smoke and the sight of burning in the distance indicated a brush fire, and soon the elephant grass gave way to scorched savannah, with isolated brush fires all around us. We drove around the fires on blackened earth, avoiding smoking tree stumps. A gazelle broke cover and bolted across our path. Farther along, we saw more gazelles sleeping under the shade of an acacia tree. Elephant tracks were clearly visible, but sadly, the animals had already headed down into Central Africa in search of water.

It wasn't long before we had to stop to change a flat tire. The P4 and the other VLRA had the same issue. We continued along and came to a small village straight out of *National Geographic*. Children playing on the outskirts of the village bolted when they saw our vehicles. Eventually their curiosity got the better of them, and they quietly came closer, hiding behind their parents until it was clear that we weren't slave traders.

The capitaine introduced himself to the village elder, a thin man who appeared to be in his seventies but was likely younger. He seemed happy enough to see us. The children watched, some wearing tattered clothing or no clothing at all, and stared at us intently. For some, it was their first time seeing white men. The elder invited us to visit his village, composed of just a dozen mud huts with straw roofs and surrounded by a fence made of tree branches.

The villagers and livestock all lived together. The men wore shorts made of animal hide, and the women were dressed in similarly made skirts. They all wore charm necklaces to ward off evil spirits.

Capitaine Martin asked the elder, "How far is it to Melfi?" He pointed and replied, "It's a five-day walk." The capitaine thanked the man for his hospitality, and we left behind rations and water for the villagers. The kids regrouped and ran behind us in the dust for a short distance, waving goodbye. We then came upon nomads travelling with their cattle and sheep and agreed on a trade. They would cook one of their young goats, stuffed with rice and potatoes provided by us, in exchange for a large carton of rations and several packs of bottled water, along with some rice and potatoes for their own consumption. My eyes had been opened to a fascinating new world that day. In the evening, I sat looking at the Chadian sky with a stomach full of delicious goat, drinking my cold beer. I was content with my surroundings.

The following day, our flat tires left us stranded. We had used all our spares. With nightfall approaching, we made camp. Smithy contacted N'Djamena by Morse code, and later that evening, we heard the distant drone of a C-160 Transall. We turned on our vehicles'

Melfi, Chad, Africa. (*Credit:* 2ᵉ Régiment étranger de parachutistes)

headlights, and the Transall made a first pass, then a second, at which point a tire attached to a white parachute appeared out of the night sky, landing some 200 metres from us. Then the crew, keen to do better, made a correction. A set of tires with glow sticks attached landed even closer. The Transall made its final pass, a low one that got all of our attention and approval. We replaced the flats and were ready for the next day's travel.

Our GPS indicated we were close to Melfi. Eventually, we found the town and spent the morning there, manually filling our water trailer and jerry cans from the town's well. A large crowd of villagers surrounded us. I watched them watching us. The African bush, the villages, the nomads, the wildlife—this stark contrast between beauty and hardship left an indelible impression on me. This trip would be the highlight of my time in Africa, just being among people going about their lives.

After ten days, we arrived back in N'Djamena, looking forward to a shower, clean clothes, and a hot meal. Abbo had his work cut out for him with our dirty combats and all the rest piled up at the end of our bunks. I had been asking Capitaine Martin (pestering, he may have said) if a trip into central Chad was being considered. As it turned out, we were soon on our way to the Abéché Garrison in the Ouaddaï region of east-central Chad. We boarded a C-130 with our parachutes and gaines. At 4500 metres, we stepped off the ramp and landed well grouped in the grass next to the Abéché runway, adjacent to the small French military camp.

The C-130 landed as we walked to the main hangar with our parachutes and gaines. We retrieved our equipment from the Herc and loaded the two VLRAs that were issued to us for our time in Abéché. We were then shown to our barracks. The camp was simple and commanded by a Legion officer, Capitaine Renouf, from the 1er REC (Cavalry), and his 2iC, an NCO from the REP. Two French regular 120mm heavy mortar teams were also present. We promptly located the camp's small mess hall and its foyer for a cold beer. I looked forward to the week ahead as I sat on the patio looking up at the stars.

Back in the C-130 the following morning, we were ready to jump onto a dirt landing strip adjacent to the old Biltine Legion Fort, another compelling piece of Legion history. In 1909, French troops invaded the Wadai Sultanate (also called Ouaddaï Kingdom), present-day Chad, and established a garrison at Abéché, among other locations. Like many Saharan forts, it was a blend of medieval and newer architecture from its time, made of mud bricks with a large gateway dominated by two imposing towers. If ever there was a place to draw comparisons to *Beau Geste*, it was here.

The exercise was to secure the landing strip and allow the C-130 to execute what is known as an assault landing, after which the 120mm mortar teams would exit the aircraft and set up their mortars ready to fire. The C-130's ramp lowered, and we jumped in two small teams, spaced apart by three seconds. As we started to descend under canopy, villagers began to gather and surrounded us when we landed. In a knee-jerk reaction, I quickly glanced over at the fort's outer walls, looking for dead légionnaires propped up in firing positions. The C-130 landed with its engines in full reverse, churning up a huge halo of Chadian sand. It came to a quick stop, with the mortar teams immediately off-loading. Exercise completed.

The C-130 cut its engines, and once the 120s were reloaded, we all flew back to Abéché. That night, we debriefed at the camp's foyer. Abéché was all right in my books, and I said to Capitaine Martin in a respectful manner, "I told ya, sir."

The following morning, I was awoken by a P4 approaching at speed, honking its horn. Shouts for a medic soon followed. I jumped out of bed, threw on my combat pants and runners, and sprinted outside. A panicked regular force caporal-chef asked me to follow him. Dimitri and I grabbed our webbing and jumped into our P4 with Smithy at the wheel. We followed the caporal-chef to the garrison's medical building, where we found several people standing around another P4. Dimitri approached the casualty, who was lying in the back of the vehicle. I could see his legs hanging out the rear door, clad in torn blood-soaked pants. My assumption was that he had been hit and dragged by a vehicle in town.

Dimitri yelled for an IV, which I prepared and handed to him. I was then able to see what we were dealing with. The victim's right arm was severed at the elbow, his bare chest was pockmarked with impacts, and his face missing from the chin up. The footwell of the P4 was filled with his blood. A quick assessment revealed that his jugular had been severed and his circulatory system had collapsed due to the massive blood loss. The military doctor arrived soon after us, pronouncing the victim deceased almost immediately. His body was quickly covered with a sheet, and we moved him from the P4 to the medical building. And that was that.

Apparently, during a live-fire exercise that morning, an AC 58 anti-tank grenade hadn't detonated on impact. The range procedure is to wait thirty minutes and then destroy the grenade in a controlled explosion. But you don't touch it. For some unknown reason, the victim had picked up the grenade and it exploded. When I heard his name, it rang a bell. He had been an NCO at the 1st Company and left behind a wife and two daughters. This tragedy was a timely reminder to all of us that if you get complacent, it can kill you.

That evening, we sat in the foyer, drinking our beer. I didn't sleep very well that night; the sight and smell of burned flesh lingered in my memory. Ironically, we were on the range the following day and a 120mm LRAC anti-tank round, which is fired from a reusable tube, fell short and failed to detonate. Capitaine Martin warned us not to touch it when we found it. He needn't have bothered. The round was found without delay and properly destroyed.

When we arrived back at camp after our range day, news awaited. The situation in the Republic of the Congo was heating up, and both REP companies in Chad were on alert. The GCP was to return to N'Djamena. Before our flight back to the capital, we met at the foyer's barbecue pit for a farewell gathering. I felt that Dimitri was ready for a Canadian tradition, so I introduced him to the art of shotgunning a beer, or three.

In N'Djamena, we prepared our kit in anticipation of a deployment into Brazzaville. Capitaine Martin was then summoned to HQ. This was good news, I thought. Would we jump into the Congo, an actual operational jump? Unfortunately, the situation in Brazzaville had calmed, and we were stood down. No jump today. With the tour at an end, we were part of the first flight to leave the country. Chad was a memorable experience with some great jumps, and I'd never forget the drive through its countryside. Before I had joined the Legion, these types of experiences were beyond my limited and immature imagination.

Abbo did well by us, too. We gave him all our civilian clothes, CDs, Discmans, and our leftover local currency.

We landed back at the base aérienne 126 Solenzara on January 20, 1999, and Corsica's views, colours, and smells were most welcomed after almost four months away from her.

CHAPTER TWENTY-FOUR

Alps

Back in Calvi, we all returned from leave, and got back into section routine. Capitaine Desmeulles informed us that we were heading to Vergio, the regiment's winter training centre in the Corsican mountains. Here we'd prepare for the *brevet skieur militaire* (BSM), the French military's primary mountain warfare course in the French Alps. Orders were given, and the section's VLRA and TRM were loaded. On April 12, 1999, we left Calvi in the early morning rain, driving several hours to the Vergio training centre. When we arrived, I was surprised to see a three-storey Alpine-style chalet— a great surprise. Inside was a large kitchen and eating area, with two smaller military-style barrack blocks adjacent to the chalet with ample bunk beds.

Once settled in, we were issued our skis, sealskins, poles, and boots. After lunch we were introduced to our 2nd Company training NCO, a Swiss national. We made our way up through the trees on our skis and sealskins to the Col de Vergio (Verghju) ski hill at 1425 metres, with its five runs. The April temperatures were low enough that the falling snow was sticking and the hill was open for business. Skiing skills varied within the section, and an evaluation resulted in the creation of three groups for the week's training program.

We gathered outside the chalet the next morning in the dark with our skis, winter Gore-Tex combats, and heavy backpacks. Following our instructors, we ascended the slope at a quick pace, and left our skis at the Castel du Vergio (ski hill chalet). In the strong wind gusts and freezing rain, we continued our ascent to the 2500-metre peak with our backpacks using our boots and poles. My legs and lungs were feeling the altitude and the pace, but by the week's end we were all accustomed to both. The Mediterranean sun eventually made a comeback, and as we worked our way into the Corsican alpine with our sealskins, several of us were left with painful burns to the eyes from the glare off the icy snow that resulted from freezing rain. Our military-issued sunglasses were absolute crap. Never again, I told myself. That was as uncomfortable as one could be.

In early March, with the training completed, we boarded a C-130 with the 2nd Company (Mountain Warfare) for the flight to southern France. On the plane, Capitaine Martin informed me that I would join the Chef d'équipe haute montagne hiver (the Winter Alpine Pathfinder Qualification). It was being run simultaneously for 2nd Company caporals who had several BSMs under their belts. I was pleased and up for the challenge.

We finished the journey by truck, arriving in Briançon in southeastern France's Haute-Alpes region, home to the 159e RIA-CNAM (Régiment d'infanterie alpine—Centre national aguerrissement combat montagne) and the Diables Rouges hockey team. I sat in the back of the TRM as we drove through the town in the chilly weather, wishing I could zip more of my body into my Gore-Tex jacket. Briançon's cafés, restaurants, and sporting goods stores were full of winter ski vacationers, and perhaps the odd hockey enthusiast. I spotted the hockey rink, which stands out like in any town, and I also noticed that the movie *Saving Private Ryan* was showing at the town's cinema. Excellent. Freezing or not, I was happy to be in the Alps again.

We drove through the 159 RIA's gates and past four-storey stone buildings surrounding a large open parade square. The garrison design was typical of many built for the military leading up to the Second World War. We were shown down the long corridors to our respective barrack rooms. The second-floor room, which would sleep sixteen of us, had large windows looking out to the Alps.

Equipment was issued from stores, and we began arranging lockers and getting our backpacks loaded with a week's worth of supplies. The ski bindings issued to me were too big for my ski boots, so I ran around trying to rectify the problem. But with everyone busy preparing, no one was that interested in my plight, and the storeroom was closed. The first day's orders were soon posted. We would meet our instructors bright and early in the morning,

Chef d'équipe haute montagne hiver, Winter Alpine Pathfinder Qualification, French Alps, heading up. (*Credit:* Joel Struthers)

then trek up the mountain to the regiment's alpine training facility. Great. My bindings problem would have to be dealt with later.

At first light, trucks transported us to the main parking lot at the base of the Serre Chevalier ski hill, at 1200 meters, with its freshly groomed runs still untouched by the day's skiers. We all split off to meet our separate training groups. I joined the others for the Pathfinder entry test. The 2nd Company caporals were all tall and fit; they looked the part, which is always encouraging. Skis and skins on, up the mountain we went in single file, following the instructor's pace, which was damn quick, virtually a straight line up the hill. WTF?!

Our spacing soon spread out, and I found myself sucking for air as I watched the instructor and a small group pull away. All I could do at that point was put my head down, dig deep, and try not to throw up on my skis. Three-quarters of the way up the hill—and a good forty-five minutes to an hour later—our instructor stopped and waited. I finally arrived third from last. Brutal. I was embarrassed. These guys were in shape. The distance between the first and last guy wasn't that big. But still, a gap existed, and I knew I was being watched; I was that guy from the GCP.

I could feel the effects of the altitude. I was short of breath, slightly dizzy, and nauseated. It wasn't my greatest moment, which surprised me at first because I had felt fine at Vergio, but the Alps, after all, were higher. Serre Chevalier's ski runs stopped at 2800 meters, well for today. The instructor then skied down the hill a short distance, and we were instructed to descend one by one for evaluation. Good; maybe I could redeem myself. I needed a decent victory after my poor performance on the ascent.

I was the stronger skier for the downhill portion, and the next evaluation was *off-piste* (to the side of the groomed hill) for a descent into powder and moguls. I waited at the top and watched the guys ski down with some difficulty. Feeling confident, I figured an aggressive descent would be impressive. Midway down, I hit a mogul and my right boot released from the improperly fitted binding. I hit the snow hard and tumbled the rest of the way down the hill in a whirlwind of powder, poles flying into the air.

I had clearly scored full marks for style and control up to that point, but zero points on my landing. I even got a few free laughs. After a drink of water and an energy bar, we put the sealskins back on and made our way up the hill to the alpine training facility. This time, the pace was a little less aggressive. At the top, three guys were quickly dropped from the course. Luckily, I survived and was still in the game.

The alpine training facility was part of the Secteur fortifié du dauphiné (the Fortified Sector of the Dauphiné), the Alpine Line extension of the Maginot Line. This region had seen some fighting between Italy's 2nd Mountain Infantry Division Sforzesca and the French during Italy's invasion of France in 1940. Our accommodations were constructed in stone and concrete, with old gun emplacements, bunkers, and tunnels built to last. My fascination with fortifications was amply satisfied here too.

The Legion's 2nd Company arrived with the section sometime after us, and we were all shown to our cramped sleeping area.

Légionnaires were chosen for kitchen duties, and a plentiful high-carb lunch was soon served. That afternoon, we were briefed on what the Pathfinder course curriculum involved and introduced to some of our safety equipment. ARVA avalanche-locator transmitters were issued, and we covered the proper techniques in finding a skier buried by an avalanche. We were also shown how to outfit our emergency sled with harness, which we loaded with extra rope, spare skis, poles, a medic pack, and a communications radio. Then we took turns skiing with the sled and making a short descent, followed by an ascent. In the evenings, our meals of pasta and red wine were hearty and quite delicious. The downside, however, was that the stone fortification we ate inside reeked, unsurprisingly, of old wet socks and farts.

Our mornings usually involved a lot of waiting outside in the dark before our instructor was ready to start the day's training. Temperatures were well below zero, and some of the guys would dress for the cold, which was problematic. Once the physical effort kicked in and the sun started its ascent, trying to take off a pair of long johns while you're making your way up a mountain on skis is tough. One of our guys overheated for this exact reason, providing us with the perfect opportunity to use the emergency sled to transport him back to the fort! The best option was to dress light and freeze your balls off early, but be a lot more comfortable later.

We were shown rescue techniques in the event of a skier falling into a crevasse. Then we climbed a narrow ridgeline using metal crampons attached to our bindings, later skiing down to a glacier avoiding crevasses. I didn't like crevasses. As a youngster skiing with my French ski school course, I fell and started sliding downhill toward a large well-marked crevasse with fast-flowing water below. The military ski instructor caught my arm not far from the ledge. That memory of trying to stop my descent and seeing the fast-approaching void stuck with me.

One day, an avalanche dog with her handler came along, and we worked with him to refine the German shepherd's skills. At lunch, we would usually find a nice vantage point to look at the amazing views or the clouds three inches from our noses, but being in the Alpine was a highlight of the course.

After a few days, and a good number of vertical metres logged, it was time for an attempt at the BSM endurance test. This was an individually timed ascent and descent on a designated course we were required to complete for our BSM/Pathfinder qualification. Following our instructor up the mountain, we trailed his usual mad pace and reached the top close behind, but fucked (tired, in soldier parlance). The instructor was always carrying additional gear, I think to show us that we were never quite at his level. We didn't argue that fact. Finally, we skied the designated downhill track as fast as we could.

We were then given a Sunday off in preparation for a live-fire shoot exercise to test our new pathfinding skills. On Monday morning, we climbed into the alpine for a night in a snow shelter, and an early-morning shoot the following day. On Wednesday, we skied the BSM exam. Leaving the start gate at one-minute intervals, I was trying my utmost to keep up a good pace, but confident knowing that there was a way to make up time—on the descent. On the descent I tucked, passing several course-mates (and offering a few words of rude encouragement), and finished strong. On the last two days we continued with the sealskins and worked on our back-country skiing, taking advantage of the Alps offerings. Week two completed.

On Saturday night, we were given a pass to hit the town, so the GCP caporals and a few of our NCOs agreed that we'd go see *Saving Private Ryan*. Excellent. Mid-movie, when the wrong Private Ryan is told his brothers were killed in the war and he's confused because one of his brothers is still in grade school, Lawson's phone rang. He left the theatre to take the call, then promptly summoned the rest of us outside. We had to return to barracks immediately. Goddamn it!

When we arrived, Capitaine Martin briefed us on the situation. A French gendarme at the French ambassador's residence in Brazzaville, Republic of the Congo, had been shot dead by a paramilitary rebel. The COS (1er RPIMa) had been sent to secure the ambassador's residence, and the GCP would relieve them. Capitaine Martin designated those of us who needed to return to Calvi the following day to prepare. I was chosen. We were dismissed and told to be ready in the morning. I handed in my issued kit, collected my FAMAS from the armoury, and packed my gear. Dimitri wasn't chosen. He

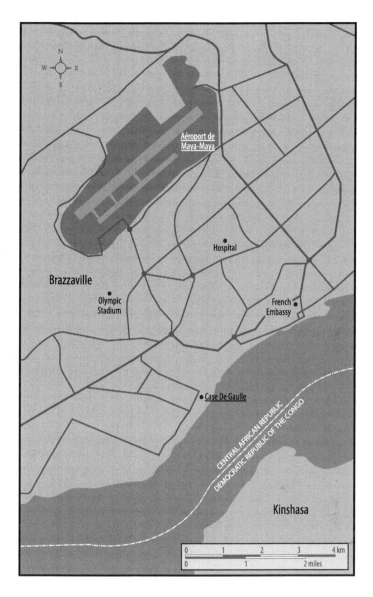

Map of Brazzaville. (*Credit:* Mike Bechthold)

looked like he might just jump from the barrack's second-storey window. I felt his pain. The final BSM exercise, which ran the entire following week, didn't inspire anyone.

I had to admit actually that I was surprised at being selected as my name had popped up in the officers' mess apparently for the wrong reasons. When I was issued the same crappy military sunglasses that left me with burned eyes in Vergio, my newly acquired civilian sunglasses actually designed to protect your eyeballs took on that new role. Early in the course, the 2nd Company CO had noticed them and pointed out that they weren't standard military issue, and I was told to wear my military-issue sunglasses.

Well, this happened on two occasions, and my apparent insubordination made its way back to Capitaine Martin. I got an earful from him, so I made certain I didn't get caught a third time. My solution was to always have both pairs of sunglasses with me, and when I was in proximity to the 2nd Company CO, I made the appropriate switch. "Cooperate, graduate," as they say. I was awarded my Chef d'équipe de haute montagne hiver qualification anyway, and more importantly, I could still see properly.

The following morning, ten of us left Briançon for Nice by train and a ferry back to Corsica.

CHAPTER TWENTY-FIVE

Case de Gaulle

With barely time to breathe, we had a fast turnaround in Calvi. Within hours, our kit and weapons were loaded onto our VLRA for another ferry trip back to the mainland, followed by the drive to the Groupement headquarters in Toulouse.

The armour-plated (COS) C-160 Transall left Toulouse Airport on April 1, 1999, with three GCP teams aboard. We wore our GCP-issued combats, jump smock, personal webbing, backpacks with section weapons, and duffel bags in hand. I awoke from my sleeping spot heaped on a cargo pallet, returned to my seat, and belted myself in. We were about to land and fuel up in Tenerife, one of Spain's Canary Islands. We then flew to Dakar, Senegal, where we spent the night at the French Air Force base, and flew on to Libreville, Gabon, the following day. The morning after, we were in the Transall again for the short flight into Brazzaville.

After an extremely steep approach, we touched down in Brazzaville, and the ramp lowered as we taxied to the terminal. All I could see from my window was the long elephant grass framing the runway and green rolling hills in the distance. As the Transall swung around on the taxiway, I caught a glimpse of Soviet-era Mig-21 fighter jets, Mil-17 helicopters, and a tired-looking T-55 tank sitting in the grass. All of them had seen better days. When we came to a stop, a few COS teammates and Direction générale de la sécurité extérieur (DGSE) greeted us.

This was terrain where Pierre Savorgnan de Brazza, a French empire builder, competed with agents of Belgian King Leopold's International Congo Association (later it became the Republic of the Congo) for the control of the Congo River basin. In the 1880s, treaties were secured with the main rulers on the river's right bank, placing their lands under French protection. Brazzaville, which was named for the Italian-born explorer, was then selected as the federal capital of French Equatorial Africa (AEF).

During the Second World War, French Equatorial Africa sided with Free French President Charles de Gaulle, and Brazzaville became its symbolic capital from 1940 to 1943. In 1944, the Brazzaville Conference heralded a period of major reform in its colonial policy,[17] including the abolition of forced labour, and giving citizenship to its colonial subjects. Postwar expansion of colonial administrative and infrastructure was beneficial, and the Congo's independence was granted in 1960.

As I stepped off the ramp, I noticed that the airport tower and terminal were stippled with impacts of different calibres from recent fighting. For whatever reason I just found these types of things to be cool. Parked next to us were a Soviet-made AN-26 Curl and a Libya-registered AN-12 Candid. We unloaded our equipment and boarded trucks for the ride to the Case de Gaulle, the residence named for French President Charles de Gaulle, who lived here at periods during the Second World War. Now it was the French ambassador's home—and soon to be ours.

Sitting on our equipment in the back of the open-bed truck, we passed government troops manning checkpoints close to the airport. President Denis Sassou Nguesso's paramilitary group, referred to as the Cobras, controlled certain neighbourhoods within the city as well as the airport. Other areas were controlled by groups with similarly absurd names like the Ninjas or the Rambos. But they were no joke. Life was cheap here, and these groups had all been involved in combat and numerous atrocities.

As we approached the city's centre, Smithy pointed out the buildings used by the Congolese army as firing positions during the ambush. He also showed us the exact area where Gilles had been killed. I could feel the weight of that section's history among my teammates, many of whom had been there that day. We then entered the Empoko neighbourhood, where the presidential palace and government buildings were located, and the area most heavily affected by the recent fighting.

Case de Gaulle, the French ambassador's residence, Brazzaville, Congo.
(*Credit:* Joel Struthers)

Empoko was a ghost town. We wove our way between scorched
and abandoned vehicles, and alongside burned-out houses. Mongrel
and malnourished dogs prowled the streets. We passed a lone police
checkpoint before the road ended abruptly at the high banks of the
Congo River. Across its churning, muddy waters was Kinshasa, the
capital of the Democratic Republic of the Congo. The fresh smell of
the river and the surrounding greenery were a reprieve from the
pervasive stench of death and rotting garbage.

The Case de Gaulle was situated in the Bacongo district overlooking the river.[18] Built in 1941, it was referred to as *la capitale de la
France libre*, or the capital of free France. This was France's land.
With its modernist architecture, the sandstone building stood out
from its surroundings. It was protected by a large, 3-metre-high
concrete wall topped with barbed wire, and each corner had observation bunkers. Construction was ongoing to reinforce the wall as
well as the main gate. Sandbags had been placed along the wall of
the main residence, and all the windows and the patio had been

protected in the same way. A .50-calibre heavy machine gun and bunker sat directly to the side of the building, covering the compound's main entrance.

The inner grounds of the Case de Gaulle were spacious. Gardens offered a clear view across the Congo River, with a vantage point on Kinshasa. Large mango trees surrounded by lush green lawns provided shade from the fierce equatorial sun.

The 8ᵉ Régiment de parachutistes d'infanterie de marine (RPIMa) team would live inside the ambassador's residence. We would move into the residence of the assistant governor, who had returned to France with his family. Our one-storey home sat in the far corner of the Case de Gaulle's inner grounds. It had been sufficiently sandbagged, with additional bunkers covering its perimeter. NCOs and caporals were split into separate sleeping quarters. Smithy, Ursa, and I shared a room. Capitaine Martin and Karine's doubled as an ops room. The residence had a small swimming pool at the back, which sat empty. It was surrounded by the sprawling lawn, which sloped down to the rear of the perimeter wall.

The real emphasis was on securing the Case's perimeter wall, but in a worst-case scenario, we could use our residence as a fighting position. The second team, the 35ᵉ Régiment d'artillery parachutiste (RAP), would move into a smaller compound closer to the French Embassy in downtown Brazzaville for its protection.

We decided to operate a twenty-four-hour roster at the Case de Gaulle, with one team on and one team off. Additional support weapons and ammunition were handed out, and a storeroom was organized with radios that were issued and tested. Then we implemented an immediate action plan and completed an exercise with both GCP teams taking up their appropriate firing positions. It was agreed that once we had settled in, we could review and reorganize our strategy accordingly.

My first guard shift was that evening. Armed with my FAMAS, NVGs, webbing, and small ops pack, I made the short walk to my observation bunker on the perimeter's wall. I was already sweating from the humidity. Days prior, we had been freezing in the Alps. Tonight, we were roasting in the Congo. I gave the correct answer to my teammate's verbal challenge as I approached the OP.

From inside the OP, I took in the view of Kinshasa's city lights across the Congo River, which divided the two countries. The bright lights of the capital of the Democratic Republic of the Congo starkly contrasted with Brazzaville's dimly lit, smoky streets. Crickets, other insects, and a tree frog somewhere made a racket that was my background noise for the next two hours.

Recently, the neighbourhood outside my OP had witnessed intense fighting and some of the worst atrocities imaginable. The odd tracer streaked across the sky, a reminder that the situation wasn't over, and it could flare up at any time. It was only a week ago that a Ninja paramilitary had snuck up on the gendarme and shot him at point-blank range from over the Case de Gaulle's front wall. These guys were fearless and unpredictable, often jacked up on narcotics or alcohol. They also believed they had magic powers, and that any bullets fired at them would miss.

The openings of our OPs were protected by wire caging to keep a hand grenade from being lobbed in; however, it wouldn't stop an RPG-7, that was certain. From my vantage point, I watched dogs roaming the streets, pawing at garbage and barking at the shadows. Smoke from cooking fires drifted across the open yard in front of me, carried by the heavy, humid night air.

Gunfire within a couple hundred metres of me caught my full attention. I heard the crack and thump of the bullet. There was some shouting, then silence. Nothing came of it. This was additional background noise you got used to. I watched the shadows, listening, and trying to get a feel for my surroundings. Then came another sudden explosion of noise. Something had hit the OP roof above me—hard.

Immediately, my heart rate went well past the red line into transient. I instinctively ducked down and took off my FAMAS's safety. What the fuck was that? As I tried to figure out what had just happened, I heard something heavy rolling on the tin roof above. The softball-sized object dropped off the ledge with a dull thud. I immediately realized what it was—a ripe mango that had fallen from the tree above. Many more mango alerts followed, but I kept my cool. After my two-hour shift was completed, I handed the OP over to my teammate, not mentioning the mango mortars. Let him enjoy that experience. I cleared my weapon, reintroduced the magazine, and climbed into my sleeping bag.

Routine was soon established. During off-duty hours, we did as we wished. We worked out, slept, and watched movies. Our food was prepared by a local cook who was hired to keep us well fed. His meals were good: chicken, fries, fish, pasta, and since we were in Africa, lots of fresh fruit. The fridge was filled with cold sodas and local beer. We ate as a team, and set aside portions for the guys on guard.

Discussions at the table soon led to the issue of the numerous mangy-looking dogs loitering around the grounds and perimeter. Since the start of conflict, many of these animals had fed off dead bodies that lay in the streets, and the idea of getting bitten by a rabid dog wasn't something anyone liked. Capitaine Martin decided that if anyone saw a dog inside the perimeter, I would be called to dispatch it with my MP5. This wasn't a task I enjoyed at all, and I made sure it was done as humanely as possible.

One evening, a call required that I use Capitaine Martin's MP5. I tracked down the poor emaciated dog and aimed the MP5's passive laser at his head. When I pulled the trigger, the round impacted the dog's midsection, which didn't kill it. I swiftly put the poor animal out of its misery and disposed of its body in a black garbage bag. Then I checked the MP5's laser to ensure the missed shot wasn't my error. It wasn't; the MP5's laser wasn't properly sighted.

I returned to the accommodations where everyone was sitting at the dinner table eating. I said, "This MP5 wasn't centred. What the fuck's up with that?" Karine, our head NCO for the tour, gave me a quick look and check, which clearly said, "Stand down, Struthers."

Our capitaine was more flight than fight. That's how I felt, anyway. The MP5 wasn't the real issue, it was the attitude. If we thought of ourselves as "elite," then we should act it. I looked at soldiering as a combination of aptitude and the access to the right training, but most importantly, one's attitude. When getting thrown into the shit, reaction comes down to a fight-or-flight instinct. I believe we're born with that—it's not taught—but it's refined with training. Just because I can run 30 kilometres with a backpack doesn't mean I'm a better soldier than the next guy, or vice versa. A soldier prepares for the fight, and it doesn't stop.

One evening, the sound of a FAMAS's full automatic fire jolted me from my sleeping bag. There's a distinct difference in the sound of a FAMAS firing and an AK-47. Grabbing my webbing, vest, and helmet, I ran to my designated bunker. The firing continued, and I waited, sweating and still breathing heavily from sprinting to my position. Word over the radio mentioned an OP at the main entrance had taken incoming rounds. Karine and Brook were sent to search a building outside the compound where they believed the shots originated from. The building was empty, and there were no signs of any 7.62mm casings.

We all remained in position for an hour or so before we were given the order to stand down. The following day, word came through that a Congolese army patrol had surprised a group of Ninjas not far from President Nguesso's palace, and the subsequent exchange of fire most likely explained last night's incoming rounds. Time for a team meeting. Proper fire control topic number one, given that a magazine and a half of ammunition was spent with no target in sight was a bit overzealous. Fair enough. I think that someone was already bored of the routine.

One afternoon, the French ambassador dropped in to say hello. He was always wearing a bow tie, which befit his ambassadorial status. On occasion he stopped and talked to us while we were on duty. He had been truly saddened by the gendarme's recent death, and I could tell he and his wife were relieved that French soldiers were on site. Every week, a military flight from Gabon or Chad would arrive with fresh provisions and equipment for both the embassy and the GCP teams. We shared the trips to the airport. It was a welcomed change of pace and a chance to get outside the Case de Gaulle's walls.

Capitaine Martin, NCOs Karine, Testaniere, and de la Chappelle, and junior ranks Bercia, Figaro, Smith, Gehrke, Holcik, and I all sat around the TV one evening watching the French news. Lasko and Brook were on guard duty. The topic of discussion was the French government posturing to deploy troops into Kosovo. In anticipation, the Groupement was given a tentative "standby." In preparation, we had biweekly lessons in Serbo-Croatian, a luxury of having teammates with homegrown language skills. We freshened up on our Soviet-era military hardware recognition, looking at slide after slide of their armoured vehicles and artillery pieces to refine our general knowledge. This kept us busy and motivated, which was much needed. I suggested learning more songs. Capitaine Martin didn't see the humour in that.

NATO eventually deployed troops into Kosovo, as did France, and we watched the COS, the Legion's 2ᵉ REI (Régiment étranger d'infanterie), 1ᵉʳ REC (Régiment étranger cavalarie), and numerous other French regular regiments participate. The REP was not involved, and even more surprisingly, neither was the Groupement. Unfortunately, this didn't help the growing stagnant feeling within the team.

The Case guard duty continued, and I was partnered with Sergent-Chef de la Chappelle, whom I found to be smart and very easygoing. His father, in fact, had spent time in a military prison for his part in the Algerian putsch.

I turned twenty-eight. There was no cake or celebration, just more guard duty, and maybe the runs.

CHAPTER TWENTY-SIX

Déjà Vu

When our three months in Brazzaville were up, a replacement team arrived. But several months later, we returned. Same job. This time, though, the rains had transformed the city into a lush mix of vegetation. The fragrant smell of new growth and ripe fruit was overpowering. The neighbourhood around the Case de Gaulle had been cleaned of rubble and garbage. And as we drove down the road, I saw that shops and bars had sprung up alongside. Brazzaville was alive once more. People were drinking and listening to loud music. Soccer fields were full of kids and adults playing. What a difference a few months of relative calm in the city made. These were happier times.

The Case de Gaulle had an improved perimeter and proper OPs with ballistic glass installed. The sandbags that lined the ambassador's residence had been removed. We were the only GCP team at the Case, so a quick guard plan was put in place. It was like we had never left. My first walk to the OP was a mental battle, déjà vu, and so I told myself, "One day at a time."

The rain was something else. Within minutes, a clear blue sky could change to slate, with accompanying thunder, lightning, and a torrential downpour. It was impressive and explained why everything was so green. Mangos were in full season, and these juicy orbs littered the grounds, leaving a pleasant, sweet smell in the air. The mango trees were also home to hundreds of large fruit bats.

One day, as I watched a local unsuccessfully try to kill a bat with his slingshot, I asked him about his experiences. Talking to the locals, I was able to better understand what life in Brazzaville was like for them, the hardships and the tragedies their families had endured over the past year. I used my MP5 to down a bat for him. The bats were the size of a large well-fed rat, with a half-metre-long wingspan and a friendly little dog's face. Actually, I felt bad after killing the bat, but the local assured me that they were quite delicious cooked over a fire. I just took his word for it.

In the evenings, a female mongoose and her little ones kept me company. She moved to and fro, using the perimeter walls between OPs. Another visitor was a large owl that perched on top of the OP, silently swooping down to catch its dinner. The ambassador's new dog, a German shepherd cross named Princess, preferred the later shifts. She made her rounds and sat with me until something caught her interest. One evening it was a snake, a big one, maybe a metre long with a midsection the size of my wrist. Princess flung it into the air by its tail, and the pissed-off snake couldn't do anything about it. The local name for that snake was a "two-step." Get bitten and it's two steps to your grave. This venomous Gaboon viper was a lot larger and much deadlier than the Canadian garter snakes I looked for as a youngster.

With the monotony, physical activity was the only way for us to keep sane and burn off plenty of negative energy. Ursa, who had become a good friend, boxed prior to joining the Legion, and he was my coach and sparring partner for the duration of the tour. Using gloves we acquired locally, our sparring sessions went full-contact. We stuck to two-minute rounds until we had enough. We even found a decent-sized plastic buoy from the river and hung it from a tree, half-filled with water, for a perfect punching bag. Another option was to go for a run outside the perimeter wall. A thirty-minute run in the Congo's heat and humidity was enough to tire me out and calm me down.

Local kids hung around the perimeter and they would try to jog with us, but they ran out of steam early on. They were good kids, keen to talk and ask about our world. Arthur, the eldest and tallest, was always leaning against something. Bonte, with his messy hair, was constantly in an argument with someone, and the smaller of the boys, Gloire, didn't say much. He watched what was going on around him, and I think he was the smartest of them all. One particular morning, Gloire pointed out a newcomer standing off to the side under a tree in the early morning shade. He said he was a

Ninja. I asked the kids to go and see if he was armed, and to find out what he wanted. They returned saying he didn't have a weapon—and that he wanted help.

I walked outside the perimeter and called out, signalling for him to come to me. The teenager, no older than fifteen as best as I could tell, approached me slowly. He looked quite weathered, and his tattered and dirty clothing hung loosely over his skinny frame. I checked his person to ensure he wasn't armed. He didn't speak French, and he wouldn't look me in the eyes. He was clearly nervous.

Over our comms, I duly informed the capitaine about our visitor. The French Embassy was called, and an NGO working with the United Nations International Children's Emergency Fund (UNICEF), which assists child soldiers, arrived soon after and took the boy to a re-education centre. Yet another experience that reminded me of how lucky I really was, and that my day-to-day bullshit problems were nothing. From what the NGO staff said, government-sponsored or opposition militias in the Republic of the Congo recruited young fighters who were poorly trained and equipped; most were killed in the fighting. Hopefully, this child soldier would be one of the luckier ones.

Général de Gaulle was right, I thought. "The better I get to know men, the more I find myself loving dogs."

Brazzaville stabilized, and we were free to visit the city when we weren't on duty. Ursa, Smithy, and I took that opportunity one evening, as did everyone. Dressed in our civilian clothes we recced the local Chinese restaurant and a popular expat nightclub not far from the city's centre. The club was small but clean, with a bar, some tables and chairs, and a large dance floor with disco lights. Loud African music kept the dance floor full. The club attracted a blend of people—local government types with money, foreign embassy staff, European businessmen, and local girls looking for money or a ticket out of Brazzaville.

The local talent was entertaining to watch. The women were dressed in the latest fashions, the highest of heels, and the biggest hoop earrings possible. And their dance moves could be described only as provocative. Ken, Ursa, and I didn't really talk much. After all, we'd been stuck in the Case together for almost two months. Our communication was reduced simply to, "Your round," as we drank our Nigerians, enjoying our little taste of freedom. Eventually, the gyrating girls would come over and talk to us. If they met our highest of standards, we would ask them to join us. To some of the women, we were clearly a dollar sign, but that wasn't always the case.

The combination of our accents, their African French dialects, and the loud music made for challenging conversation, but they made me laugh. They all had big brown eyes, big laughs, and some were quite attractive. When it came to flaunting their curves, we had some pros. We bought them beer or juice; some of them were Muslim. It made for new discussions and some much-needed laughs. When we left the club's main alley to walk to our vehicle, women were lined up along the building's walls, asking to go home with us, or spend a few minutes in our vehicle—whatever it took—for our money.

As with most short-term remedies, alcohol and these nighttime diversions led to problems. Sergent Prigent, while returning from town late one evening, made a condescending comment to Selak, who was on guard duty. At breakfast the following morning, Prigent's black eye was a topic of great discussion. It wasn't long before Capitaine Martin warned all of us that if something like this happened again, both participants would be flown back to Calvi and charged, regardless of who was at fault. This made me start to consider my life long term. Thirty years of age was just around the corner. Did I want to be a légionnaire for the better part of it? I wasn't convinced that I did.

Two Russian-made Mil-24 Hind gunships, hired by the local government and flown by foreign pilots, appeared over the Case de Gaulle every few days. I always made an effort to get out onto the grass field and watch them fly over. The upper portions of the fuselage were painted in jungle camo, the underbelly was light blue, and they made a hell of a racket. One afternoon as I stood looking up at one fly over at a low level, I thought to myself, "I want to fly helicopters."

Our last month passed without further fisticuffs, and we were eventually replaced. For me, it couldn't have happened soon enough.

CHAPTER TWENTY-SEVEN

Salade Niçoise

With the arrival of the new millennium not that far off, I spent my post-Congo three weeks' *permission longue durée* (PLD) snowboarding at Tigne in the French Alps. Once again, it's an awesome place. I also started researching helicopter training programs in Canada, something I knew nothing about. The eventual post-leave depression was offset somewhat by the idea that I had a tentative plan in place. Back in Calvi, routine took over in the form of training and more training, and all of us hoping something operational was going to happen that would require either the regiment or the Groupement. The downtime, however, allowed me to start planning my Legion exit strategy. I completed the administrative application process for the Vancouver Island Helicopters (VIH) flight-training program in Victoria, British Columbia.

Soon, a container arrived with new Cagiva VMX motorbikes, which were being introduced to the GCP as a reconnaissance tool. Lasko, a motocross enthusiast, ran our Cagiva training program. We left the regiment's gates on our motorbikes with our backpacks and FAMASs, headed for the Corsican roads and countryside. It wasn't long before the team started racking up some serious injuries. A directive from the Groupement followed, telling us to leave the motorbikes alone.

I survived the Cagiva. I stood on my own two legs, able to use both my wrists inside the phone booth outside the CEA company's building for my interview with VIH. When I told the lead flight instructor exactly where I was calling from, there was a noticeable pause in the conversation. Otherwise, the interview seemed to go OK. Time would tell whether I'd be flying helicopters, or just continue jumping from them.

Exit. (*Credit:* Lieutenant Dimitri Leloup)

The team was issued the new French G9 parachute, and after a mid-air fatality within another GCP team, safety measures were added. We travelled to the ÉTAP for our G9 and Ralentisseur-Stabilisateur-Extracteur (RSE) certifications. The RSE was basically a small drag-shoot deployed immediately once in stable free fall to minimize lateral drift. The RSE wasn't a very popular addition; it meant we weren't really in free fall.

During the evenings, some of us returned to Le Triangle, but the atmosphere was different from my days on course. And at this stage of my life, to be honest, hanging out in bars wasn't really a priority. With G9 and RSE certifications completed, on the journey back to Calvi, Capitaine Martin designated ten demonstration jumpers for the upcoming Camerone Day. I was fortunate enough to be chosen, and as usual a lot of preparation and importance went into marking the event. We were to jump on the regiment's parade square (likely my first and last opportunity to do so). A Casa 235 (like a small Transall) arrived, and for several days we jumped, working on our team groupings. The pressure was on not to miss our mark or hit the regiment's buildings or the parade square's rose bushes.

April 30, 2000, Camerone Day, the weather wasn't co-operating. Winds were gusting, so we had to exit the Casa at low altitude, with a quick opening. That meant there would be very little time to regroup. Thankfully, we all landed on the parade square, but our grouping wasn't great. My parents were in the crowd that day, visiting the island of Corsica and the regiment, which I'd described to them in detail during my time here. The event felt like a fitting way to share my time in the Legion with them, so I was happy I didn't impact a building or do a face plant on the regiment's parade square. After our jump, we lined up on the parade square for review by both the French military and the Legion's commanding generals.

Strolling back to our building afterwards, with my parachute on, gaine on my shoulders, and FAMAS in hand, I walked past Capitaine Raoul, and he quickly noted that our jump was shit. Once I had stored away my kit in the section building, I went to our small bar to get myself a bottle of water. Sitting on the couch alone, with her long legs crossed and her large hat at her side was Laetitia Casta, the French supermodel. Any beautiful brunette with legs like hers wasn't the norm in our section, but she was on a whole other level. Casta was the regiment VIP guest for the day's parade. Her chaperone, the regiment CO, was in our capitaine's office. Knowing who

G9, parachute final. (*Credit:* 2ᵉ Régiment étranger de parachutistes)

she was, I said hello in both French and English, and asked if she wanted a juice or something. She replied, "Bonjour," and declined my drink offer. That was the end of our deep conversation. I felt that

if I told her I was in love with her, after only a few seconds of knowing each other, it might have gotten weird.

That evening, veteran légionnaires joined us for the company
dinner and shared our wine. As the night progressed, the singing started. Many of the veterans joined in (former German Wehrmacht or other nationalities), veteran légionnaires of the Indochina
and Algeria campaigns. In post–Second World War France, German POWs were given the option of joining the Legion, and this
influx had far-reaching influences on the organization. To this day,
the REP's 2nd Company song is the former Wehrmacht marching
song, "Edelweiss." It was sung several times during the night, and
brought up emotions for our veteran guests. During the evening,
some of them shared their experiences, recounting past exploits in
vivid detail. Others just listened, content to sit among fellow légionnaires, paratroopers, again. As German paratrooper Major Rudolf
Böhmler said, "The secret of a paratrooper's success can be summed
up in three words: comradeship, esprit de corps, and efficiency."

It wasn't long before summer vacationers arrived on the island once
again, and the tire (shooting), mines, explosives (TME) cell returned
from Paris after a training program with the Groupe d'intervention
de la gendarmerie nationale (GIGN). The GIGN's method of clearing
buildings was considered one of the best. Our team's training then
began so that we could learn the latest tools of the trade and benefit
from the GIGN's current expertise and experience.

I passed before Capitaine Desmeulles not long afterwards and
was asked if I was resigning. I needed to confirm yes or no. I duly
informed Capitaine Desmeulles that I wasn't extending past the
six-year mark. I had given it a lot of thought, and I told him that I
had applied to a Canadian helicopter flight-training program, and
that I had been accepted, which was true. Six years in the Legion
wasn't just something you walk away from easily; nevertheless I felt
I needed to move on. Capitaine Desmeulles gave me some flak, considering the regiment's commitment to train GCP team members,
but ultimately he understood the decision was mine to make.

I then passed in front of the company capitaine, explaining the
same, and he countered with a two-year posting to the French military's commando course in Djibouti, East Africa. This was completely

Camerone Day, review by both the French military and the Legion's commanding generals, in Calvi, Corsica. (*Credit:* Joel Struthers)

unexpected. But standing in that office, my kepi at my side, the pull to move on was stronger. I was almost twenty-nine and at a crossroads. I respectfully declined. The capitaine accepted my choice.

Our work continued, and on May 11, 2000, we loaded vehicles for the ferry ride and drive to a French regular military camp in Fréjus in southern France for Cooperative Lantern 2000, NATO's Partnership for Peace Programme (PFP). It was France's first PFP exercise, which involved six hundred military personnel from twenty-two countries. Our role was to demonstrate how to recover a hostage from a building. We would rappel from a helicopter, clear the building, and then extract with hostage by grappe.

Grappe, also referred to as special patrol insertion/extraction (SPIE), was developed to rapidly insert or extract a team from an area that does not allow a helicopter landing. A specially designed rope is lowered from a hovering helicopter. Team personnel, each wearing a harness with attached carabiner, hook up to a D-ring inserted in the rope. The helicopter then lifts vertically until the personnel are clear of obstructions, then proceeds in forward flight to a secure zone.

The officers planned the trip over extremely well, and we arrived in Fréjus early to prepare, but also right before the long weekend started. It was an opportunity for some of our teammates to visit home. For those of us légionnaires who couldn't, on a late-Friday afternoon we boarded a train in our summer dress uniforms, destined for Cannes, which was hosting the Festival de Cannes (international film festival). Dimitri, Ursa, and I walked down Cannes's main boulevard, with the sun setting over the Mediterranean coast and the yachts of the festival elite docked at the main pier. We managed to pass the port's security checkpoint unchallenged; it was cocktail hour, real cocktails. As we strolled the pier, we glanced into the luxurious yachts where parties were going on with actresses, fashion models, and the festival's elite. Sadly, no one invited three REP men aboard. Their loss.

Afterwards, we retreated to a local nightclub and mingled in our world. We had no problem getting into nightclubs wearing our uniforms since légionnaires weren't the norm in these parts. Inside the club, we got a variety of attention. Some people were wary of us; others were interested. And inevitably, my kepi was stained by a dirty table.

Early Monday morning, we were back at work—our reality— preparing a hostage-recovery demonstration. It was simple enough, and when our day was done, a few of us ran to town, each carrying our civilian beach attire in a small backpack. The run took about an hour, which usually gave us about another hour or two at the beach before sunset. Then we'd grab a meal at one of the beachside restaurants. Salade Niçoise was a favourite of mine, accompanied with a glass or two of chilled rosé or a dark beer. Later in the evening, someone from the section would drive down in a P4 to pick us up. One evening, while walking along the main avenue with a teammate, we passed a group of young French Arab guys. A comment was directed our way. I stopped in my tracks. I don't recall the exact words uttered, but it was his tone and delivery that was clear to me, and I wasn't going to let it go unchecked.

I replied, "Do you think you've got what it takes to back that up?" Some of them did. One of the braver guys approached, and I put him on his ass with a straight left. Another tried the same, and then three of them circled. We were backing up at this stage, and two of the guys were focused on me. One was a big kid, taller than me. They spoke to one another in Arabic, but the tall one said to me, in French, "You can fight, German." Evidently, my anglophone accent had confused him.

From street-side garbage cans, they retrieved their weapons—glass Orangina bottles—which they started to hurl at us. We ran back a short distance, then stood our ground. I noticed two French Tahitian military soldiers in civvies passing by a distance away; it was hard to miss the military haircuts and particular way of walking. I called out, saying we were with the REP, and they ran over to assist. At the same time, a car arrived and out poured half a dozen more French Arabs, who joined the fray. We did what we could, but one of the French Tahitians was quickly knocked down and kicked unconscious. I had taken a solid punch—or maybe a bottle—to the side of the head, and blood was getting into my right eye, making it hard to see.

How long this went on for, I don't recall. But we backed our way down the main avenue, fighting as they circled, some running at us with flying kicks or punches. My left hand was starting to hurt from the number of times I connected with their heads. A police car finally arrived and the guys split, running into the side streets. The police quickly apprehended two of them. An ambulance was called, and the French Tahitian was looked after while the rest of us were given some basic first aid.

Unknown to me, Lawson and another NCO had driven by and seen the melee. To my surprise, they were standing by with the police. We drove to the local precinct and when it was just my teammate and me in the room, the police officers left the young men handcuffed on their chairs, saying, "We'll be back in two minutes, and no earlier." But we just let it be. Personally, I wasn't in the mood or state for any revenge. Capitaine Desmeulles was soon present to witness our official statements, and the police informed us they were familiar with the two individuals they had apprehended. Both were minors who had been in and out of youth detention centres. The police couldn't do much, considering. They were disillusioned youth.

The following day after my night in the hospital, Lieutenant Monicault was briefing the guys on the day's demos, responsibilities, and timings. He was new to the section after recently completing his SOGH course. I showed up at the briefing late, but it was clear that I wasn't a part of the demo, which made total sense considering, but I took my exclusion the wrong way, and Lieutenant Monicault listened to my short, concussed reaction. And in all fairness, he let it go and ordered me to relax and to go take a look at my head. Indeed, I had an impressive black eye, which I already knew, obviously. He finished by saying that if I felt better soon, he would reintroduce me to the demos.

We visited the French Tahitian fellow in the hospital and thanked him and the other guy for helping us out. We had been lucky they were walking by and willing to assist us when they did, otherwise the outcome could have been a lot uglier.

Capitaine Desmeulles later made a passing comment that I should stop playing "le gros bras," the big arms. Noted. He also told us all that an upper-ranking regular force officer had asked him, "Why are légionnaires allowed out?" When I heard that comment, it bugged me to no end, concussion or not. Legion officers know the score, but not everyone in the French military does. After all, we weren't "society's undesirables" who joined the Legion and couldn't be trusted outside a regiment's walls. On the contrary, I believe we performed our roles with integrity.

Hearing that statement or that type of attitude only reinforced my decision to part ways with the Legion. More to the point, it was clear to me that it was France that had a problem, one that lay outside the regiment's walls. I eventually rejoined our demonstrations and decided I wouldn't run into town any more. On our final demonstration, the team's English-speakers were sent to man a static display with our weapons, communications gear, surveillance optics, G9 parachute, and OP's gaine spread out for all to see. Capitaine Desmeulles said a few words in English, and then we answered questions directed to us by NATO military personnel and guests.

The Norwegian major-general commanding NATO Forces West approached and asked me directly about the section's role. I answered the general as candidly as I could. He finished by commenting that my English was excellent, glancing slightly at my black eye. "I'm Canadian, sir," I said. He replied with a slight smile, "Ah yes, the French Foreign Legion."

CHAPTER TWENTY-EIGHT

Civile

That following month I was tasked to assist with the pre-selection process. Selection was being run by Karine, and the candidates were standing next to our section at morning parade in their combats ready for the TAP tests. I recognized Ivan Gambier among them, the Frenchman from my medic's course. I also spotted Hetny, returning for his second attempt. Unfortunately, he had an accidental discharge on the range that first week of pre-selection, which was his demise. That type of error can't be ignored.

The reality was that these légionnaires' ability, toughness, and commitment to soldiering wasn't in question. Everyone arrived in good shape. You didn't get to the pre-selection if you weren't physically fit. Plus, candidates were approved based on their abilities within their individual combat companies beforehand. A company capitaine wouldn't send a candidate to selection unless it was warranted. Making it to GCP pre-selection was a coveted opportunity, and selection was based on whether you could learn the required skills quickly enough and mix in well within the team. Candidates were pushed to see how badly they wanted it.

Later in the pre-selection candidates were grouped in binômes, or pairs, and given a jerry can three-quarters full of water to carry while locating a dozen GPS coordinates. Once they reached the final set of coordinates several hours later, they were told to stand down for a few hours of sleep. While crashed out in their sleeping bags in a field, they were secured, blindfolded, and given a few kicks before being loaded into the back of the section VLRA.

The candidates were then taken to the amphibious centre, their combat vests removed, feet tied, and arms secured behind their backs—this is referred to as *crapaudine* in *Beau Geste*—while the jerry cans of water were emptied on them as they lay on the cement roadway. Adding to the physical and mental discomfort of the biting early morning Mediterranean cold wind were muzzled 1st Company war dogs mauling them. Stress by dog drool.

We then walked the shivering guys to the Zodiac dock and pushed them into the frigid waters. After being allowed to panic for a moment, candidates were helped to their feet. The guys stood in shoulder-deep water shaking. Gambier was smiling, and that was the right type of attitude, and one that got you into the section.

News followed that the Groupement des commando parachutistes would be part of the Bastille Day military défilé. A C-160 Transall arrived in Calvi early July, and we flew to an air force base outside Paris to meet the other GCP teams from mainland France. We were shown to our short-term air force accommodations and issued the new SF recce vehicle, perhaps a new addition after the Cagiva motorbike failure. We familiarized ourselves with the new vehicles and, using the runway, quickly worked on formation driving in preparation for July 14.

With an afternoon free, a few of us junior ranks, wearing our summer dress uniforms, took a taxi to the city's 7th arrondissement to visit Les Invalides. Initiated in 1670 by Louis XIV as a home and hospital for war veterans, the building now encompasses Musée de l'Armée, France's National War Museum, among other museums and monuments. The Dôme des Invalides, a large domed church, houses the tombs of some of France's war heroes, most notably Napoléon Bonaparte.

It was fascinating walking the long halls, looking at many of Bonaparte's campaign flags and cannons used in battle. This time, I paid more attention to the Battle of Waterloo exhibits. I think some of the museum's visitors found our Legion uniforms and kepis interesting too. I felt like I was behind a glass window myself at times.

After paying our respects to Bonaparte, we walked to a café on Rue de Grenelle, careful not to step in the dog poop that's ever-present on Paris streets, and we enjoyed an expensive beer, with our kepis all neatly piled together away from dirty tables. Pretty Parisians walked by on their way to and from work or other activities,

Congo team in Paris, with the Arc de Triomphe in the background. (*Credit:* 2ᵉ Régiment étranger de parachutistes)

totally ignoring the best smile any of us could manage. Even an accented "Bonjour, mademoiselle" did nothing. We were ghosts.

Early in the morning of the 14th, in our brand-new jump combats, medals, and green berets, with Capitaine Martin sitting shotgun in the Jeep, I drove from the air force base to Paris's downtown core. Military police were positioned at the main intersections, directing the French military vehicles along the required route. As we neared the city centre and its cobblestoned streets, shopkeepers were starting to open their cafés, bakeries, and newspaper stands before the morning rush. I enjoyed the drive, surrounded by Paris's history and culture, circling the Arc de Triomphe with its huge tricolore hanging from the massive arch and France's Tomb of the Unknown Soldier, then continuing down the famous Champs-Élysées.

As daylight made its appearance, and a few early spectators found spots on the sidewalk to watch the parade, we took a team photo, which included Capitaine Martin, NCOs Karine, Testaniere, de la Chappelle, Laskowski, Brook, and junior ranks Bercia, Figaro, Smith, Gehrke, Holcik, and me. Then we split off to find a *café crème* and wait. Like my last défilé with the CEA and 1st Company, the orders eventually blared over the loudspeakers, and President Jacques Chirac made his way down the Champs with his Imperial Guard. The order to start our engines soon followed, and we got into position. Then, at a walking pace, GCP officers standing in the vehicle saluting, we drove down to the Place de la Concorde, and the défilé was complete. It was a somewhat more laid-back and uneventful défilé compared to my last, but because of these two experiences, I would always see Paris in a different way compared to most people who visit the City of Light.

Our evening was free before our flight back to Calvi the following day. Dimitri's SOGH course-mate from the GIGN invited a few of us to visit the compound at Satory, a Paris suburb. The GIGN's main headquarters building included a large vehicle bay with numerous unmarked station wagons and SUVs. A Puma helicopter outside sat on standby. The main floor held the armoury, radio communications room, and an operations centre. We handled a wide variety of assault weapons—sniper rifles and sidearms—like kids in a candy store, really. I was most interested in handling the AK-47 recovered from the hijacked airbus at the Marseille Airport, and a team member's revolver that took an AK 7.62 round during the initial assault. The round had disabled his weapon and severed his finger, at which point he dropped the short (revolver) and went to his long (FAMAS). I put on the Kevlar helmet with ballistic visor that had also taken a direct 7.62 round, saving the gendarme's life, albeit knocking him out cold in the process.

In the basement's range, we fired the HK-P-7, SIG P-226, MP5 with M-Point quick-target acquisition systems, and the Smith & Wesson revolver. The mock-up rooms and various targets allowed them to train as a team or individually whenever they felt the urge. Our host's speed and grouping in the quick-reaction drills was tight. I was impressed with both their skills and overall set up, and if I were a Frenchman, I'd want to be a member of GIGN.

Paris défilé, Groupement GCP. I'm driving in the foreground, right-hand side of photo. (*Credit:* 2ᵉ Régiment étranger de parachutistes)

We were then invited to our host gendarme's family living quarters for dinner with his wife and a few other GIGN teammates. They were down-to-earth, smart, and switched-on guys. I could see why they were a respected organization within the anti-terrorism community.

The next day, we flew back to Calvi, landing on a sunny and hot Corsica.

My last week in Calvi was finally upon me. Before heading to Aubagne for the departure formalities, I spent my time finalizing the administrative requirements and handing in my kit. On my last evening, a handful of us—Lasko, Dimitri, Ursa, Maguire, Lawson, and Brook—went to a restaurant in town for a meal. As the evening progressed, a few of us decided to venture farther afield to a smaller, less popular nightclub on Algajola Beach east of Calvi. As we walked inside the club, I quickly noticed an attractive girl on the dance floor. She had a Mediterranean look to her, with long, dark curly hair and a petite dancer's body. She was with friends, from what I could tell, and they were all dancing, talking, and laughing among themselves in the small club, which was only partly full. She noticed me watching her.

I eventually introduced myself, and after minutes of trying to make conversation over loud techno beats, we agreed to talk outside. She told me she spent her summer days on the beach and evenings in the local nightclubs. And that if I came looking, she would be there. Something about her struck me. Her eyes were truthful. It was as if this island was trying to tell me something. Maybe Corsica was enticing me to stay.

Despite the captivating nature of my new dark-haired female friend, and the island, whose landscapes and lifestyle I had gotten to know intimately, it was time to close the chapter on my life in the Legion. The following morning, as per my orders, I passed before Capitaine Desmeulles, and he gave me a GCP section plaque and wished me good luck. I thanked him for the opportunities given to me in the section, and I really meant it. Later, I passed in front of the company's and regiment's commanding officers. I messed up my presentation in the regiment CO's office, mixing up the order of my lines, damn it, but I recovered. Nerves, I guess. Lieutenant-Colonel Prevost looked at me sternly and said, "Bonne chance, Caporal Struthers, dans la vie civile." Good luck in civilian life.

His administrative clerk handed me a regimental crest on my way out, showing me the door.

I said goodbye to my teammates, and wished them a safe but operational future. It felt like I was betraying them somewhat, but everyone has to make choices and I had made mine. I boarded the ferry in Bastia on August 31, 2000, leaving behind Corsica. It had been my home for five years. I'd miss it and the days I spent swimming along the beaches, hiking and running the wooded trails, skiing the carved mountains, driving the narrow roads, and embracing Corsica's unique approach to life. It was a place I wouldn't forget anytime soon.

Arriving at the 1er RE Quartier Vienot in Aubagne, where my journey had started six years ago as a younger man with a less worldly outlook and experience, I joined a group of twenty-five other légionnaires from various regiments. They were also going civile in a few days. We were subjected to a final medical and more administrative protocols before presenting ourselves in the offices of a colonel. He asked if I was certain about my decision to leave the Legion. It felt like a lifetime ago that I stood in front of that white-washed three-storey building in Strasbourg, staring at the words *Legio Patria Nostra*. On that September day in 1994 almost six years ago, my hand hovered over the push-button doorbell as I hesitated, unsure if I could commit to what lay ahead. Today, however, my resolve was firm.

During our last few evenings as légionnaires, we were free to submit titres de permissions, but I decided to burn off my restless energy in the gym where I had spent my post-EMPS days working at the regiment's sports bureau. As the days ticked by, I watched the clock and the *engagé volontaires* being marched around the regiment. I was thankful that was behind me, and waited in anticipation of when I could leave the regiment's front gate as a civilian.

That day finally arrived. One by one, we entered the office of the Legion's commanding general, Général Grail, and presented ourselves. His office was quite large, so most of the time was spent walking to and from the spot where we were to present ourselves. It was a quick "Yes sir, no sir" affair. The commanding general wished me good luck. And that was it.

Our group was then taken to the Legion museum to see Capitaine Danjou's wooden hand and we finished up by joining Général Grail for a group photo in front of the Monument aux Morts. When I got back to the barracks, I took off my uniform for the very last time and changed into my civilian clothes. With my bags packed, I walked to the regiment's front gate, perhaps a little faster than normal. I had a train to catch. I presented my authorization slip to the duty sergent at the front gate, looked down at my new light-blue Nikes, and walked outside. I was a civilian once again.

Epilogue: *Système D*

I boarded my train inside the busy Gare Saint-Charles station, and soon left Marseille's crowds behind for the expansive French countryside. I reflected on my goals and accomplishments over my six years serving in the French Foreign Legion. I had made it to the 2ᵉ Régiment étranger de parachutistes — Le REP — earning my place within a team of like-minded individuals. But more importantly, the Legion had changed the course of my life.

My personal pursuit of becoming a soldier meant I had become part of something bigger than what the Canadian military was able to offer. It's a testament to the French Foreign Legion, and to France, to be able to take people from such diverse backgrounds and shape them into one of the world's finest military units, true to its motto, *Honneur et Fidelité*, Honour and Fidelity. I owed the Legion, and France, a lot.

I watched the landscape go by outside my window, which reminded me of my history lesson at Château des Julhans all those years ago. I had read years after that the château was frequented by a young artillery officer named Napoléon Bonaparte, who was courting the château owner's daughter, Désirée Clary. I would miss France and its history.

Before I returned to Canada, I needed to pay my respects. After several hours on a train and a short taxi ride, I arrived in the village of Reviers. Here, I walked the length of 2049 headstones at the Bény-sur-Mer Canadian War Cemetery, where Canadian soldiers who fell at Normandy had been laid to rest. On its rolling hills, I looked at the soldiers' names and ages, and was humbled by their sacrifice. I then walked along Juno Beach, where my paternal grandfather landed on June 6, 1994 — D-Day. Not far away was Sword Beach, where my maternal grandfather drove his Sherman tank off the boat only a few days later. On that day, more than half a century later, I was prouder than ever of my family's military heritage and Canadian history.

On my flight back to Canada, I wasn't celebrating my return home. My future was uncertain. But the Legion's *Système D—Demerde—* which basically means "work shit out," was ingrained in me. Within weeks, I started flight training in Victoria, British Columbia. Adjusting to civilian life took time. There were no more whistles or night jumps over a Mediterranean island. The uncertainty of employment and novelty of paying bills were my new reality.

Throughout my helicopter training, I visited both sets of grandparents, who still lived in Sidney on Vancouver Island. During a conversation with my grandfather, Major-General (Ret.) A. James Tedlie, DSO, he mentioned Indochina and flying into Diên Biên Phu only weeks after France's surrender. I was blown away. I hadn't known about this before joining the Legion. He had been sent there as Canada's military adviser to the International Control Commission (ICC) to oversee the gradual transfer of power between France and the Viet Minh, and the subsequent partition of the country.

I didn't ask my grandfather enough about his experience. At the time, I felt that he would share more if he really wanted to discuss these things. Sadly, he passed, and my hero was lost. In his memoir, entitled *An Amateur Soldier*, my grandfather doesn't say much about Diên Biên Phu. However, he wrote: "Any kind of flying in 1954 was a novelty to me, but flying first class on Air France was something else again. I was served a hot toddy of brandy and milk by a super stewardess, and delicious meals are things I long remember."

I guess that after years of war your immediate priorities change. Why focus on the negatives? My grandfather also wrote: "People often ask veterans what feelings they have when they know that they survived the horrors of a dreadful war. Surprisingly enough, a good many answer 'a sense of guilt.'"

Before his passing, my grandfather suggested that I put my memories to paper because if I didn't, I would regret it one day. I took his advice and began the process of writing from my container room while working on a drilling platform in Algeria's Sahara Desert.

Flying helicopters commercially meant that initially, limited opportunities were afforded to low-time pilots, along with low wages. So, in the slower winter seasons, I worked as a security contractor for a British firm based in London, England, supporting exploration efforts in North Africa and, later, government contracts in Iraq and Afghanistan. Over the years working alongside the Algerian, US, and British military was interesting, to say the least, notably the differences from my Legion experience. In my travels while working in Algeria, I had the opportunity to visit Sidi Bel Abbès — La Maison mère de la Légion étrangère — the Legion's home. Today it's an Algerian gendarme training centre.

There, a gendarme kindly offered to show me the inside and I quickly accepted. From a French *poste de guard* inside its front gate, I looked at its famous parade square, which I had seen in numerous black-and-white photos. This was where Le Monument aux Morts, a globe flanked by four légionnaire statues, originally stood. We used the same statue as our backdrop in the final photo taken with Général Grail at the 1er RE in Aubagne the day I left the Legion.

I also took the opportunity to visit Diên Biên Phu in present-day Vietnam, which had the biggest effect on me. I saw the sky from which légionnaires had jumped. Flying in via Hanoi and working from a battle map I had downloaded from the internet, I searched for Beatrice. It was one of seven French strongholds built around the Muong Thanh Valley and the first to fall to the Viet Minh. Apparently, all the strongholds were named after the mistresses of French Forces CO, Colonel de Castries. I found Beatrice hidden in the tall grass and trees, virtually intact. Walking through its well-built and preserved trenches, I entered the main bunker. There in the ceiling was an obvious hole, letting sunlight stream inside. It was the remnants of a Viet Minh mortar round that killed légionnaire commander Major Paul Pegot and his entire staff. "Alles tod." "All dead." The last message from Beatrice.

To show my respect to the légionnaires killed fighting, I buried my Médaille de bronze de la défence national and my Médaille outre-mer in her hillside and in the process took its dark soil — earth stained with Legion blood — into my hand.

I then visited the Viet Minh war museum in the town of Diên Biên Phu. The photos of dead légionnaires and recovered green berets

Nzerekore, in Guinea, West Africa, 2015. Waiting on passengers while providing flying support for the UN's World Food Program in its effort to stop the Ebola virus outbreak there and in Sierra Leone and Liberia, Africa, I am joined by little locals, who decided to sit with me. (*Credit:* Mike Bridson)

and weapons certainly was strange to see. I had never really considered the other side. I then pondered what my grandfather's experience had been; dealing with both the French and the Viet Minh soon after the battle must have been something else.

I left the museum thinking about my family's historical connections. Perhaps all those words typed years ago in that container meant something, and there was an actual story to be shared.

Years later, in 2015, while flying support for the United Nations' World Food Program's efforts to stop the Ebola virus outbreak in Guinea, Sierra Leone, and Liberia, I had the opportunity to work with the French military's Health Service. When liaising with its French officers, their vocabulary and mannerisms brought back memories, and a much needed push to finish efforts and share *Appel*.

When we'd fly in to various regions, the locals would gather to watch our helicopter land in a storm of brown dirt, tossing into the air the small, coloured garbage bags that were everywhere. Their stares were skeptical, even judgmental, perhaps. The kids were always keen to talk to or touch a white person. A friendly "hello" in their native tongue always got a reaction. Africa is a tough place to grow up, and I respected the kids I talked to for their resiliency. I would answer their questions, including what was generally the first: "Where are you from?" followed by "Did you fly that helicopter all the way from Canada today?"

The final act to complete this story came during two separate trips to France, with both my children in tow, and notably a return to the island of Corsica in 2017—their introduction to my Legion past. Leaving the Bonifacio Citadel in our rented blue Peugeot having explored the south (and enduring my son's early complaint that I couldn't drive a standard), we drove north. Our plan was to visit the regiment, an invitation offered in 2016 by its then commanding officer, Colonel Monicault (formerly Lieutenant Monicault, GCP).

Dimitri Leloup, who worked his way up through the Legion ranks and was recently promoted to lieutenant, had invited us to visit Fort de Nogent, where he was stationed. A REP delegation happened to be staying at the fort. While inside the sous-officer mess foyer for an aperitif—a proper one; my children drank Orangina—Colonel Monicault approached us.

An officer and a gentleman, he introduced himself to my children, shaking their hands. The kids quickly got bored and went off to sit somewhere. Colonel Monicault and I discussed the regiment's efforts in the global fight against fundamentalism, notably in Mali, North Africa. Colonel Desmeulles (formerly Capitaine Desmeulles, GCP) had led the regiment during Operation Serval in 2012, which included an operational jump on Tombouctou. The section managed a number of operational SOGH jumps in support of the same fight. I could see this was a proud moment for Colonel Monicault— and so it should be. I mentioned how deeply saddened, more so angered, I had been by the recent terrorism in France, but confident that the right people were dealing with it. The conversation finished with him inviting me and my children to visit the regiment, including accommodation within its perimeter fence.

Driving the final stretch of Corsica's coastal road, we descended into Calvi Bay on the same road I had taken all those years ago as

Camp Raffalli, 2ᵉ Régiment étranger de parachutistes, Calvi, Corsica. (*Credit*: Joel Struthers)

a young légionnaire. After several "Are we there yet?"s, I told my kids, "Ferme ta gueule" (Shut your mouth) and put on your kepis.

Approaching the regiment's front gate, I slowed right down, looking into its parade square in passing. The emotions I felt at that exact moment are difficult to explain. We drove past, checked into our Calvi hotel, and spent the rest of the day swimming at Rocher Beach. The next morning, after some delicious fresh croissants, *pains au chocolat*, orange juice, and two strong café crèmes (for me) at one of the citadel's cafés, we drove to the regiment.

Parked outside the regiment's gates, noting the new REP insignia painted on its water tower, I asked my kids what they wanted to do — Visit the regiment or go snorkelling at the Rocher Beach? Perhaps they could sense the answer I was looking for. The REP was in my past and the regiment was busy doing real work. My focus now was on my son Carter (twelve), and daughter Kyle (nine), and snorkelling.

Vive la Légion étrangère.

—Fin—

Notes

1 *The Comprehensive Guide to the Victoria & George Cross*, http://www.vconline.org.uk/george-a-ravenhill-vc/4587982658.

2 Douglas E. Harker, *The Dukes* (N.p.: British Columbia Regiment, 1974).

3 Colonel G. W. L. Nicholson, *Canadian Expeditionary Force 1914–1919* (Ottawa: Minister of National Defence, 1962).

4 French Foreign Legion Recruitment, http://en.legion-recrute.com/index.php.

5 Douglas Porch, *The French Foreign Legion: A Complete History of the Legendary Fighting Force* (New York: Skyhorse Publishing, 2010).

6 Ibid.

7 Ibid.

8 Pierre Sergent, *Cameron* (Paris: Fayard, 1980).

9 4ᵉ Regiment étranger, *Les fortes têtes* (Lavaur, France: Légion étrangère, 1994.

10 Alistair Horne, *A Savage War of Peace: Algeria 1954–1962* (New York: Viking Press, 1978).

11 Ibid.

12 Erwan Bergot, *Les 170 jours de Dien Bien Phu* (Saint-Amand [Cher], France: Presses de la Cité, 1979).

13 Andrew Roberts, *Napolean: A Life* (New York: Viking, 2014).

14 Pierre Dufour, *2ᵉ REP, Action Immédiate* (Paris: Lavauzelle, 1994).

15 Jean-Paul Gourevitch, *La France en Afrique* (Saint-Amand-Montrond [Cher], France: Acropole, 2008).

16 Ibid.

17 Ibid.

18 *La France au Congo, Ambassade de France à Brazzaville*, https://cg.ambafrance.org/Case-de-Gaulle-Case-ouverte.

L'Envoi: About the Author

Today my life is a balance of fatherhood and work, no different than most. Langley, British Columbia, is home, and I still run the same trail in Fort Langley that I used when training for the Westies. Flying helicopters commercially is both challenging and rewarding. I wasn't a natural by any means, and initially I didn't trust or understand these machines. Unlike free fall, I had a lot of mechanical moving parts around me that I wasn't too sure about. But I think flying fills my need for excitement and constant movement, a part of my genetic engineering perhaps.

I do miss the jumping at times. While supporting British Columbia's Para Attack Crews (fire jumpers) during the summer fire season, watching its young men and women fight fires from the air brings with it an inevitable wave of nostalgia. I had tried a jump or two at a local para club, but it just wasn't the same.

Writing *this story* was definitely an effort. I couldn't have done it alone. I was a soldier, not a writer, after all. Thank you, Janet Gyenes, for your understanding of the English language and editing skills. We sure spent a lot of time on that. Thank you, family and friends, notably my dad, Jen, Mark, Smithy, and Chris, who helped me shape *Appel*'s narrative. I also have to thank a fighter pilot from my dad's era who took interest in my story and pointed me in the right direction. Lastly, thank you, Colonel Desmeulles, Lieutenant Leloup, and the Legion for your support and assistance, which gave this story its legitimacy. I not only felt that this book was a much-needed positive account from the Legion's ranks, but it also had to have the Legion's approval. And if this book helps to educate people on the facts regarding the French Foreign Legion, well then, all that singing was worth it.

Index